EGYPT
AND THE
HOLY LAND
YESTERDAY AND TODAY
LITHOGRAPHS AND DIARIES BY DAVID ROBERTS R.A.

Text by Fabio Bourbon

Photographs by Antonio Attini

Project editor
Valeria Manferto De Fabianis

CONTENTS

WHITE STAR PUBLISHERS

WS White Star Publishers® is a registered trademark
property of Edizioni White Star s.r.l.

© 2010 Edizioni White Star s.r.l.
Via Candido Sassone, 24
13100 Vercelli, Italy
www.whitestar.it

Translation: A.B.A., Milan - Antony Shugaar

ISBN 978-88-544-0555-4
1 2 3 4 5 6   14 13 12 11 10

Printed in Thailand

Taken from:
Egypt yesterday and today, lithographs by David Roberts
© 1996 White Star S.r.l.

The Holy Land yesterday and today, lithographs by David Roberts
© 1993 White Star S.r.l.

EGYPT

AND THE

HOLY LAND

YESTERDAY AND TODAY

LITHOGRAPHS AND DIARIES BY DAVID ROBERTS R.A.

WHITE STAR PUBLISHERS

After a long search and some hard bargaining, Roberts's ambitious project eventually found the right publisher in Francis Graham Moon. In order to finance the printing of the monumental work, Moon recruited private subscribers who would receive the large, hand-colored deluxe edition of the lithographs.

Between 1842 and 1849, on the basis of sketches made on the spot and aided by his excellent memory, Roberts produced drawings that Louis Haghe gradually turned into prints published monthly. The complete work consisted of six folio volumes, comprising 247 lithographs, including six frontispieces. The first three volumes, dedicated to Queen Victoria and entitled The Holy Land, Syria, Idumea, Egypt and Nubia, mainly contained the subjects Roberts had drawn during the second half of his journey, from the Sinai peninsula to Beirut; the original text was written by Rev. George Croly. The other three volumes, dedicated to King Louis Philippe of France, appeared under the title Egypt and Nubia, From Drawings Made on the Spot by David Roberts, R.A. The lithographs portrayed the monumental sites of pharaonic Egypt and the mosques of Cairo, and the text was written by William Brockedon.The lithograph shown here depicts Roberts's meeting with the pasha of Egypt on the 16th of May, 1839, when he stopped over in Alexandria on his return from Beirut. Logically, this illustration should have concluded the previous volume, The Holy Land Yesterday and Today; however, in view of its geographical location and incompatibility of form with the rest of the works, we considered that it was more logical to include it as a separate plate in this volume. The informal meeting arranged by the British consul in Cairo, Colonel Campbell, lasted about 20 minutes, and left an indelible impression on the artist. Roberts did not have pencil and paper with him, and had to reconstruct the scene from memory. The pasha, on the left, is sitting cross-legged, while the senior members of his entourage stand behind him; the men sitting on the sofa on the right are Colonel Campbell, Lieutenant Waghorn, Roberts himself leaning slightly forward, and two English officers.

3

THE LIFE, WORKS, AND TRAVELS OF DAVID ROBERTS R.A.

*T*he son of a humble cobbler, David Roberts was born on the 24th of October, 1796, in Stockbridge, a village near Edinburgh, Scotland. His natural artistic talent soon became apparent, encouraged by his mother, who used to tell him stories about her own birthplace, Saint Andrews, where the remains of a famous cathedral and a monastery stood. Inspired by some colored posters advertising a circus, the young Roberts covered the walls of the kitchen with processions of animals and other figures in red chalk, so bringing his surprising ability to the notice of his father. The family's economic situation did not permit the boy to be sent to school, but Roberts, who is today considered one of the greatest landscape artists of the nineteenth century, was a brilliant self-taught student who had learned all the academic fundamentals to become a painter by the age of forty.

In all probability, the only person to have taught him any of the rudiments of design was Gavin Beugo, a cantankerous and authoritarian decorator who was suggested to the family by the Trustees Academy of Edinburgh and for whom Roberts worked as an apprentice for seven years. An anecdote that confirms the artist's innate qualities refers to this period: Beugo had given the boy a one-pound note with which to pay a supplier, but as the latter was not at home, Roberts had enough time to copy to perfection the astonishing subject - something he had never been able to look at closely before. Some time later, while tidying up her son's drawings, his mother found the false bank note and, terrified, thought she had raised a thief before she understood her mistake.

4 *Although he spent most of his life in London, Roberts was always very attracted by Scotland. This view of the castle of Carlaverock appears in* Scotland Delineated.

5 *This 1844 portrait of David Roberts by C. Baugniet was used in the first edition of* The Holy Land, Syria, Idumea, Arabia, Egypt & Nubia.

In 1815, the young Roberts moved to Perth, where he had his first paid job as a professional decorator. He returned to Edinburgh the following year and was employed as a scene painter in a second-rate touring theater company, the Pantheon, with which he traveled widely around Britain. During the tour, he also had occasion to try his hand at acting, though only in small parts. Later on, he wrote that his contact with the astounding world of theater had allowed him to achieve his greatest ambition, which was to be able to travel to distant lands; as a result of watching performances of Aladdin and the Forty Thieves, it seemed to him that Baghdad had become familiar territory, with its minarets and spice-scented nights. At that time, however, he had no idea that travels in the East would be part of his future.

In 1819, he became the official scene-painter at the Theatre Royal in Glasgow, and later moved with the same job to the Theatre Royal in Edinburgh. His marriage in 1820 to Scottish actress Margaret McLachlan ended after a short and tempestuous period made even more difficult by his young wife's heavy drinking. Yet Roberts was a considerate father, and always close to his only child, Christine, born on 4th June 1821.

He was deeply fond of her and she repaid his kindness in later life by ordering his works and copying his travel diaries, which remain in manuscript form in the National Scottish Library of Edinburgh, unfortunately mostly unpublished.

Having become well-known in theater circles, Roberts was engaged by the Drury Lane Theatre of London during the last months of 1822, together with his friend and rival Clarkson Stanfield, who was also to become a famous landscape artist. Having moved to London, Roberts exhibited his first oil painting, a view of Dryburgh Abbey, at the Society of British Artists in 1824. That same year, he traveled to France, and during his journey he made several drawings of the Gothic cathedral in Rouen. On his return to England, he had the chance to show for the first time one of his canvasses at the British Institution. Soon after his move to Covent Garden Theatre in August 1826, the fifteen scenes he produced for the London production of Mozart's Abduction from the Seraglio met with resounding success.

This was about the time when his View of Rouen Cathedral was presented to the public at the Royal Academy and his art began to receive critical acclaim; even The Times published a sincere appreciation of his work.

It is interesting to note that the Scottish artist continued to collaborate closely with Clarkson Stanfield, alongside his efforts at Covent Garden Theatre. For example, together they painted a couple of large panoramas, later accidentally destroyed. To the world of that period, the term "panorama" referred to paintings of landscapes so large that they were hung as though on the inside of a cylinder so that the public could stand inside and view them by walking around. The sensation of being in a real landscape was heightened by the use of lighting and such features as bushes, earth, stones, grass, and even running water to simulate streams.

After years of intense effort as a landscape artist and encouraged by the growing approval of the public, Roberts left his job as scene-painter at Covent Garden in 1830 and restricted his professional activity to the much more lucrative occupation of studio painting. In 1831, he was elected president of the Society of British Artists, of which he had been one of the founding members in 1823. Despite obligations to his growing number of private clients, Roberts was able to make several trips during the early part of his career, from which he would usually bring back sketches, drawings, and watercolors that he would use as subjects for his paintings.

In addition to famous views of places and monuments in France, Germany, and the Low Countries, he did not neglect to illustrate his country of birth, and during his frequent visits to his parents' home, he was able to study the greatest of Scotland's historical heritage, which inspired him to paint some of his best canvasses. Another product of his explorations was an excellent series of copperplates depicting Scottish monasteries that, unfortunately, was never reprinted after the first edition. During the same period he also put together a collection of drawings entitled Pilgrims of the Rhine, commissioned by Sir Bulwer Lytton.

8 On his return journey from Italy, in 1851, Roberts stopped in Vienna, in Austria where he painted this picture of the interior of St. Stephen's Cathedral.

9 Entitled The Grand Entrance to Rouen Cathedral and dated 1831, this large oil painting is similar in subject to the view Roberts exhibited in 1826 at the Royal Academy, of which unfortunately no trace remains.

On the advice of his friend David Wilkie, Roberts decided to visit Spain in October 1832. The country was little known in Britain at the time but was to prove a source of profound inspiration. During the trip, which lasted a full year, Roberts managed to visit nearly all the main Spanish cities, including Madrid, Toledo, Granada, Malaga, Seville, and Gibraltar, as well as a few sites in Morocco. In the meantime, he tirelessly drew a series of ruins and monuments from a number of periods, paying particular attention to Moorish art and the local Gothic style. The results of his trip through Spain were numerous canvasses, all exhibited to the public to great acclaim, plus three series of lithographs published between 1835 and 1837 in various editions of Jenning's Landscape Annual. In 1837, a selection of 37 large format lithographs of beautiful views of Spanish monuments appeared under the title Picturesque Sketches of Spain. In only two months, 1,200 copies had been sold, which would have brought Roberts a small fortune if he had not been cheated by his publishers. If nothing else, the long Spanish episode brought Roberts a solid international reputation and the acquaintance of Louis Haghe (a young Belgian engraver of outstanding talent, despite missing his right arm) with whom Roberts was to enjoy a long and rewarding professional relationship in the years to come. In the meantime, the artist had not neglected his painting, and several of his canvasses were hung in the Royal Academy between 1835 and 1837. The success with which these paintings were met meant that Roberts was welcomed as a member of the prestigious institution in early 1838.

Roberts' visit to Morocco during his Spanish trip sparked his interest in new and wider horizons. Having gathered all his savings and studied in great detail the uses, customs, and social and political situations in Egypt, Palestine, and Syria, he set out in August 1838 on the long expedition that was to make him famous and ensure his name a place in posterity. After heading for Paris, he continued down the Rhône valley to arrive at Marseilles on the 11st of September, where he boarded a steamer. After making stops in Malta and the Cyclades, he disembarked in Alexandria at the end of September.

Roberts had neither the time nor the financial resources to allow himself the luxury of dallying; on the contrary, he was fully aware of the fact that his artistic achievements, and consequently his future, depended on the success of his undertaking.

So he headed straight for Cairo, where he hired a boat to carry him up the Nile toward Abu Simbel, stopping briefly at various temples and monuments on the way in order to take meticulous measurements. It was only after he had safely reached his coveted destination - the temple excavated from rock by Ramesses II in the heart of Nubia - that Roberts permitted himself to continue his journey at a more leisurely pace. He started back up the Nile, concentrating on his artwork but without stopping too long in any one place. The artist's documentation of the ancient sites has assumed an even greater importance today, especially the depictions of the Nubian temples that had to be dismantled, relocated, and reassembled, often a long way from their original location, after the construction of the High Dam at Aswan. Once the valley above the dam was flooded, many of the landscapes recorded by Roberts were destroyed forever.

12 On the 24th of September 1838, Roberts described his arrival in the port of Alexandria with these words in his travel diary: "The bay was crowded with a large number of vessels, many of which were warships; our boat was soon surrounded by the most picturesque boatmen I have ever seen."

13 This famous 1840 portrait of Roberts in oriental dress was painted by Robert Scott Launder. The clothes and accessories were souvenirs he collected during his trip to Egypt and the Holy Land.

14-15 *This watercolor over a pencil sketch is dated 1839. It was made in preparation for the lithograph that appeared in the third volume of* Egypt & Nubia *under the title* Cairo, from the Gate of Citizenib.

On the 21st of December, Roberts arrived once more in Cairo with more than a hundred drawings and paintings. He stayed six weeks in the capital, during which he became the first European to be allowed to enter a mosque to depict its interior. He dedicated much of his effort to the masterpieces of Islamic architecture, which he had decided in advance he would reproduce in the same detail as the ruins of pharaonic Egypt.

It should be mentioned that Roberts, like many of his professional colleagues, made use of a camera lucida (light chamber), an instrument that used a prism to reflect any object onto a drawing sheet so that it could be traced.

In Cairo Roberts met Hanafee Ismail Effendi, a young Egyptian Christian convert, who was to accompany the Scot as far as Jerusalem.

It was during these days that Roberts met two English travelers, Jens Pell and John Kinnear, with whom he decided to set off in February 1839 for Sinai then Petra and Palestine. Petra was the legendary Nabataean rock city that had been rediscovered only in 1812 by the Swiss orientalist Johann Ludwig Burckhardt.

Roberts reached the rock city on the 6th of March 1839, and, thanks to the good offices of his local guides and the payment of a hefty toll, he was given leave to stay for five days in what was then the territory of a rather warlike Bedouin tribe.

He did not have much time, but he used it well; although he was able to turn out only fourteen drawings, his views of the extraordinary monuments cut from the rock are among the best any artist has ever produced.

Leaving Petra to head for Palestine, Roberts left Kinnear at Gaza and continued to Jerusalem, which he reached on Good Friday. He wanted to visit all the monuments in the City of David, including the superb Mosque of Omar, the Holy Sepulchre, the excavated tombs in the Valley of Kidron, and the Damascus Gate. During his trips around the city, he was able to execute a large number of drawings, which he was to use in the years to come for subjects in a whole crop of lithographs, watercolors, and oil paintings. Walking along the external perimeter of the walls and climbing the surrounding heights, he was able to see the city from many different viewpoints, which inspired him to produce several panoramic views of great effect. During his stay in Jerusalem, Roberts had the opportunity to make a short but interesting side-trip in the company of an exceptional host: Achmet Aga, the governor of the city, had invited Roberts to accompany him while he escorted a caravan of Christian pilgrims to the River Jordan for Easter. After visiting the important places in the area (including the Dead Sea, the monastery of Saint Sabas, and Bethlehem) and then taking his leave also of Jens Pell, he returned to Jerusalem and then started north via Lake Tiberias and the principal cities along the coast of Lebanon. At Baalbek, however, he went down with an insistent fever that prevented him from reaching Palmyra and forced him to turn back to Beirut, from where he set sail for England on the 13rd of May 1839.

Once back in Britain after an absence of eleven months, Roberts presented the results of his efforts to numerous publishers until he found adequate interest in his work with Francis Graham Moon. In 1840, Moon offered Roberts £3,000 to publish his work and supervise the complex task of engraving the plates. The lithographs were produced by Louis Haghe, assisted by his brother and a few others, from the pile of drawings and detailed observations that Roberts had made about each monument. The complete work, of which the number of copies made is unknown but was certainly limited, finally made up six large-format volumes in folio that contained 248 plates, including six frontispieces and a portrait of the artist by C. Baugniet. The first three volumes appeared between 1842 and 1845, with a dedication to Queen Victoria and entitled The Holy Land, Syria, Idumea, Egypt & Nubia. They contained the illustrations Roberts had made during the second half of his trip, from Sinai to Beirut,

and the pictures were accompanied by a commentary by the Reverend George Croly. The other three volumes, this time dedicated to King Louis Philippe of France, appeared between 1846 and 1849 under the title Egypt & Nubia. *These lithographs illustrated the temples and monuments of pharaonic Egypt and the mosques of Cairo. William Brockedon provided the commentary. The technique used by the engraver for the luxury edition - published in a limited number following subscription by leading figures of the day - was particularly painstaking, as each plate was printed in black and white then colored by hand. The cheaper version was printed in black, ocher, and white highlighting. This was followed in 1855 by a reprint in a smaller format entitled simply* The Holy Land and Egypt.

SIDON.
Looking towards Mount Lebanon.

TYRE

16-17 In the years subsequent to the publication of The Holy Land *David Roberts enjoyed a growing success with the public as well as great critical acclaim. Fascinated by Biblical subjects and by the remarkable views of archeological sites with an "exotic" flavor, such as Petra and Baalbec, a number of private clients commissioned him to do paintings based on the lithographs. Among the most illustrious of his private clients were Queen Victoria, the Countess of Warwick, and many other members of the British aristocracy and upper class. The ink sketches shown here (depicting Tyre, the Church of the Nativity in Bethlehem, Sidon, Jerusalem seen from the Mount of Olives, and Baalbec) accompanied a short note which indicated specific features, size, and price of every painting - a sort of "technical file" presented by the artist before completing the painting. These sketches are particularly interesting because they allow us to guess at what the preparatory drawings - sketched on the spot by Roberts during his journey through the Holy Land - must have looked like.*
The watercolor illustrated in the following pages illustrates Petra.

17

The rewards reaped by Roberts as a result of his efforts were mostly in terms of fame and glory, as the sum paid by Moon represented little in comparison to the enormous volume of work he had undertaken, besides the discomforts of the trip. In any case, the paintings he made for private clients earned him enough money to establish himself in a luxurious building in Fitzroy Street, where he had a special well-lit room built that he used as a studio. Two years after his return to England, Roberts was finally made a statutory member of the Royal Academy.

In 1841, Queen Victoria commissioned Roberts to paint a picture of The Bridge at Toledo, which is still kept in the Royal Collection. Other paintings were to follow, including one of A Fountain in Madrid and several views of the Great Exhibition held at Crystal Palace in 1851. While he continued work on the drawings for Louis Haghe in 1842, Roberts presented his diploma painting to the Royal Academy. It was a view of Baalbek entitled The Gateway of the Temple of Bacchus, which was later to

appear as a lithograph in The Holy Land, Syria, Idumea, Egypt & Nubia.

By 1845, both his parents were dead and his daughter had been married for four years, so Roberts, feeling lonely, took his sister into his home for a while. During the next two decades, the artist visited many European countries, views of which were later worked up into paintings and engravings that were exhibited with great success in the most important English galleries and abroad. His huge

clientele included many influential persons of the day and his friends numbered famous poets, writers, and artists, like William Turner, William Thackeray, and Charles Dickens (to whom he gave The Arrival of the Simoon in 1850, a painting adapted from one of the lithographs in Egypt & Nubia).

Between 1847 and 1852, Hogarth published a series of lithographs with the title Scotland Delineated that included fifteen views by Roberts.

18 The southern face of the ruined Melrose Abbey, a masterpiece of Scottish Gothic architecture.

19 This watercolor of a fountain in the Prado in Madrid has almost the same subject as the oil painting commissioned from Roberts in 1842 by Queen Victoria as a gift to Prince Albert, which now forms a part of the Royal Collections.

David Roberts, R.A.

20 top In all probability, it was
Roberts's friend William Turner who
suggested he should paint a series of
views centered on the Thames, but the
project was only begun ten or so years
later, in 1860. This view, The New
Palace of Westminster, Seen from the
River is dated 1861.

20-21 Roberts painted this view of
Rome from the monastery of San
Onofrio on Monte Gianicolo in 1856.
The warm Roman light at sunset
reproduced faithfully by the artist was
judged unreal by some English critics,
who were perhaps accustomed to
the more subdued colors of London.

In 1847 the Rotonda, a building constructed in Leicester Square especially for exhibitions, displayed a huge panorama of Cairo based on Roberts' drawings. Roberts achieved another formidable success in 1849, when he exhibited the painting The Destruction of Jerusalem by Titus *in the Royal Academy, and the following year Louis Haghe produced a lithograph of this famous painting.*

Roberts visited Italy for the first time in 1851 and stayed four weeks in Venice; two years later he spent an entire winter in Rome, taking the opportunity to visit Naples, Pompeii, and Paestum. Many views were produced over the following years as a result of this experience. In particular, a large canvas entitled Rome Seen from the Monastery of San Onofrio *was very well received by critics and public alike.*

By this time, Roberts had created a solid international reputation for himself that brought him important awards and recognitions: one of the most prestigious was bestowed on him at the International Exhibition of Paris in 1855 and that same year Roberts became an honorary member of the Royal Academy of Amsterdam.

In 1860, he began a series of oil paintings of the River Thames that he was to continue until his death. As his health was getting worse and worse, he asked Louis Haghe, with whom he had developed a strong friendship, to accompany him on his last trip, to Belgium in 1861.

Testament to his continuing celebrity was the fact that nearly all his work by this stage of his life was executed on commission, which of course also proved highly remunerative.

He returned to his beloved Scotland in 1861 and continued to exhibit at the Royal Academy as well as other public and private galleries. In 1862, he was one of the most highly praised artists at the International Exhibition in South Kensington.

22-23 *John Ballantine painted his* Portrait of David Roberts in His Studio *around 1862, just two years before the death of the great Scottish landscape artist. It has been suggested that the boy posing as a painter was Roberts's youngest grandchild, Gilbert Elhanan Bicknell, born in 1859. It has been confirmed that the painting on the easel is* A View of St. Paul's from Fleet Street, *which was never completed and is now part of a private American collection.*

Surrounded by the love of his daughter and his friends and still riding high in the esteem of art critics, David Roberts died of a heart attack on the 25th of November 1864, at the age of 68 and was buried in Norwood cemetery. Just a few weeks earlier, he had presented two views at the Royal Academy. The many drawings, sketches, and watercolors he had never wanted to be separated from were sold at auction at Christie's in 1881 and today form part of many public and private collections around the world; his oil paintings, however, are mostly to be seen in the main English and Scottish galleries and art museums.

In 1866, James Ballantine published the first biography of the great Scottish landscape artist, a work to which many of these pages are indebted. The book was dedicated to Roberts's childhood friend, Clarkson Stanfield.

After his death, David Roberts was soon quite unjustly forgotten, along with many other British artists of the Victorian age. He has only recently been "rediscovered" by the critics, and the interest of art collectors has seen the value placed on his work skyrocket. Today he is unanimously considered one of the masters of the nineteenth-century British school of Romantic art and is well known for the epic majesty and extraordinary descriptive detail with which he imbues all his views, even managing to endow humble subjects with nobility. His admirable illustrations of the Forum in Rome and the Moorish buildings in Spain, the impressive perspectives of the French Gothic cathedrals, and the drawings of his native Scotland are as well known to art connoisseurs as they are to those simply appreciative of beauty, who recognize the quality of his work almost by instinct.

Despite his vast artistic output, Roberts's fame is still essentially linked to the lithographs produced as a result of his long trip through Egypt and the Holy Land. Although narrow in judgment, that celebrity is not undeserved, as this monumental work - today universally famous as The Holy Land and Egypt - is a masterpiece that still inspires awe. The result of his extraordinary journey in the Holy Land is today considered a great work of art that has survived the critical scrutiny of time and fashion unscathed.

As for the three volumes that dealt with the valley of the Nile, the documentary value of Roberts's illustrations is incalculable. Although many westerners had visited Egypt before him on the trail of ancient ruins, Roberts was the first to make systematic exploration of the largest Egyptian and Islamic sites for educational purposes a priority. No one before him had portrayed so carefully the temples, necropoli, mosques, and minarets, reproducing every detail with a precision that today we would call photographic.

The pages in these volumes offer not only an example of the technical and figurative virtuosity that conferred upon David Roberts a leading place in British art of the nineteenth century but also allow the reader to savor atmospheres and sensations that today, in the era of technology, have been irredeemably lost.

Fabio Bourbon

EGYPT

YESTERDAY AND TODAY

INTRODUCTION

David Roberts was unfairly forgotten soon after his death, like many other British artists of the Victorian era, and only rediscovered recently by art critics. However, collectors' interest in his work has never flagged, and his pictures fetch very high prices. Unanimously described as one of the masters of the 19th-century British romantic school, Roberts is now known to the general public for the epic grandeur and incredible detail of all his views.

Despite his extensive artistic production, Roberts's fame is still mainly due to the lithographs based on the drawings he made during his long pilgrimage to Egypt and the Holy Land. Though unjustifiably limited, this fame is not undeserved, as this monumental work constitutes a masterpiece that is still of great interest. Although many other Westerners had visited the archaeological remains of Egypt before him, Roberts was the first whose priority was systematic exploration of the major Egyptian and Islamic monumental sites, with a view to publishing a popular work.

No one had ever drawn temples, necropolises, mosques and minarets with such scrupulous care, reproducing every detail with a precision that today would be called photographic.

The 124 lithographs reproduced here, made with extraordinary skill by Louis Haghe with the aid of his brother and a few other assistants, appeared in the hand-painted deluxe edition, which was published by Francis Graham Moon in London between 1842 and 1849 and supplied on subscription to a number of dignitaries of the period; the number of copies printed is unknown, but it was certainly a very limited edition. The second edition was printed in black, white and ocher, and was followed by numerous reprints in a smaller size.

We consider that apart from the artistic value of the lithographs reproduced here, the main interest of this volume lies in the fact that they are arranged in the strictest possible chronological sequence, from Roberts's arrival in Alexandria on the 24th of September 1838 to his departure from Cairo on the 6th of February 1839.

In an attempt to reconstruct the author's experiences, we have divided his itinerary into three separate stages, shown in different colors on the map opposite, each of which corresponds to one chapter.

Roberts had neither the time nor the money to be able to afford any delay; he was also fully aware that his artistic success and his future in general depended on the outcome of the venture. From Alexandria, he therefore traveled to Cairo, and from there in the direction of Abu Simbel, without delay; as he sailed up the Nile he only stopped when strictly necessary. Having arrived safe and sound at his long-awaited destination, the fabulous rock temple excavated by order of Rameses II in the heart of Nubia, Roberts embarked on the return journey with a calmer spirit, though he never stopped very long in one place. His long stay in Cairo was entirely devoted to the masterpieces of Islamic architecture, which he had decided to document with the same precision with which he had just portrayed the magnificent ruins of pharaonic Egypt. As a matter of fact, the work he accomplished during those weeks spent in the Egyptian capital before his departure for the Holy Land exceeded even his own expectations. In view of all these factors, we have opened each chapter of this volume with one of the three frontispieces that appeared in the first edition of the work published by Graham Moon, depicting the places that most impressed Roberts - Abu Simbel, Karnak and Cairo - and the three different emotional experiences he underwent there. The original division of the work into three volumes encouraged our attempt at a chronological reinterpretation of Roberts's very unusual artistic and human experience. The method we followed in reconstructing his itinerary basically involved a detailed study of Roberts's travel journals (which are now housed in manuscript form at the National Scottish Library in Edinburgh) and a geographical reconnaissance of each location. Our purpose, in the quite frequent cases in which there were gaps in Roberts's written notes, was to establish the feasibility of the schedule and the logic of the sequences we have devised. Especially in the Cairo chapter, we faced considerable problems because the basic information was incomplete and great changes have occurred in the city in the meantime; as a result of earthquakes, collapses and demolition, no trace remains of some buildings, while the appearance of others is greatly altered, sometimes making it impossible to match the lithograph with its exact photographic equivalent. Equally, Roberts published his prints without following any chronological order, and the fact that many of the lithographs are undated (or incorrectly dated as a result of errors by the engraver) presented considerable difficulties in composing the most reliable possible sequence of pictures; however, we trust that our attempt has at least partly succeeded in recreating the fascination of Roberts's remarkable journey.

Fabio Bourbon

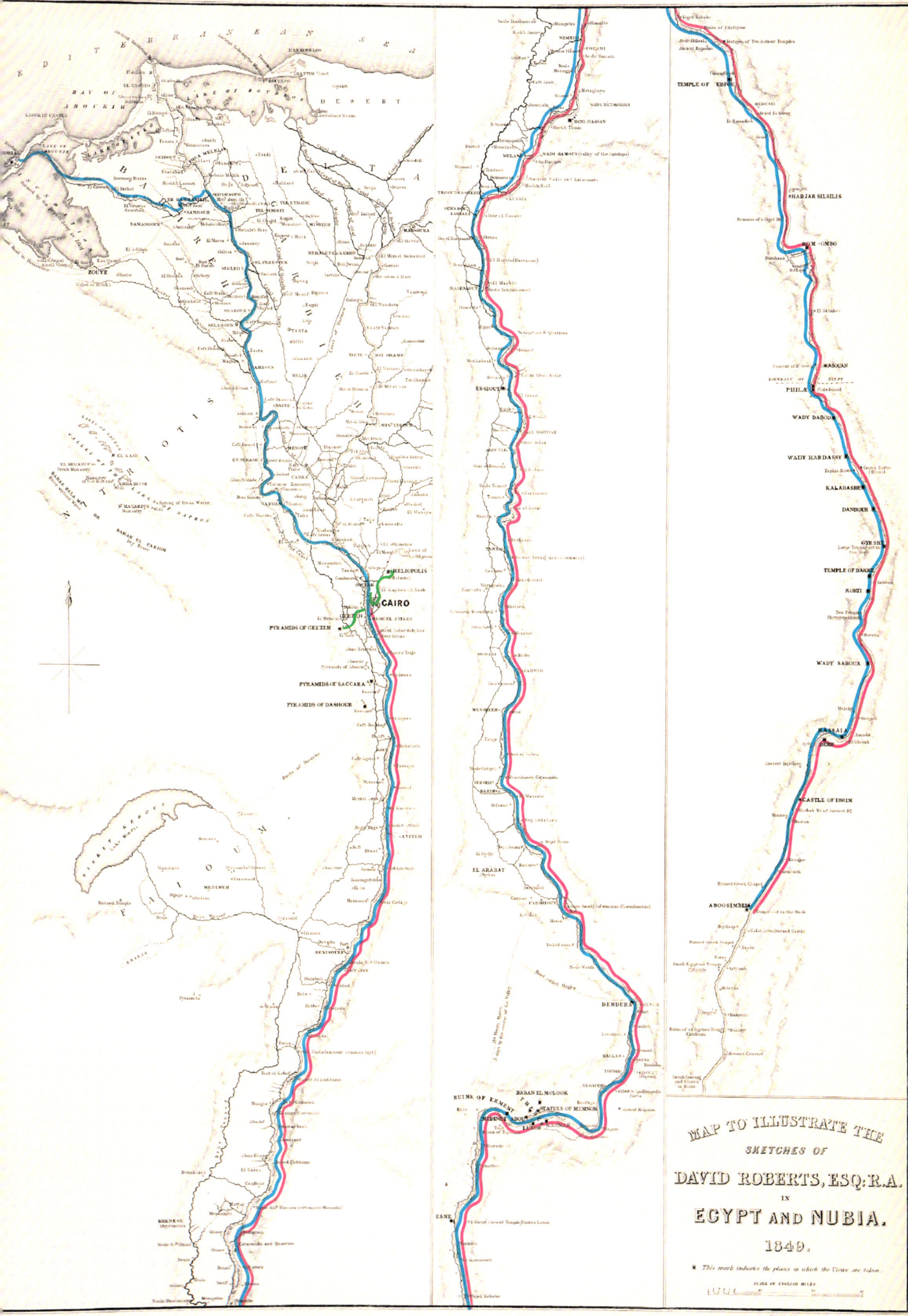

MEDITERRANEAN SEA

DESERT

DELTA

BAHR EL GHARBIEH

NATRON or NITROTIS

FAIOUM

CAIRO
HELIOPOLIS
PYRAMIDS OF GEEZEH
PYRAMIDS OF SACCARA
PYRAMIDS OF DASHOUR

BENI HASSAN
WADI GAMOUS (valley of the Antelope)
MELAWI
MANFALOUT
ES-SIOUT
TAHTA
GIRGEH
BARDIS
EL ARABAT
FARSHIOUT
DENDERA
BALLAS
KOUS
NEGADEH
BABAN EL MOLOOK
RUINS OF ERMENT
STATUES OF MEMNON
MEDINET ABOU
LUXOR
ESNE

TEMPLE OF EDFOU
HADJAR SILSILIS
KOM-OMBO
ASSOUAN
PHILAE
WADY DABOD
WADY KARDASSY
KALABSHEE
DANDOUR
GYRSHE
TEMPLE OF DAKKE
KOSHTI
WADY SABOUA
MASSALA
DERR
CASTLE OF IBRIM
ABOOSIMBEL

MAP TO ILLUSTRATE THE

SKETCHES OF

DAVID ROBERTS, ESQ: R.A.

IN

EGYPT AND NUBIA.

1849.

This mark indicates the places in which the Views are taken.

SCALE OF ENGLISH MILES

FROM ALEXANDRIA TO ABU SIMBEL

24th September - 10th November 1838

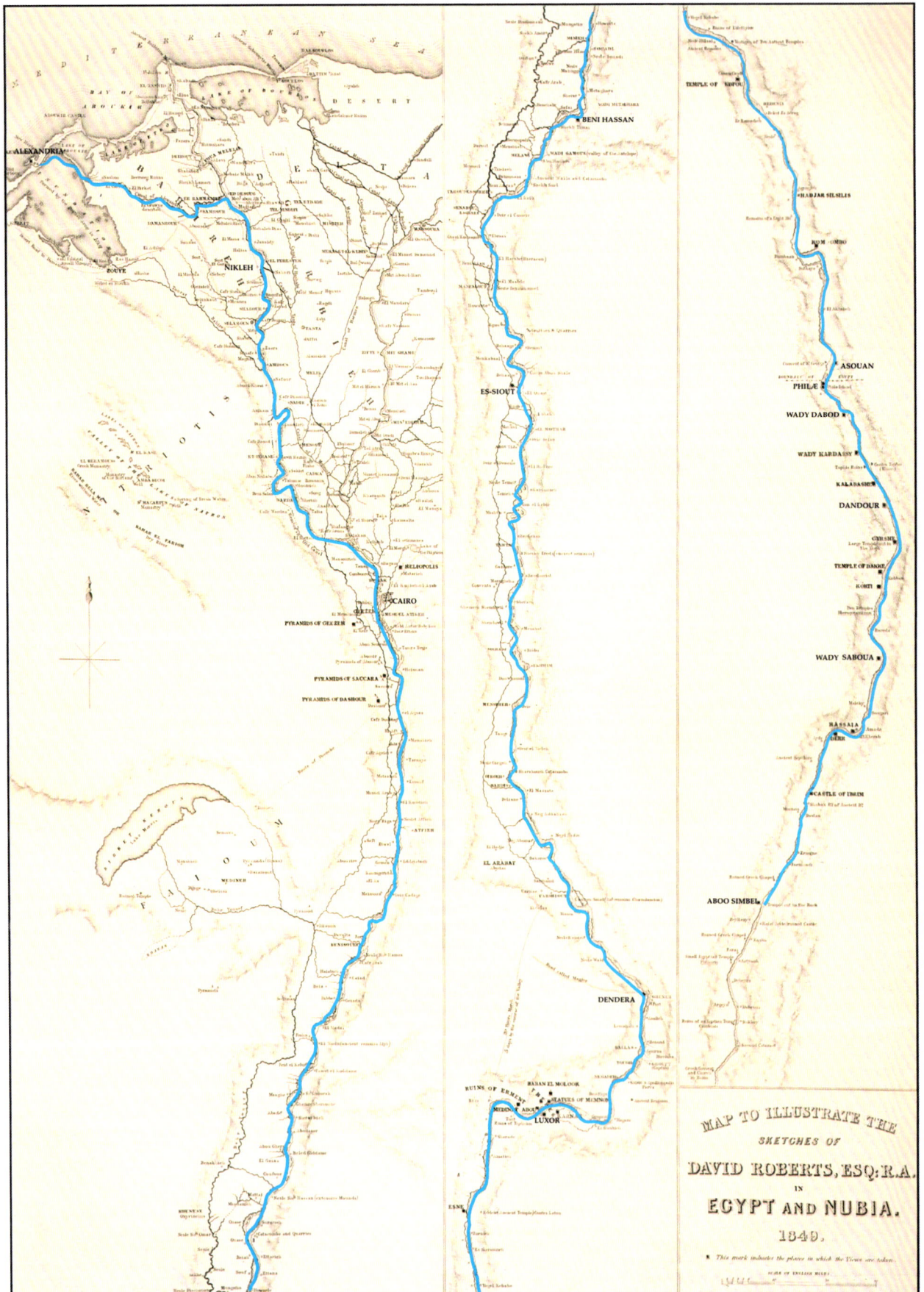

MAP TO ILLUSTRATE THE
SKETCHES OF
DAVID ROBERTS, ESQ: R.A.
IN
EGYPT AND NUBIA.
1849.

EGYPT & NUBIA

David Roberts, R.A.

WILLIAM BROCKEDON, F.R.S.

LOUIS HAGHE.

VOL. 3

F. G. MOON, 20, THREADNEEDLE STREET,
PUBLISHER IN ORDINARY TO HER MAJESTY.
MDCCCXLIX.

THE PORT OF ALEXANDRIA

Plate 1

24th September 1838

*A*fter spending a great deal of time planning the journey that was to take him away from home for nearly a year, David Roberts left London on the 31st of August 1838. Following stopovers in France, Italy, Malta and the Cyclades, he eventually reached Alexandria on the 24th of September. The sight of Alexandria left him speechless, it was so different from any other city he had ever seen. He was particularly amazed by the crowds that thronged around the ship and on the wharves: boatmen vociferously offering their services, others transshipping goods and passengers, black porters who would shoulder huge loads for a small reward, and camel drivers who rushed around getting their animals into line amid the most appalling din. On entering the city Roberts saw, mingling together in an indescribable confusion, magnificently dressed Turkish gentlemen, stark naked black slave girls, Greek and Jewish merchants and people of every nationality heading in one direction or another, apparently aimlessly. Though dazed by all this novelty, the Scottish artist remained sufficiently objective to observe that despite the glorious relics of its past, the ancient splendor of Alexandria had long ago declined. The city, with its 600,000 inhabitants, looked more like an anthill than anything else.

From David Roberts's journal:

24th September - This morning we rose early. Alexandria was right in front of us, with mosques and palm trees that gave it a different atmosphere from any I had ever breathed before...
The bay was crowded with a large number of vessels, many of which were warships; our boat was soon surrounded by the most picturesque boatmen I have ever seen...

CLEOPATRA'S NEEDLES IN ALEXANDRIA

Plate 2

24th-26th September 1838

As soon as he disembarked in Alexandria, Roberts set to work to arrange a voyage up the Nile to Abu Simbel. First of all he chartered a boat that would take him by river to the Delta, from where he intended to travel to Cairo. Preceded by a letter of introduction from the foreign minister that he had obtained at home with the aid of friends in high places, he contacted Colonel Campbell to obtain all possible assistance. Colonel Campbell gave him a very cordial welcome, obtained the documents authorizing him to travel unhindered in Egypt and Nubia, and gave him a great deal of advice that was to prove very useful in the coming months. Egypt, governed by Pasha Mohammed Ali (who had taken power in 1805 after driving out the Turks and had inflicted a resounding defeat even on the English), was an unpredictable country where Western travelers had to cope with every kind of discomfort.

Though absorbed by the numerous preparations for his imminent expedition, Roberts could not suppress his natural artist's curiosity, and on the very day of his arrival he visited the main sights of the great port. This first contact with the monuments of ancient Egypt was not a great success, however, because of their ruined condition, so that only two of them provided suitable subjects for his inspiration: the obelisks of Tuthmosis III and Pompey's Column. Two days later he made some sketches after measuring them accurately; this practice was of great importance in order to reproduce the proportions of the monuments and every structural and decorative element with the greatest precision.

At the time when Roberts visited Alexandria, only one of the two great obelisks, known as Cleopatra's Needles was still standing on its pedestal. This name, though evocative, had no historical foundation but was of popular origin, partly based on the fact that in Arabic these ancient symbols of the generating power of the sun god were generically called messalah (needles).

The two great monoliths were erected by Pharaoh Tuthmosis III in front of the Temple of Amun at Heliopolis, from which they were transferred over fourteen centuries later, by order of Augustus, to decorate the temple erected in Alexandria in honor of Julius Caesar. Of the two obelisks, which stood some 70 feet tall, the one that Roberts saw lying on the ground was taken to London and erected on the Victoria Embankment on the 13th of September 1878, while the other, donated to the United States in 1869 to mark the opening of the Suez Canal, was erected at Central Park in New York on the 22nd of January 1881.

POMPEY'S COLUMN AT ALEXANDRIA

Plate 3

24th-26th September 1838

On the evening of the 24th, accompanied by a local guide and some Europeans he had just met, Roberts, riding a donkey, reached the ancient citadel of Rhakotis to see the famous Pompey's Column.
It did not particularly impress him, but rather suggested neglect and desolation.
The column, which stands 100 feet tall, is erected on an older base made of spoil. The shaft, made of a single piece of red granite, supports a white marble Corinthian capital.
The attribution of this monument to Julius Caesar's great rival Gnaeus Pompeus is based on legend, although it belongs to the right historical period. The column was actually part of the extension to the Serapeum, ordered by Mark Antony to provide new premises for the famous library, which was destroyed in the fire following Caesar's siege of Alexandria.
After numerous trials and tribulations and the permanent ruin of the second library, this surviving element of the great portico was re-erected in AD 296 in honor of the Emperor Diocletian, who had put down a rebellion against the power of Rome. On that occasion a statue may have been placed on the capital.
Generally, according to the notes in his journal, Roberts seems to have been more struck *by the local color than the very modest antiquities to be seen in Alexandria. In particular, he was horrified by the sight of the slave market, where lovely Circassians and half-naked black girls were auctioned under the scorching sun.*

From David Roberts's journal:

24th September - Pompey's Column consists of five parts: the pedestal, the plinth, the base, the shaft and the capital. It may originally have been surmounted by a statue; alternatively, it may have been part of the colonnade of a temple, which I think is likely, as it stands on a pile of rubble.

Pompey's Pillar, Alexandria.   David Roberts R.A.

An ancient well near Nikleh

Plate 4

In Alexandria, as well as Colonel Campbell, Roberts met the consul, Robert Thorburn, well known to British travelers of the period because of his unrivaled helpfulness. With their assistance, the Scottish artist was introduced to French explorer and geographer Louis-Maurice-Adolphe Linant de Bellefonds, who accompanied him in his excursions around town and some Britons, two of whom decided to join his expedition. In Roberts's journal, one of them (a Mr. Vanderhorst) is always referred to as Mr. V; he was a clumsy, chubby gentleman accompanied by a Maltese servant and an Italian chef, who said he was traveling for the sake of his delicate health. Roberts's second traveling companion was the jovial Captain Nelley of the 99th East Middlesex Regiment, who made himself very useful as an interpreter and was certainly the liveliest of the small group of adventurers. A third member, whom Roberts met in Cairo, later joined the expedition;

Roberts never revealed the identity of this mysterious Mr. A. The group was completed by Ismail, a young Egyptian converted to Christianity, hired by the artist as his personal servant. After taking on provisions for four months and safely stowing away the letters of introduction addressed to the pasha of Egypt, Mohammed Ali, Roberts left Alexandria at dawn on the 27th. The next morning the party reached the village of Asfeh, on one of the arms of the Nile. They then transferred to a more spacious boat, heading for Sa el-Hagar, the ancient Sais. On the 29th the boat put in at Nikleh, where a fair was underway. In his journal, Roberts wrote that people were flocking to the village from all directions, bringing with them goods of some kind or flocks of sheep and goats. In the artist's eyes the surrounding region appeared to be very fertile, partly because of the numerous wells (saqiyah), whose operation was highly ingenious despite their bizarre appearance.

From David Roberts's journal:

29th September - The waters of the Nile are thick and muddy; the region is intensively cultivated and dotted with villages, usually surrounded by palm trees which, by contrast with the whiteness of the minarets, make a very picturesque sight. The corn fields are irrigated by wells from which water is raised with earthenware pitchers secured to a rope which winds round a wheel pulled by an ox or a camel.

A Persian Wheel,
used in raising Water from the Nile.

THE GIZA FERRY IN THE PORT OF CAIRO

Plate 5

30th September-7th October 1838

After leaving the village of Nikleh and covering some more equally picturesque stages on their journey, Roberts and his traveling companions eventually came in sight of the Pyramids at around midday on the 30th, and a few hours later landed at Boulak, the port of Cairo.

After booking into a hotel and calling on the British ambassador, Roberts visited the city and its amazing monuments. He was particularly impressed by the mosque of Sultan Hassan, whose extremely elaborate decorations took his breath away.

On the 3rd he traveled to the Pyramids by donkey. At first sight they did not look particularly huge, but he changed his mind when it came to climbing them. In any event, as he wrote in his journal, he was far more impressed by the sight of the Sphinx.

On the 5th he explored the tombs of the Caliphs, many of which were ruined by that time or inhabited by paupers and beggars, in striking contrast with the splendor of the magnificent mosaic floors, the finely painted walls and the domes studded with mother-of-pearl and semi-precious stones.

Enthusiastic about all these sights but ever mindful of his organizational responsibilities, he managed in the meantime to charter a fishing boat complete with its eight-man crew and captain, and drastically cleared it of rats by sinking it in the shallows for a few days.

Vanderhorst, Captain Nelley and Mr. A. were to follow him on a second craft.

On the 6th of October, he finally embarked after proudly hoisting the Union Jack, but was forced to spend the night on board in the port of Boulak because of the unfavorable wind. The next day, while he waited for the mainsail yard to be replaced after a slight rigging incident, he passed the time by drawing the Giza ferry, with the Pyramids in the background.

From David Roberts's journal:

1st October - From the heights of the Alcazar or the Citadel there is a magnificent view of Cairo: below lies the city with its domes and minarets, then the suburb of Boulak and the labyrinth of the Nile, while the Pyramids of Giza and the mountains of Libya stand out on the horizon.

THE ENTRANCE TO A TOMB AT BENI HASAN

Plate 6

8th-11th October 1838

During the night of the 7th, Roberts had his first unpleasant encounter with the local mosquitos, as a result of which he could not sleep a wink; unfortunately, he would have to get used to their company. The first few days of the trip were totally windless, so the crew had to man the oars most of the time.

The surrounding countryside passed slowly by with a continuous range of hills, and the monotony of the cornfields was only broken up here and there by poor villages of sun-dried mud or thick groves of date-laden palm trees. On the morning of the 9th, the boat landed at Beni Suef, where a market was in full swing. Roberts, always interested in details and anxious to see as much as possible, mingled with the crowds. The women, wearing ankle-length indigo blue cotton dresses, carried baskets full of fruit or cages of pigeons on their heads, while the men drove flocks of sheep and goats in front of them. All this formed a very picturesque setting, which he enjoyed very much.

The next day the boat put in at Sheikly, the ancient Cynopolis, where the sand dunes reached down to the banks of the great river. In order to stretch his legs, the artist decided to continue on foot to nearby Onaseh. During his walk he noticed that the local people did not bury their dead (probably because the tombs would have been flooded when the Nile periodically bursted its banks) but laid the bodies in small niches of unfired bricks that were soon damaged by the elements, with the result that macabre heaps of whitened skeletons, wrapped in the remains of their burial garments, were scattered all around.

Roberts spent the night at Minieh (present el-Minya), in the middle of which stood the ruins of an attractive mosque with marble columns. The next day the voyage continued, amid magnificent scenery, to Beni Hasan, where Roberts sketched the ancient ruins. The rock tombs of this district are named after an Arab tribe which occupied a number of neighboring villages, now abandoned and ruined.

The necropolis was excavated during the Middle Kingdom, and is considered to be of great interest, not only for its architecture but also for the splendid scenes of domestic life that decorate the tomb walls. The sepulchre illustrated by Roberts is that of the monarch Ammenemes, the front of which presents two interesting proto-Doric pillars.

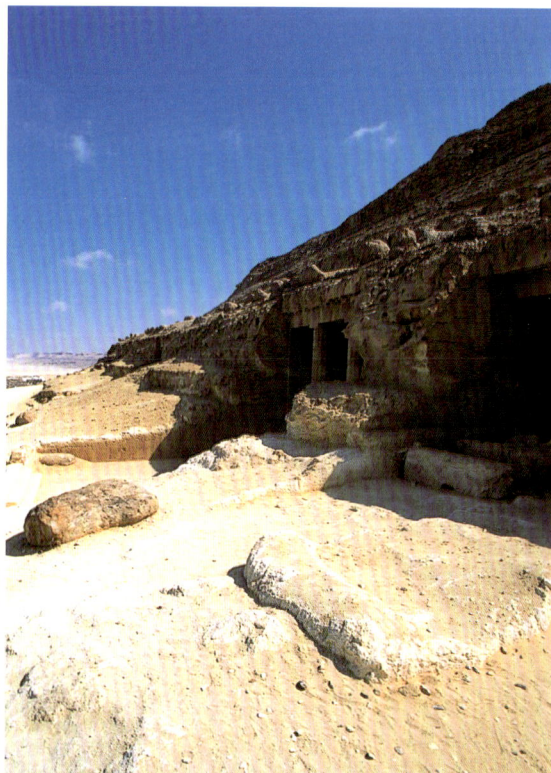

From David Roberts's journal:

11th October - The main tomb has two Doric columns on the façade, and is entirely covered with hieroglyphics; inside, in a niche, are the remains of a large statue and two smaller ones, carved in the living rock. Other tombs are excavated in the rock walls that rise above the left bank of the Nile; nearly all of them are aligned at the same height. Each one has a well or a deep cavity which is perpendicular to the floor or slopes steeply.

SIOUT

Plate 7

11th-13th October 1838

*A*fter spending
a few hours at Beni Hasan,
Roberts set off for el-Sheik
Ibadah, the ancient Antinoe.
However, he was greatly
disappointed, as hardly a trace
remained of the glorious relics
described some years earlier by
other travelers. Here and there a
few columns still stood amid
rubble and piles of soil, but no
trace remained of the marble
triumphal arches of the Roman
period, which had almost
certainly been dismantled by the
local people to make lime.
Roberts consoled himself by
buying some ancient coins very
cheaply. His interest in
collecting coins is often
mentioned in his journal, where
he meticulously listed similar
purchases made in numerous
places.
On the 12th, the boat put in at
Manfalut, a declining town
whose bazaar provided six
chickens for the galley. The next
morning the expedition reached
Siout, known in ancient times
as Sauti, and now as Asyut. In
the past, the town had amassed
great wealth because of its
favorable position at the center
of a huge fertile plain, but
Roberts remarked that, as
elsewhere, little remained of the
ancient monuments but a few
heaps of rubble and some burial
areas.

THE MINARET OF THE GREAT MOSQUE AT SIOUT

<u>Plate 8</u>

13th October 1838

iout was once the center of the worship of Upuauet, the war god in the form of a desert wolf or lycaon, thus its Greek name of Lycopolis. It was the birthplace of neo-Platonic philosopher Plotinus in the 2nd century BC, and was later known as the city where the Holy Family stayed when they had to flee to Egypt to escape Herod's persecution. Converted to Christianity in the 4th century, it is still one of the largest Coptic centers in Egypt, although it also has a major Islamic university. Roberts described it as the largest city he encountered after leaving Cairo; a prosperous, well-kept town with numerous bazaars offering all sorts of goods. The solemnity of the merchants seemed rather absurd to him, however, because of their evident reluctance to take their chabouks (a kind of long pipe) out of their mouths to answer his questions. This and similar comments, which are by no means infrequent in his journal, give a faithful picture of the difficulties sometimes encountered by Roberts, although he often proved quite adaptable, in his contacts with such very different ways of life from his own. In any case, any misunderstandings must have been mutual.
Though puzzled by certain attitudes, the Scottish artist was genuinely fascinated by Islamic architecture, and unhesitatingly pronounced that the most outstanding monument in Siout was the Great Mosque, with its soaring minaret, which he lost no time in sketching.
After visiting the capital, Roberts walked to the rock necropolis, famous for the great tombs excavated halfway up a tall rock face. Though impressed by the magnificent tombs, the Scotsman could not conceal his irritation at the sight of evident traces left by mummy seekers who, during their sacrilegious operations, had scattered mutilated, shriveled human remains all around. This profanation was due to the widespread use of parts of mummies by Arab and European apothecaries from the Middle Ages onwards to prepare remedies that were popularly believed to have miracle-working properties. In pharmacological use this fashion reached its height in the 17th century, disappearing entirely around the turn of the 18th century, but mummies were still used in esoteric practices until the early decades of the 20th century. Needless to say, the damage caused by the tomb robbers in their frenetic excavations represents an incalculable loss to archaeology.

One of the Principal Mosques
Siout, Upper Egypt

THE TEMPLE OF DENDERA AND THE SO-CALLED TYPHONIUM

Plate 9

14th-20th October 1838

As mentioned in the Introduction, Roberts had planned his journey carefully in order to minimize the number of stops made and consequently the expense. He had decided to reach Abu Simbel as soon as possible, then sail back down the Nile to Cairo and begin the sketches, watercolors and oils that he would complete when he returned home. On the outward trip he therefore stopped only as long as absolutely necessary at the main archaeological sites, combining these stops (with laudable thrift) with the practical requirements of the expedition. While he measured façades, columns, funeral chambers and statues and recorded his data and personal impressions in his notebook, the crew restocked the galley and attended to the numerous other tasks required to ensure the success of the expedition.
At this stage, Roberts preferred merely to observe the spectacular remains of the pharaohs' Egypt, though with a technical eye, as if he wished to drink in the atmosphere of the extraordinary land he had long dreamed of before tackling the difficult task he had set himself. Only when he became accustomed to all this grandeur did he intend to commit the shapes and colors to paper. In fact, as can be seen from the pages of his journal, during the first weeks of the trip, until

Abu Simbel, Roberts produced very few complete drawings; he preferred sketches, details, perspective studies and the inevitable measurements. The only exceptions are views of some minor sites at which he decided not to stop on the return journey, and a few other lithographs mentioned in the journal, perhaps painted when he had more time to spare. However, it is reasonable to assume that in some cases he was carried away by enthusiasm, as in the case of this view of the Temple of Dendera and the adjacent Typhonium. Five days after leaving Siout on the 14th, Roberts reached the famous sanctuary of Hathor, following stops at Abutig, Antæopolis (where he saw a magnificent sunset over the ruins of the Roman amphitheater), el-Maragha, whose sheik welcomed him with great honors, and Girgah. On the 18th, while the boat was underway, he saw a group of huge crocodiles sniffing the morning air on a sandbank; they did not seem to be at all disturbed even by the rifle shots fired at them by the crew. Although the imposing ruins of Dendera had greatly impressed Roberts, he was plunged into a state of melancholic prostration at the thought of the transience of earthly things.

From David Roberts's journal:

19th October - I rose at dawn and betook myself to the ruins of Dendera accompanied by Captain Nelley, who acted as my assistant while I took measurements. On entering the temple I was amazed to see the marvellous state of preservation of the entire structure (with the sole exception of the points where it has been damaged intentionally) and the immense amount of work since the surface is covered with hieroglyphics, both inside and out. To the north-west stands the Typhonium, named after the figures of Typhon which appear frequently there.

From David Roberts's journal:

23rd October - The air is so pure and the plain on which it stands so large, that it is impossible to realise the size of the temple until you are really close to it; only the contrast with the homes that now surround the structures enables their majesty to be fully appreciated. The main columns, whose circumference is 30 feet, give some idea of the proportions of the complex; the capitals, carved to the shape of lotus flowers, must have a maximum circumference of 30 feet.

The Temple of Luxor seen from the Nile

Plate 10

20th-23rd October 1838

Roberts reached Dendera on the 19th of October and set off again the next day, after completing a view of the temple and eating a good lunch. On the morning of Sunday the 21st, the two boats tied up near Goorna, a small village where visitors to ancient Thebes could spend the night and buy food and fresh water. The adventurous party wasted no time, but hired donkeys and set off for the great Theban necropolises that stretch along the west bank of the Nile. Here, in the plain dominated by the Theban Heights, the mountain sacred to the goddess Mertseger (She who loves Silence), stand the eternal resting places of pharaohs and royal brides, princes and princesses, officials and courtiers. The artist was particularly struck by the impressive appearance of what is known as the Memnonium, the funeral temple of Rameses II, in which lay the remains of the huge monolithic statue of the sovereign.

On the way back to the boats, various local inhabitants came to meet the newcomers, offering to sell them a number of exceptionally well preserved ancient mummies. On Monday morning the party visited the Valley of the Kings, where a number of unfinished tombs enabled Roberts to study the construction techniques and the methods used by the decorators. A few laconic words written in his faithful journal indicate that the evening reserved a pleasant surprise for the tired traveling companions: a performance by some young dancers, who were "very elegant and graceful." The Scotsman particularly liked a very tall girl with ebony skin, whose perfect features seemed the most expressive he had ever seen in his life. In his descriptions of the dancers and the women he had admired in Egypt in general, Roberts is certainly the most reserved of his contemporaries; perhaps he censored his notes later so as not to scandalize his daughter, or perhaps the modest Christine cut certain passages of her own initiative when recopying her father's memories. On the 23rd, the moment finally came to visit the spectacular ruins of Luxor, which took the artist's breath away; the notes in his journal clearly indicate that the dimensions of the complex almost obsessed poor Roberts, who spent hours measuring columns, capitals, reliefs and walls in a paroxysm of amazement and admiration.

49

Point of Luxor from the North Sept.

THE TEMPLE OF LUXOR
SEEN FROM THE SOUTHWEST

Plate 11

23rd October 1838

Luxor, now a flourishing tourist resort on the east bank of the Nile 450 miles south of Cairo, is universally famous for its majestic ruins, which were explored and described in detail as early as the period of Napoleon Bonaparte's expedition. Here, in the fertile plain that occupies a vast loop of the river, one of the greatest religious and political centers in the ancient world developed in the 2nd millennium BC: *a city so rich and influential that at the height of its glory it had the astonishing population of half a million inhabitants.*

by the regional capital. The god Amun, associated with Mut and Khonsu in the Theban Triad, was worshipped with great ceremony in the huge metropolis. The spiritual rule of the triad was imposed on every other town in the country by extensive proselytizing work carried out by the powerful priestly caste of the district. The Great Temple of Luxor was the main satellite of the huge sacred complex of Karnak, with which it was closely linked for reasons of worship and by architectural and ornamental characteristics due to the same

As a matter of fact, the present town is only part of ancient Thebes, several times capital of Egypt during the Middle and New Kingdoms, which developed from the original urban nucleus located near present-day Karnak, and rapidly grew until it included the area now occupied

historical events. Already greatly excited by the sanctuary of Luxor, Roberts described Karnak, where he arrived on the afternoon of the 23rd of October, in almost astonished tones, again emphasizing the formidable size of those temples that had survived the millennia.

ASWAN AND THE ELEPHANTINE ISLAND

Plate 12

24th-29th October 1838

*R*oberts left Karnak on the afternoon of the 23rd of October, and reached Aswan six days later after calling at the places of greatest historical interest. On the 24th the artist first visited the picturesque ruins of Hermonthis, then stayed for a few hours at Esna to view the remains of the temple of Khnum. At dawn the next day he strolled on the plain around ancient Eilathia, surrounded by mighty walls, and on the 26th he decided to visit Edfu, whose temple interested him greatly because of its size and the supreme elegance of its bas-reliefs. On the 28th he was at Kom Ombo, where the ruins of the sanctuary dominated the lazy waters of the Nile like giants half-buried in the sand.

As usual, Roberts wrote detailed descriptions of each monument, but the pages of his journal are fascinating not so much for his architectural notes as for his brilliant landscape descriptions, which, in a few words describe sceneries, often with a wild beauty, that are now lost forever. For example, before reaching Edfu, he wrote, "About midway we found a sheik's tomb, in which were jars of water for the thirsty traveler. A lean hungry dog and two immense white eagles were gorging themselves on a dead camel, and they scarcely stopped when we approached them."

On the 27th, he spent the whole day on board, and wrote, "Scarcely a breath of wind. Crocodiles lie sunning themselves on the banks. The cooing of the wild pigeons, and the notes of numerous birds, are heard from the groves of palms, and the solitary crane stalks along by the river-side."

Aswan, called Syene by the Greeks, once famous for its granite quarries, is situated under the First Cataract of the Nile, where the great river branches, and is studded with a myriad of granite rocks and some larger islands. The entire area surrounding the present-day city was known in ancient times by the name of Yeb, or "Land of Elephants," perhaps because the Egyptians saw the huge animals there for the first time, or because of the fact that many of the rocks molded by the water resemble elephants; only later was the name restricted to the strategically located Elephantine Island and the town that developed up there. Roberts was ferried there, but discovered with some disappointment that only a few slight traces of the ancient ruins remained.

29th October - On reaching Aswan we wandered among the ruins of the city, which stands on a rise overlooking the river. All that remains of it are a few brick walls, so after making a drawing of this section of the Nile, I crossed it to visit Elephantine Island. Here I found no sign of ancient temples apart from a few columns and heaps of rubble. However, I saw a solitary statue, and on examining the wall next the stream I found it composed of stones covered with hieroglyphics.

THE SO-CALLED HYPAETHRAL TEMPLE ON THE ISLE OF PHILAE

Plate 13

30th October-1st November 1838

On the morning of the 30th of October, after hiring a number of donkeys, Roberts and his tireless traveling companions set off southward in search of a boatman who could ferry them across to the Isle of Philae, the "pearl of Egypt," where pilgrims congregated in ancient times to pay homage to the mysterious, benign goddess Isis. The magnificent ruins of the great sanctuary still survived in all their splendor, and the artist was greatly impressed. The island, which he described as a corner of paradise in the midst of boundless desolation, somehow recalled the green land where he was born and the happy times of his youth, a pleasant sensation that he was never to forget. The time passed quickly as the four gentlemen roamed around the ancient walls, and the time to take their leave of this delightful spot came all too quickly. The next day, while preparations were being made for the crossing of the First Cataract, a messenger reached Aswan bearing an invitation from the bey himself. The lord of the district welcomed Roberts and Captain Nelley into his tent with great courtesy; as he offered them coffee and good tobacco he told them he had been ordered by the pasha to give them all possible assistance, but Roberts politely declined the courteous offer. This answer was perhaps too hasty, because crossing the rapids with the two boats proved very laborious, and took up the whole of the 1st of November. The artist therefore decided to spend the time available at Philae, where he drew what is known as the "Pharaoh's Bed," which he described as a "hypaethral temple" because it had no roof. In fact, the pavilion was erected by Trajan in AD 105 as a shelter for the sacred boat of Isis on which the statue of the goddess was carried during processions to the temples of southern Nubia. The elegant structure consists of a quadrangular kiosk formed by 14 columns united at the base by intercolumnar walls, mostly devoid of decoration. The capitals, no two of which are alike, are the floral type. The unusual cubes surmounting them were to have been carved with the effigy of Hathor. Though incomplete, the kiosk has become the very symbol of Philae because of its beauty, and still remains the best example of the taste and skill of Egyptian architecture in the Roman period.

The monument became famous as the "Pharaoh's Bed" because it was wrongly believed in ancient times that the sovereigns of Egypt resided there during their visits to the great sanctuary.

From David Roberts's journal:

30th October - There are four temples on the island. The first I visited, with lotus-shaped capitals, is the southernmost one. It gives the impression of being unfinished. It is made of very fine sandstone, and the details of the decorations are so clear as to suggest that the stone cutters have only just finished work. I can hardly convince myself that I have seen a 2,000-year-old monument. We set off again, and at sunset we finally entered Nubia.

THE TEMPLE OF WADI DABOD

Plate 14

2nd November 1838

On the morning of Friday, the 2nd of November, Roberts and his traveling companions went ashore near Wadi Dabod, in a place where a small temple with very elegant proportions stood. Like many other Nubian sanctuaries it was never completed, as demonstrated by the fact that the two outer columns on the façade are unpolished. Their irregular surface and the roughly hewn capitals confirmed to the artist's eyes the supposition that Egyptian craftsmen carved the hieroglyphics and smaller details of the decoration after the various blocks of stone had been assembled in their correct positions.

The oldest part of the temple was built in the first half of the 3rd century BC by King Adikhalamani, who dedicated it to the god Amun; during the next century it was reconsecrated to the goddess Isis, and extended on various occasions by Ptolemy VI and Ptolemy VIII. The construction of the left wing and the addition of the façade, with its four great columns, were ordered by Roman emperors Augustus and Tiberius, who were portrayed with the attributes of the ancient pharaohs on the walls built up to halfway up the intercolumniations. As in the case of the more famous temples of Abu Simbel and Philae, the small temple of Wadi Dabod also risked being submerged by the waters of Lake Nasser when the Great Aswan Dam was built, but was saved by the intervention of UNESCO; it was dismantled between 1960 and 1961, and the pieces were temporarily stored. Later, the Egyptian government donated them to Spain in gratitude for that country's help during the salvage operations, and the monument was reconstructed in 1968 on a hill not far from the heart of Madrid, in the Parque de la Montaña. After taking notes and drawing the site, Roberts walked on to Wadi Kardassy, where he found a temple similar to the one he had just seen; however, as sunset was imminent he decided to postpone a more detailed visit until his return.

From David Roberts's journal:

2nd November - This morning we put in at Wadi Dabod, where a small unfinished temple stands. In the adytum there is a red granite votive chapel which probably contained the statue of Isis; the type of decoration suggests that it is much older than the temple.

From David Roberts's journal:

4th November - Today we stopped below the small temple of Dandour. The building, which stands just under the line of the Tropic, is formed by a portico with two columns on the front, followed by two rooms and finally by the actual cella. *Here there is a small stele, probably dedicated to Isis. The winged solar globe appears on the architrave, while the walls of the* pronaos *are decorated with the figures of Isis and Osiris offering sacrifices.*

THE TEMPLE OF DANDOUR

Plate 15

3rd-4th November 1838

After a few hours at Kalabsha, a village on the west bank of the Nile near which stood a magnificent temple, Roberts spent the night of the 3rd of November on board, and went ashore near Dandour at daybreak. As he himself admitted, the small temple in this area might appear trivial by comparison with the grandiose buildings he had seen up to this point. Nevertheless, the monument possessed an intrinsic historical value as it was built by Augustus in honor of the local divinities Peteese and Pihor. Augustus, who was strongly attracted by Egyptian culture, always considered Egypt as his private possession, and this preference (shared by many of his successors) led to a fashion based on pharaonic art in Rome. Even after his death, one of the characteristic features of Roman rule in Egypt was that local building styles continued to be used. Threatened by the waters of Lake Nasser, the Temple of Dandour was dismantled in 1963 on the initiative of UNESCO, and donated by Egypt to the United States. It is now on view in a special room of the Metropolitan Museum of Art in New York. The presence in this plate of a number of people intent on measuring the temple façade is interesting; the fact that one of them is wearing European dress suggests that Roberts could not resist the temptation of depicting himself, the loyal Ismail and some members of the crew.

THE TEMPLE OF WADI SABOUA

Plate 16

5th-6th November 1838

On the night of the 4th of November, the boat passed alongside the temples of Gyrshe and Dakke, and by dawn was close to the island of Derar, which Roberts described as being intensively cultivated. The rising sun shone down on stretches of gleaming white sand, in the middle of which, at a certain point, the outline of the Temple of Offalina stood out. This place is also known by the name of Maharraqa. The Scottish artist went ashore for as long as necessary to visit the great complex, which greatly impressed him, and returned on board in the early afternoon. The next day the heat was oppressive, and the total absence of wind slowed the progress of the boat, with the result that the majestic ruins of Wadi Saboua did not appear on the horizon until the early hours of the 6th of November. The temple, which Roberts much admired, met the same fate as nearly all the other Nubian monuments; it was dismantled into great numbered blocks and was later rebuilt some two and half miles from its original location in a place called New Sabu, on the banks of the great reservoir. The sacred building was erected by Rameses II and consecrated to Amun and Ra-Harakhti, the supreme divinities of Egypt under Rameses; the founder also had himself worshipped, with the result that the temple was known as "The House of Rameses-Meryamun in the dominion of Amun." That is why the sphinxes and statues erected in front of the pylon bore the features of the deified sovereign. In his journal, Roberts wrote that the most spectacular feature of the complex was the long dromos, a kind of avenue lined with sphinxes and preceded by two huge statues of the pharaoh, which led to the temple. It was the sphinxes that suggested to the local people the modern name given to the site, namely Valley of Lions. This plate is of great historical value, as most of these sculptures have sadly been lost.

From David Roberts's journal:

6th November - Yesterday the thermometer read 96.8°F in the shade, and there was not a breath of wind. After sunset a slight breeze rose, and this morning we woke not far from Wadi Saboua. The ruins of the temple lie on the west bank of the Nile, 1,485 feet from the river, in the middle of what must once have been a fertile plain. Now great heaps of sand have covered it, burying the portico of the temple; a few stunted bushes are the only signs of plant life, and there is not a single hut in sight.

The Temple of Wadi Saboua
SEEN FROM THE COURTYARD

Plate 17

6th November 1838

The entrance to the temple proper consists of a reddish sandstone pylon 60 feet tall, once preceded by two huge statues of Rameses II, only one of which is still in its original place. The central portal, decorated with bas-reliefs portraying the sovereign offering sacrifices to the gods, leads to the courtyard, bounded on two sides by porticoes with five pillars each; a huge statue of the pharaoh rests on each pillar. The bas-reliefs carved on the walls portray the usual scenes of offerings.

From the courtyard a staircase leads to a narrow terrace onto which opens the portal leading to the main hall; this was converted into a church in the Christian era after many of the reliefs had been covered with frescoes. This large hall, only partly roofed by a ceiling supported by pillars, is followed by a room built crosswise to it, entirely excavated in the rock, which linked to various other rooms.

The numerous reliefs show Rameses II making offerings to the gods and to his own deified image. In the back wall there are three chapels; the central chapel was the actual naos. Here, some of the images decorating the walls represent the pharaoh taking flowers to Ra-Harakhti's solar boat, decorated with hawks' heads, and to Amun's, decorated with rams' heads. A niche contains the statues of the three divinities worshipped in the sanctuary, which were badly damaged by the early Christians.

When Roberts reached Wadi Saboua, the hypogean part could not be visited, as it was blocked by a great mass of sand that also partly obstructed the courtyard. He also noticed that the friable material with which the building was constructed was showing evident signs of erosion, and that many blocks were loose, perhaps because of earth tremors. In fact, when the sanctuary was reconstructed, it required extensive restoration work.

From David Roberts's journal:

6th November - Much of the temple is buried under the sand, the smooth surface of which is only broken by the trails left by snakes and the tiny tracks of a few lizards. The words of the Biblical prophecy really seem to have come wholly true, "I will make the land of Egypt utterly waste and desolate, from Migdol to Syene and even unto the border of Ethiopia."

Temple of Wadi Saboua, Nubia

Two colossal statues in the Temple of Wadi Saboua

Plate 18

Two enormous statues stood guard in front of the pylon, terminating the long access dromos to the temple, and two more, portraying Rameses II with the headgear and emblems of the god Osiris, stood at the start of the avenue. Only the Colossus, which Roberts portrayed standing, now survives; the others have been stolen or destroyed. The statue portrays the sovereign with the symbol of Amun-Ra, a long stick that ends in a ram's head surmounted by the solar disk and the uraeus, the sacred cobra that symbolized light and sovereignty. Rameses is wearing the Nubian hairstyle of fine plaits, with a narrow band around his head and the uraeus on his forehead. The Temple of Wadi Saboua is the only Nubian sanctuary whose dromos has survived, though only in part.

Before the temple was rebuilt in an area 198 feet higher than the original site, this avenue led directly from the bank of the Nile to the sanctuary. Roberts stayed at Wadi Saboua all day on the 6th of November, and set off the next morning for Abu Simbel after measuring and drawing properly the ruins of the sanctuary. On several occasions the Scotsman wrote of how much he enjoyed the long hours spent sailing down the great river, and not only because of the splendid landscape; he was also exceedingly proud of leading a crew of such skilled men. He often observed the bright Union Jack fluttering from the mast with equal pleasure, especially when they passed other vessels flying weatherworn flags or the crescent of the pasha of Egypt.

From David Roberts's journal:

9th November - This morning I finally reached Abu Simbel, the great temple excavated in rock that has so often been described. Carved on the mountain face are four colossal human figures in a seated position.

THE ARRIVAL AT THE TEMPLES OF ABU SIMBEL

Plate 19

7th-9th November 1838

On the morning of the 7th of November, the two boats moored near Kosocko, a pleasant looking town where it was decided to spend the entire day. The rest was very welcome after such a long navigation, and Roberts spent the time observing local customs with his usual interest. At sunset the crew went back on board, and a few hours later, Hassaia and Derr were already receding into the distance.

In the early hours of the next morning the Scottish artist viewed the magnificent ruins of the fortress of Ibrim, which he decided to examine with greater attention on the return trip as the destination of his voyage was now only a few miles away.

Abu Simbel appeared on the horizon as night was falling, and only the increasing darkness could delay the long-awaited moment. After a few hours' sleep, David Roberts finally arrived in front of the two huge temples excavated in the rock: it was dawn on Friday, 9th November 1838.

Abu Simbel had been discovered only 25 years earlier, in March 1813, by famous Swiss explorer Johann Ludwig Burckhardt, but its fame had already spread far and wide. Englishman William John Bankes and Italian Giovanni Finati, attracted by the description of the fabulous site, had managed to enter the smaller temple, dedicated to Hathor and Queen Nefertari, in 1815, but were unable to shift the great mass of sand that obstructed the façade of the large temple. All they could see of it was the bust of one of the four great statues of Rameses II. After a similarly fruitless attempt by Piedmontese Consul Drovetti, Giovanni Battista Belzoni finally managed to enter the temple on the 1st of August 1817 after spending more than a month in the difficult undertaking of removing the sand.

When Roberts reached the spot, the gorge that separated the two rock temples was still partly blocked by a great sand dune that reached down to the waters of the Nile, but the two monuments were mostly visible. Roberts was the first to depict them correctly in all their splendor, with his usual meticulous attention to architectural proportions and details.

9th November - It is appalling to see these masterpieces of ancient art not only massacred by souvenir hunters but actually covered with the signatures of every Tomkins, Smith and Hopkins. One of the hands of the best preserved colossus has been literally destroyed by these vandals who, not content with having taken a finger of the great statue as a souvenir of their deplorable exploit, have then had the gall to carve their stupid names on the very forehead of the god.

THE GREAT TEMPLE
OF ABU SIMBEL

Plate 20

9th November 1838

*R*oberts
*described Abu Simbel as
"the monument which alone
makes the trip to Nubia
worthwhile." The colossi were
in an exceptionally good state
of preservation, undoubtedly
due to the long period they
had spent buried in the sand,
which sheltered them from the
ravages of time and the elements.
However, in the few years that
had elapsed since their discovery,
the stupidity of Western travelers
had already left its indelible
mark; dozens of signatures
carved in the stone ruined
their solemnity, and the same
vandals had removed numerous
fragments to show off as
souvenirs on their return
home. Disgusted at the sight
of this vandalism, Roberts
expressed the hope that the sand
would providentially return
to cover the magnificent
sanctuary. It is therefore curious,
to say the least, that in the
lithograph the signature
of none other than Roberts himself
appears right on the instep of
the first colossus. However, the
blame for this embarrassing
incident can be attributed to Louis
Haghe, who probably thought
that the artist would be pleased
if he added this unfortunate
detail. This hypothesis is borne
out by the fact that the signature
is followed by the initials R.A.
(Royal Academician), which
Roberts would not have added
himself since he did not actually
become a member of the Royal
Academy until two years after his
return home.*

The Colossi of Rameses ii at Abu Simbel

Plate 21

9th November 1838

Even today, the temple's gigantic proportions are astonishing: its façade is 125 feet wide and 100 feet high, the equivalent of a modern nine-storey building. The four statues, which stand over 65 feet tall, finely reproduce the features of the sovereign, adorned with the crowns of Upper and Lower Egypt and the cobra symbol, the uraeus, the attribute of Osiris. From the purely static point of view the architects of the period solved the serious problem of the stability of the complex by using the four colossi as load-bearing pillars, against which the enormous load of the rock mass behind was equally distributed. A multitude of slaves under the orders of head sculptor Pyay, whose name is recalled in an inscription, completed the elaborate front of the temple, framed by a convex molding called a torus, surmounted by a cornice with uraei, above which runs a high-relief strip depicting twenty-two seated baboons, each over eight feet tall. Below the torus runs a molding carved with dedicatory hieroglyphics, and further down, in a niche in the middle of the façade, is the great statue portraying Ra-Harakhti with a sparrow hawk's head.

As the god rests his right hand on the scepter with the head of the jackal (User) and his left on the scepter with the figure of Maat, goddess of truth and justice, the three figures form the name User-Maat-Ra, adopted by the pharaoh when he ascended to the throne. At the sides, two large bas-reliefs portray the features of Rameses II. Between the legs of each colossus stand other smaller statues that portray the members of the royal family; there are pictures of black and Asian prisoners on the plinth and on the sides of the chairs. The work of stone masons and sculptors was followed by that of painters, but time and the incessant ravages of wind and sand have entirely cancelled out what at the time of Rameses must have been a very rich range of colors. The ruthless work of nature attacked the temple even in ancient times; in fact, the most serious damage was caused by earth tremors. One of the colossi, the third from the left, was repaired in the time of Pharaoh Sethi II, around 1200 BC, while the upper part of the second, which fell during the 34th year of Rameses' reign, has lain on the ground ever since.

*9th November - The beauty and size
of the temple are not surpassed by any
other Egyptian monument, even the
Theban sanctuaries. If it is compared
with the heads of Isis decorating the
capitals of the Temple of Dendera, the
most elaborate and best finished of the
Egyptian temples, the poor goddess
actually seems coarse. And to think
that Dendera is far more recent than
Abu Simbel!*

THE INTERIOR OF THE GREAT TEMPLE AT ABU SIMBEL

Plate 22

9th November 1838

The rock sanctuary of Abu Simbel symbolizes the boundless ambitions of the most powerful pharaoh of ancient Egypt. Dedicated in theory to the triad of divinities consisting of Amen-Ra, Harmakhis and Ptah, the temple was actually built to glorify over the centuries the name of its builder, Rameses II the Great, who reigned for 67 long years, from 1290 to 1224 BC. The images of the Pharaoh, repeated some hundred times on the façade and the walls of the several rooms, show him at various moments of his life: son, husband, proud father, victorious warrior and, finally, worshipped as a god on earth. However, it would be a mistake to consider Abu Simbel as the embodiment of a megalomaniac's dream, because Rameses II was actually a great sovereign, skilled diplomat and brilliant strategist whose self-deification was the last stage in a plan aimed at making his rule totally stable. From the architectural standpoint, the sanctuary is nothing other than the magnificent transposition of the architectural features of the classic Egyptian temple into the living rock. Thus, while the façade was designed as a pylon, the succession of rooms built behind rather than above it involved the mammoth task of penetrating layers of sandstone. The experience of moving from the outside, flooded with blinding light, to the silent darkness of the pronaos, is an indescribable one that greatly moved the Scottish artist. The ceiling of the huge rectangular room, 60 feet long and 50 feet wide, is supported by eight pillars, 30 feet tall, arranged in two rows, on each of which rests a statue representing Osiris with the features of Rameses II. The giants on the left wear the white crown of Upper Egypt, while those on the right wear the pschent (double crown); the hands crossed on the chest hold the heka (scepter) and the nekhaka (scourge), both symbols of power and royalty. A great vulture, the emblem of the goddess Nekhebet, protectress of Upper Egypt, is painted on the ceiling of the nave, while the ceilings of the aisles represent a starry sky. Most of the wall paintings illustrate scenes from the Battle of Kadesh, which victoriously concluded the pharaoh's military campaign against the Hittites in the fifth year of his reign. Many scenes show the sovereign sacrificing prisoners to the gods, and the bas-relief that shows the pharaoh standing in his war chariot seizing his bow is an absolute masterpiece. Six more rooms, in which the votive offerings were placed, surround this room to the right and left. The pronaos is followed by a second hypostyle room supported by four square pillars on which pictures of the pharaoh seated in front of various divinities are painted. Note the blunder made in the dating of the plate by Haghe or one of his assistants; the day and month are correct, but the year is wrong.

The naos of the Great Temple at Abu Simbel

Plate 23

10th November 1838

The sacrarium, the most remote and secret part of the temple, is situated 215 feet from the entrance, in the heart of the mountain. In this small room, which measures 13 feet wide and just over 23 feet deep, stand the statues of Amun-Ra, Harmakhis, Ptah and Rameses II. Careful observation of the arrangement of the temple revealed as early as the 19th century that the complex was built in accordance with a precise plan, in which nothing was left to chance. Twice a year, at the solstices, a ray of sunlight penetrates the corridor separating the entrance from the naos at 5:58 a.m. and floods the left shoulder of Amun-Ra with light. A few moments later, having touched the image of the sovereign, it concentrates on Harmakhis. The "sun miracle" lasts for around 20 minutes. It is very significant that the statue of the last divinity is never touched by the sunbeam, as Ptah was the Lord of Darkness. However, the fascination of Abu Simbel is not limited only to this ingenious system. In order to understand the significance of the Nubian temple fully, it should be remembered that this was the sanctuary in which Rameses II decided to deify himself. The pharaoh originally worshipped Horus, son of Isis and Osiris and Lord of Meha; he later began to identify with the god himself, and decided to excavate a temple in the same mountain of Meha, now called Abu Simbel. The gradual illumination of the three divinities takes place between the 10th of February and the 1st of March, and from the 10th of October through the 30th.

On the 21st of February and the 21st of October the first rays of the sun are exactly on the axis of the temple; the second date corresponds to the first jubilee, celebrated after 30 years of Ramses II's reign. Here, Rameses II is identified with a solar divinity the equal of Amun-Ra and Harmakhis. When it became necessary to dismantle the temples of Abu Simbel and rebuild them in a higher position to save them from the waters of the artificial Lake Nasser, special attention was paid to the orientation of the main sanctuary so that the "miracle of the sun" could still take place.

The work began in spring 1964 under the sponsorship of UNESCO, and was completed four years later. The Great Temple was cut into 807 blocks with an average weight of 20 tons each and reassembled on a huge reinforced concrete skeleton.

The great illumination event was repeated in February 1969, taking place just as it did 3,000 years earlier, and continues to this day.

From David Roberts's journal:

9th November - In the cella there are four plaster-covered, painted deities; opposite them stand the remains of an altar, also excavated in the living rock. The corners are intact and regular, but the top is damaged. It is the only thing of the kind I have seen so far, and it is truly fascinating. Some 24 inches in front of the altar there are grooves and holes in the walls on both sides, perhaps left by a kind of gate that prevented worshippers from entering the room.

FROM ABU SIMBEL TO CAIRO

11th November - 21st December 1838

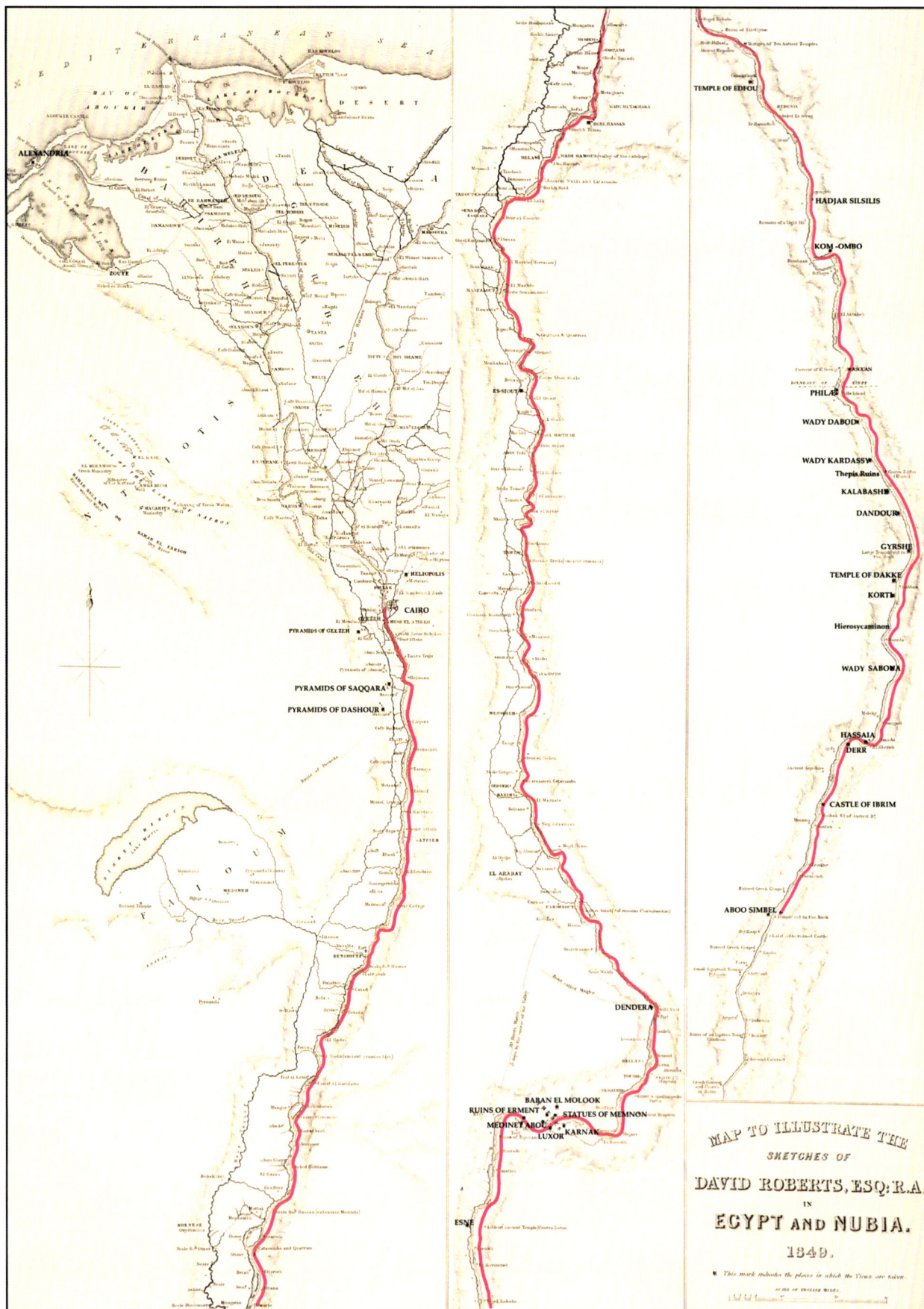

MAP TO ILLUSTRATE THE SKETCHES OF DAVID ROBERTS, ESQ. R.A. IN EGYPT AND NUBIA. 1849.

EGYPT & NUBIA

David Roberts R.A.

WILLIAM BROCKEDON

LOUIS HAGHE

Entrance to the Great Temple of Aboo-Simbel, Nubia.

LONDON, F. G. MOON, 20, THREADNEEDLE STREET.
PUBLISHED BY ORDINARY TO HER MAJESTY.
MDCCCXLVI.

THE NILE IN THE VICINITY OF THE FORTRESS OF IBRIM

Plate 24

11th-12th November 1838

*A*bu Simbel, 530 miles from Cairo, was usually the southernmost point reached by European travelers of the day, and Roberts was no exception. While the artist was busy with his pencils and watercolors, the other members of the expedition continued as far as Wadi Halfa to see the Second Cataract of the Nile; however, their description, far from interesting him, persuaded him to go no further. He decided that it would be far more convenient to finish his last drawings (which demonstrate his great preference for the Great Temple over the Sanctuary of Hathor and Nefertari, inhabited by swarms of bats and other "beasties") and immediately commence the return journey. On the 11th of November, as evening fell, the two boats began to descend the river, and a few hours later tied up near the Fortress of Ibrim. These few notes written by the author reveal the feeling of relief felt by the entire party at that change of horizon: "Thank God our vessel's prow now faces the north and civilisation." For weeks Roberts and the others had borne the most intolerable heat, eaten dates and drunk brackish water, suffered from mosquito and horsefly bites and often slept in uncomfortable conditions, wrapped in their jackets to protect themselves against the damp of the night, so the mere thought of the comforts of Cairo must have seemed like heaven.

From David Roberts's journal:

11th November - The rubble lies in layers, and it seems clear that the village which grew up around the fortress was built on the ruins of the previous ones. The fortress must have been very powerful and well defended; some ruins here and there indicate its very remote origin.

THE FORTRESS OF IBRIM

Plate 25

12th November 1838

*A*fter waking at sunrise, Roberts spent the early hours of the 12th drawing. The ruins of the Fortress of Ibrim, which stood alone on a tall promontory jutting out over the river, made a very attractive sight, and to some extent recalled the Moorish castles he had visited during his journey to Spain. The origins of the fortress date back to the period of Roman rule, when the place was known as Primis and occupied one of the most strategically important positions in all Nubia, standing guard over the traffic along the Nile. In the 16th century the fortress was occupied by the Bosnian contingent sent by Sultan Selim I to conquer the region; it was held in 1812 by the Mamluks fleeing from the army of Mohammed Ali's son Ibrahim, but was retaken and destroyed by him. Sadly, the majestic ruins of the fortress are now submerged by the waters of Lake Nasser, so that Roberts's work has a unique historical value. From this point on the artist makes no explicit mention of his traveling companions, so it is probable that Captain Nelley, Mr. V. and Mr. A. decided to return directly to Cairo.

THE TEMPLE OF AMADA
AT HASSAYA

Plate 26

12th-13th November 1838

During the night the boat reached Derr, the capital of Nubia, which Roberts described as a large city whose houses were certainly better built and more attractive than those of Lower Egypt. Oddly, the walls of the buildings sloped inwards, so that the houses were shaped like truncated pyramids. Roberts was particularly impressed by a huge sycamore that stood right in the middle of the capital. He also visited the small rock temple located nearby, but did not draw it,

hovels; the pronaos was surmounted by the unwieldy bulk of a mud and straw dome, almost certainly built when the temple was converted into a Christian church.
The sanctuary, which was founded by Thutmoses III and continued by Amenhotep II in the 15th century BC, is not particularly large, but its proportions are very elegant and it is entirely covered with reliefs of exquisite workmanship.
During the campaign to save the Nubian monuments,

certainly because it must have seemed very modest by comparison with Abu Simbel. The next day he visited the Sanctuary of Amada, near Hassaya. The building was partly buried by sand and surrounded by various ruined

the Temple of Amada was entirely enclosed in a steel and cement framework weighing 990 tons and moved to its new site, nearly two miles away and 200 feet higher, by a three-rail rack railway built expressly for this purpose.

From David Roberts's journal:

13th November - The temple is still intact, and its walls, like those of the two rooms communicating with it, are covered with tiny hieroglyphics of exquisite workmanship, carved with far greater expertise than those generally seen in similar buildings. Their colours are bright, and in almost perfect condition.

THE TEMPLE OF
WADI MAHARRAKA

Plate 27

14th November 1838

After spending the whole night sailing down the river, in the early hours of the 14th of November, Roberts came in sight of the Temple of Maharraka, which he had already visited ten days earlier. The small building was in an advanced state of disrepair, but 14 of the 16 columns in the inner courtyard were still standing. Because of the roughly hewn capitals and almost total absence of wall decorations, the artist easily deduced that the building, like most of the Nubian temples, had remained unfinished because of the spread of Christianity in the region; in addition, the numerous frescoes depicting Biblical subjects that were still visible clearly demonstrated that the sanctuary, originally dedicated to Isis and Serapis, had been converted into a church. The temple, of which all that remains is the hypostyle room illustrated by Roberts, stood in the ancient Hierasykaminos (City of the Sacred Sycamore), which marked the southernmost border of the Roman Empire from 23 BC to AD 297. The spiral staircase in the north east corner leading to the portico roof constitutes a unique exception in Egyptian architecture, and can only be explained by the fact that the temple was almost certainly designed by a Roman architect.

The Temple of Maharraka, restored in 1908, was dismantled during the campaign to save the Nubian monuments and rebuilt at New Saboua. After the construction of the Great Aswan Dam, inaugurated on the 15th of January 1971, no less than 20 temples standing on the banks of the Nile between the First and Second Cataracts ran the risk of being submerged by the waters of the great artificial Lake Nasser. In order to save them, UNESCO devised one of the most extraordinary international salvage programs ever undertaken to preserve architectural and art treasures, which concluded with the recovery of most of the sanctuaries in the preservation areas. Five of the minor temples were donated by Egypt to countries that had generously participated in the huge project (the United States, the Netherlands, Germany, Italy and Spain) and reconstructed in those countries. The main ones were assembled in three different areas: New Kalabsha, where the rock temple of Beit el-Wali is also located, New Saboua and New Amada. However, despite these mammoth efforts, not all the Nubian monuments could be saved, and some of them lie forever beneath the waters of the Nile.

Nubian Women at Kortis, on the Nile

NUBIAN WOMEN AT KORTI

Plate 28

14th November 1838

This lithograph, generally omitted from modern reproductions of Roberts's works as no monument appears in it, provides insight into the tastes of the period in which he lived and worked, which were already quite chaste, but not yet fiercely repressed by Victorian morality. The scene shows young Nubian women carrying water near Korti, a village where the boat tied up on the afternoon of the 14th of November; however, the author pays more attention to the beauty of the girls than to local customs.

Roberts was evidently equally susceptible to the charms of the exotic and the charms of women, and in this rare case his temperament as a man and an artist led him to take an unaccustomed liberty. Many other contemporary artists, like Emile Prisse d'Avennes, were dazzled by the sinuous grace of the local girls, especially the most scantily clad, who constituted an excellent subject in the name of art. This subject could also be enjoyed without embarrassment by the purchaser of the work, on the pretext of learned ethnological interest. Various entries in Roberts's journal mention the beauty of the local women with great enthusiasm; it is a pity that these accounts were censored in several places by the prudish Christine, who evidently considered certain passages too licentious to be made public, as she thought they might show her famous father in a dubious light. This is a pity, because the portrait of the artist would certainly have gained in humanity and become less antiseptic if these passages had been presented in their entirety.

A GROUP OF ABYSSINIAN SLAVES AT KORTI

Plate 29

14th November 1838

*N*ear Korti, Roberts came upon a group of Abyssinian slaves, mostly young women, who were waiting in the shade of a few stunted palm trees to be taken to the Cairo market. The girl in the middle of the lithograph is preparing the dourra *flour needed to make bread in accordance with a thousand-year-old method. Like all Europeans, Roberts was upset and revolted by the inhuman practice of slavery and, despite the bucolic appearance of this lithograph, he found the scene horrifying. Nearly all the slaves were frightened-looking young women and children; some appeared to be suffering from fever, and two, who lay at some distance from the others, seemed to be close to death. In Egypt, Abyssinian girls were quite expensive because of their good character, intelligence and great beauty.*

The poor girls suffered greatly during the journey, but once purchased by their new masters were well fed and clothed, and treated kindly. They usually joined the harems of the middle classes or a wealthy man. The merchants in the lithograph were handsome Nubians, apart from one brute with violent manners, certainly a drug addict, who for a while insisted on tormenting Roberts and his men in the vain attempt to conclude a deal. This lithograph, which represents invaluable evidence of an age that fortunately is no more, is of historical interest for a second reason. In the background, Roberts inserted a general view of the Temple of Amun at Wadi Dabod, actually several miles from Korti; the sanctuary was then practically intact, but a few decades later, around 1894, the first of the three pylons was swept away by the Nile.

From David Roberts's journal:

14th November - At Korti there are the remains of a very small temple which is hardly worth a visit. However, the town is quite interesting. On our arrival the inhabitants seemed very frightened, especially the women and children, who actually ran away. We were told that this strange behaviour is due to the fact that many of them are often carried away as slaves, and the mere appearance of a white man has the power to terrify them.

THE TEMPLE OF DAKKE

Plate 30

14th November 1838

*T*wo hours'
march from Korti stood the
magnificent ruins of the Temple
of Dakke, a gem of architecture
and sculpture that Roberts
hastened to reach before sunset.
The sanctuary, of moderate but
very well balanced dimensions,
was consecrated to the god
Thoth of Pnubs, an Ethiopian
town that the Greeks called
Paotnuphis. The building
which, unlike all the other
Nubian temples, is oriented
from north to south, was
erected in the late 3rd century
BC by order of Ethiopian
King Arqamon and his
contemporary, the Macedonian
Pharaoh Ptolemy IV Philopator.
Later, Ptolemy VII Evergete II
added the pronaos, but the
temple only acquired its final
appearance during Roman rule,
after the construction of the
great pylon inserted in the outer
boundary walls, which have
almost disappeared.
Some reliefs and numerous
inscriptions in Greek and
Demotic by ancient visitors
appear on the front façades
of the two towers; the habit
of leaving one's mark on
monuments evidently dates
back to a very early age.
The colonnaded courtyard,
which originally stood between
the pylon and the pronaos,
has been entirely destroyed,
whereas the rear of the temple
is well preserved.
The sanctuary of Dakke
had to be dismantled after
the construction of the Aswan
High Dam and rebuilt at New
Saboua; during the work it was
discovered that some blocks,
evidently reused, had belonged
to an older temple dating from
the age of Queen Hatshepsut
and dedicated to the god Horus
of Baki. That town, from which
trails led to the gold mines
of Umm Garayat, is now
submerged under the waters
of Lake Nasser.
Note the clearly incorrect date
in the bottom right-hand corner
of the lithograph, probably due
to a mistake by Haghe or his
assistants.

From David Roberts's journal:

14th November - The Temple of Dakke is of such exquisite workmanship that anyone wishing to take a perfect specimen of the beauty of Egyptian art back to Europe need travel no further.

THE ROCK TEMPLE OF GYRSHE

Plate 31

15th November 1838

*R*oberts left Dakke in the late evening, and reached Gyrshe (which later became known as Gerf Hussein) in the middle of the night. Tireless as ever, at sunrise he was already on the way to the rise where a rock temple, excavated during the reign of Rameses II, stood. This lithograph and the description of the place in his travel journal now appear to be permeated by an aura of tragedy, for the sanctuary of "Rameses-Meryamun in the Dominion of Ptah" is lost for ever. The poor state of preservation of the structures, the crumbling rock, high costs and lack of time made it impracticable to save this monument during the UNESCO salvage campaign. Thus in the mid-sixties it fell victim to the waters of Lake Nasser together with countless burial grounds, rock tombs, votive shrines, chapels, and the ruins of fortresses, churches and Coptic monasteries.

The temple, consecrated to Ptah, Hathor, Ptah-Tatjenen and the deified Rameses II, was built by Setau, viceroy of Kush, the name by which Upper Nubia was then known; Lower Nubia was known as Wawat, while the Greeks called the whole region Ethiopia. A pronaos with columns built onto the rock wall preceded the hypogeal part, which was some 100 feet deep and consisted of the hypostyle room portrayed by Roberts, a transverse room and the cella containing the statues of the divinities. The artist noted that the various rooms, inhabited by a myriad bats, had already deteriorated badly because of the fires lit by shepherds who had used the temple for shelter over the centuries. Many of the reliefs and hieroglyphics were by then indecipherable, but the hypostyle room, supported by six colossi portraying Rameses the Great with the headdress of Upper Egypt, maintained all of its mysterious fascination.

From David Roberts's journal:

15th November - We reached Gyrshe last night, and by daybreak this morning I was on my way to the hill where the temple is excavated. The ascent seems to have been originally a flight of steps, on each side of which the sphinxes now lying scattered about have been placed. Only two of the 12 columns of the portico are still standing, supporting a trabeation that projects from the living rock. There are various rooms, colossal statues and wall decorations in the temple, but all is badly damaged, and the figures on the walls are barely recognisable.

Excavated Temple of Gyrche - Nubia

D. Roberts RA

Temple of Kalabshah - Nubia - Novr 1838

THE TEMPLE OF KALABSHA

Plate 32

15th November 1838

Satisfied by his visit to the Temple of Gyrshe, by the late afternoon on the 15th of November, Roberts was already at Kalabsha, where he ordered the tents to be pitched for the night. As there was enough light and the sketches he had drawn on the outward journey were quite detailed, the artist had time to complete two views of the great sanctuary. The temple, considered the most grandiose Nubian monument after Abu Simbel, was built in the Ptolemaic period on the foundations of an older one, dating from the time of Amenhotep II and consecrated to the local god Mandulis, associated with Isis and Osiris. Rebuilt during the reign of Augustus, it remained almost entirely bare of decorations, and the little decoration there appears unfinished.

The 245-foot-long building could be reached from the Nile along a processional route that climbed to two huge platforms built at different levels, both in front of the pylon. The façade of the pylon has no reliefs, and its plainness is only relieved by the usual grooves in which the flagpoles of the sacred banners were fixed. The impressive size of the temple was justified by the strategic importance of Talmis, the ancient name of Kalabsha, which stood guard over a narrow stretch of the Nile; the building was converted into a church and fell into ruin after the Arab conquest.

In the lithograph, humble mud dwellings seem to huddle around the massive bulk of the temple, and even cluster on the roof of the naos, as if seeking protection, to form a scenario common to nearly all the Egyptian archaeological sites in the 19th century. The place drawn by Roberts no longer exists today, as it was submerged by the waters of Lake Nasser; all that survives is the temple, which, between 1961 and 1963, was dismantled and rebuilt 25 miles further south at New Kalabsha, at the western end of the Great Aswan Dam.

From David Roberts's journal:

15th November - After leaving Gyrshe, towards evening we were again in sight of the Temple of Kalabsha, the loveliest in Nubia. Situated in a loop of the river in the middle of a stretch of barren rocks, surrounded by palm and acacia trees, it is only seen to be ruined from close by. The reliefs have such clear-cut edges that they seem to have been recently carved, and the whole, with its elegant proportions and delicate details, is in no way inferior even to Philae.

The pronaos of the Temple of Kalabsha

Plate 33

15th November 1838

*B*eyond the pylon is a courtyard surrounded on three sides by a portico, most of whose columns had fallen and been buried by debris when Roberts saw them. The end wall is constituted by the façade of the atrium, in the middle of which is an impressive portal. According to the canons of Egyptian Ptolemaic and Roman art, the intercolumniations are partly closed by screens covered with bas-reliefs portraying, among other things, the gods Thot and Horus performing libations by pouring holy water onto the sovereign. On one of the columns, a long inscription in Meroitic (the language spoken by the Nubians under Ptolemaic and Roman rule) recounts the victory of King Silko over his eternal enemies the Blemmyes; the epigraph is translated into bad Greek on one of the intercolumnar walls. In the atrium, 12 columns with capitals featuring plant designs support the ceiling, much of which has now collapsed. Of the various reliefs present here, two are of some interest; the first shows one of the Ptolemies making offerings to Mandulis, while the other portrays the founder of the first sanctuary, Amenhotep II, offering wine to Min and the patron god of the temple. The atrium is followed by the sacrarium, formed by three successive chambers that leave enough space around them for a corridor inside the perimeter wall, built as a continuance of the side walls of the courtyard. The complex was enclosed by a high embankment that formed a corridor similar to the previous one. This plan simplifies the elements of the typical Ptolemaic-Roman temple, while still retaining its general layout.

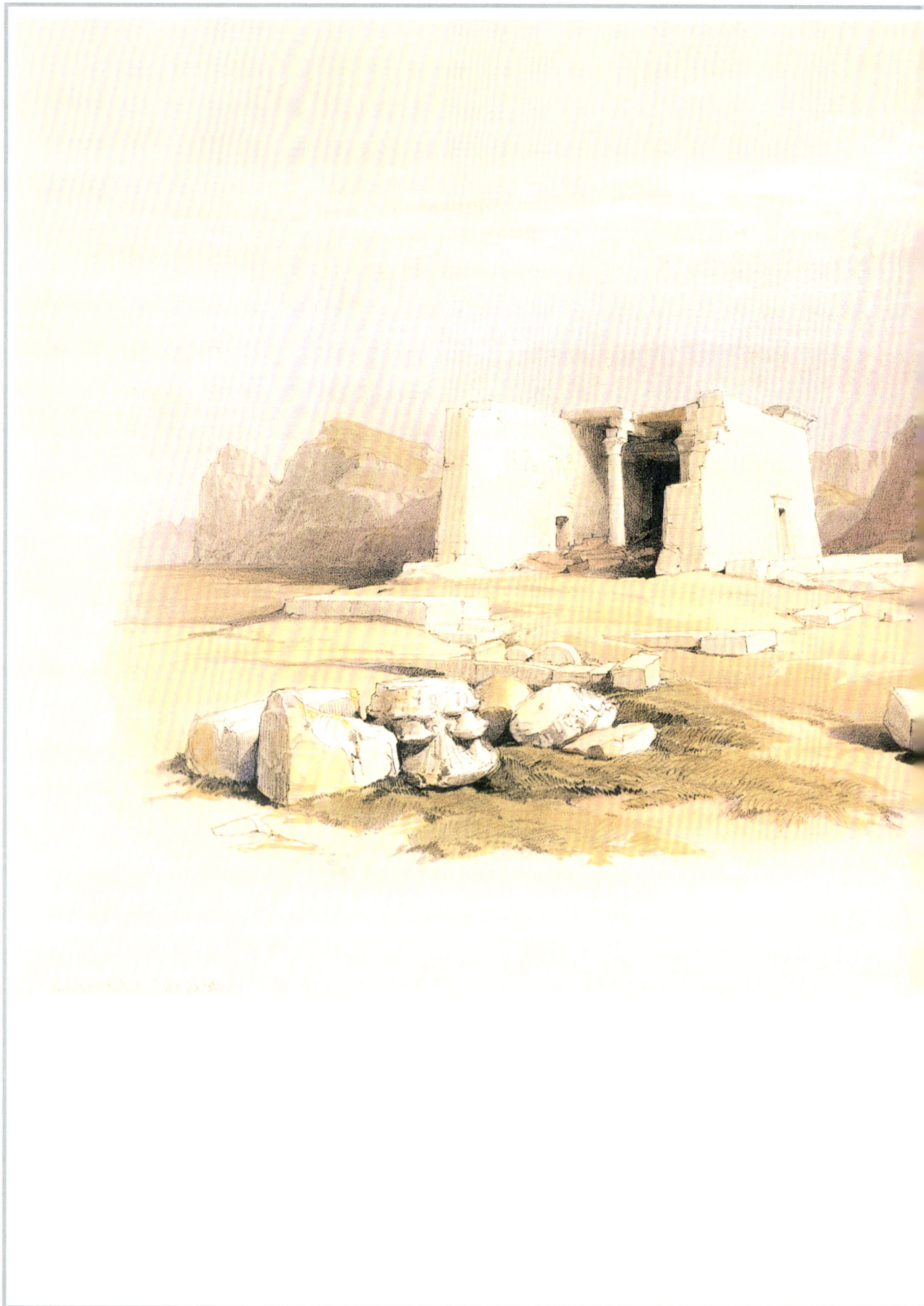

THE RUINS OF THE TEMPLE OF TAFA

Plate 34

16th November 1838

From Abu Simbel onwards the Scotsman ordered his men to stop frequently, not only so that he could draw the ruined monuments in the various places but also to enable him to buy ancient coins, swords, amulets and small antiques, or to ask the most attractive girls to pose for him. These breaks were welcomed by his men, who were becoming increasingly lazy as a result of women's company and banquets. In the preceding few days he had often had to resort to threats and flattery to make them row faster, but whenever he became engrossed in sketching his supervision ceased, and the crew returned on board even less eagerly than before. The same thing happened at Kalabsha, and Roberts had a certain amount of trouble persuading the crew to depart for Tafa, where he arrived on the morning of the 16th of November.

Here, not far from Wadi Kardassy, stood two small temples very similar to others he had already seen in the region. It is fortunate that Roberts decided to draw this, the most badly damaged one; while the north temple, which was almost intact, was donated to the Netherlands and has been on display at the National Museum in Leyden since 1978, the south temple was used as a source of reusable materials from 1870 onwards, and was entirely dismantled.

The sanctuary, which together with its neighbor formed the religious center of the Roman settlement of Taphis, was founded in the late Ptolemaic period and extensively rebuilt during the Roman occupation of Lower Nubia. Roberts described it as a building of rather modest manufacture and unharmonious proportions, surrounded by architectural fragments scattered over the adjacent plain.

The Little Temple of Wadi Kardassy

Plate 35

16th November 1838

As the day was not too hot, Roberts continued on foot from Tafa to Wadi Kardassy. On his way he passed through various villages, whose inhabitants crowded around him curiously. In the early afternoon he finally came in sight of the rocky plateau on which stood a small kiosk, consecrated to the goddess Isis, that was similar in layout to the one on Philae. At that time the building, which overlooked the Nile, constituted one of the most impressive scenes in all of Lower Nubia. Sadly, following the construction of the Sadd el-Ali (High Dam) at Aswan, this site disappeared, engulfed by the huge mass of water of the reservoir, which, with an area of 2,100 square miles and a length of 316 miles, is the second largest in the world. Lake Nasser has brought undeniable financial advantages to Egypt, but at the same time has upset the ecological balance in the region and inflicted untold damage on the archaeological heritage and landscape of Nubia.

Temple of Wady Kardassy
Nubia

Ruins of the Temple of Kardassy, Nubia

THE LITTLE TEMPLE OF WADI KARDASSY WITH THE NILE IN THE BACKGROUND

Plate 36

16th November 1838

The little temple, or rather the kiosk, of Kardassy is a small building only about ten square yards, built in the late Ptolemaic period and completed during Roman rule. It was originally formed by ten columns connected by low intercolumnar walls, only six of which are still standing; the two on either side of the portal are surmounted by elegant capitals with the face of the goddess Hathor, while the others support capitals of floral inspiration.

It is interesting to note that the two Hathor capitals in turn support two stylized altars, containing an asp.

As can be clearly seen in the lithograph, this building, unlike the Temple of Philae, which was never finished, was roofed with huge monolithic slabs, all but one of which have been destroyed. The intercolumnar walls are bare, apart from the long row of uraei surrounding the upper strip and the winged solar disks appearing immediately below it.

As demonstrated by a number of crosses carved inside it, the building was used as a church until the advent of Islam. The Roman legionnaires built a fortress near the temple to guard traffic along the Nile and the nearby stone quarries. The kiosk of Kardassy was dismantled during the campaign to save the Nubian temples and reassembled near the Temple of Kalabsha, some 25 miles away from its ancient site. Unfortunately, its new location is far less spectacular than the original one.

From David Roberts's journal:

16th November - It is hard to guess at the age of the building from its condition, as the devastation which has spoilt it seems to have been wreaked but yesterday. The temple is dazzling in the sunlight against the deep blue of the sky, and it almost seems as though the hand of its destroyers had just ceased its work. Because of the total absence of moisture, the stones ring like bells at the slightest touch.

A GROUP OF NUBIANS NEAR THE TEMPLE OF WADI KARDASSY

Plate 37

16th November 1838

*A*t Wadi Kardassy, Roberts bought some copper coins from a woman, while a man offered him a long sword (which he described as being similar to those carried by the Scottish Highlanders) and another smaller one that he wore hanging from his belt. Keen to strike a bargain like all self-respecting tourists, Roberts also bought from the same man an attractive bracelet that he saw on his left arm, a small hippopotamus-hide shield and a water bottle with a hide cover decorated with shells, all for only 30 shillings, which was a very reasonable price even for that period.

Especially at first, Roberts had no great respect for the Nubians, who to his Western eyes seemed little more than savages. Only long acquaintance with the two Nubians in the crew, both called Hassan, and the slowly dawning realization of how much those people suffered from harassment by slave traders and compulsory conscription by Pasha Mohammed Ali, led him to mitigate his opinion considerably. Above all, he truly admired the physical appearance and sincere friendliness of the Nubians, "with their well-proportioned bodies and frank, intelligent expressions." However, he was appalled by the women's habit of smearing themselves with butter or castor oil to soften their skin and keep away parasites, mainly because of the nauseous smell that ceaselessly issued from their bodies; otherwise, he considered them splendid, indeed desirable. Far less prejudiced than he had been only a few days earlier, at Wadi Kardassy Roberts decided to immortalize a group of local inhabitants, many of whom wore a singular hairstyle of very ancient origin. Of the weapons they held, only the spears were part of their usual equipment; they had brought the long swords and shields to sell.

THE NILE NEAR WADI DABOD

Plate 38

16th November 1838

Roberts left Wadi Kardassy in the afternoon, and came in sight of the heights of Wadi Dabod at sunset. As the boat sailed along, following the placid current of the river, his attention was attracted by a number of crocodiles basking on the sandy shores, as if to absorb the last rays of the sun. These formidable reptiles, up to 20 feet long, with an array of lethal teeth, were the true rulers of the Nile for centuries, feared and respected by the local people to the extent of being worshipped as the earthly manifestation of a deity, Sobek of Kom Ombo. The cult of this god had some interesting features. In various regions the crocodile was worshipped in ancient times as the supreme deity, but later began to be identified first as an ally and then as the actual personification of Set, the god of evil and enemy of Osiris, so that the crocodile itself became less and less important. However, the danger represented by the great predator was still sufficient to win it the terrified respect of those who had to cross the river every day; its sly movements, exceptional strength and speed made it a formidable enemy.

There were numerous crocodiles between Gebel el-Silsila and Kom Ombo; they lived in large family groups on the sandbanks and in the shallows in the middle of the river, taking a heavy toll of human lives every year. It is therefore easy to understand why Sobek continued to be worshipped with particular fervor in the region, and his image was frequently evoked as a propitiatory totem by boatmen. Even in the 19th century, blood-curdling tales were told about crocodiles, and the local people were terrified of them. They only lost their supremacy on the river after the construction of the first Aswan Dam, and they have now almost disappeared from the part of the Nile that flows through Egypt. Although the lithograph is very effective, it is highly unlikely that the artist ventured very close to the lethal creatures; he probably left this doubtful privilege to the herons shown in the plate, who earned their safety and food by picking parasites off these descendants of the prehistoric dinosaurs.

107

General view
of the Island of Philae

Plate 39

17th-18th November 1838

On the 17th of November, when darkness fell, Roberts was back on the Island of Philae, where he spent the next two days drawing the temples that had so impressed him less than three weeks earlier. This stop was welcomed with great enthusiasm by Hassan Amoris (so called to distinguish him from a fellow crew member also called Hassan), as the beautiful wife who had won him his nickname lived in the region of the First Cataract. This magnificent view shows the entire complex, seen from the of heterogeneous elements of different periods, although most of the buildings date from the Ptolemaic-Roman period. On the far right of the lithograph is the Kiosk of Nectanebo and the neighboring obelisk, both dating from the 4th century BC; opposite them are the two wings of the colonnade built by Augustus. Next to the first pylon is the portal of Ptolemy II, evidently surviving from an older building; in the background is the great Kiosk of Trajan. Between the two pylons is a large courtyard:

heights of the nearby island of Biggé. The temple, consecrated to the goddess Isis and her son Harpocrates, a local form of the god Horus, stands on the site of an older sanctuary, probably built by Nectanebo, the first pharaoh for whom dated remains have been found on the site. The complex presents a succession the side overlooking the river is closed by a mammisi, whose rear façade can be seen here. On the wharf opposite it, overlooking the Nile, stands the great portal of Hadrian. The Temple of Isis proper, consisting of an atrium and the naos, surrounded by some secondary rooms, stands behind the second pylon.

Ruins Temple on the Island of Bigga, Nubia

THE RUINS OF A LITTLE TEMPLE ON THE ISLE OF BIGGÉ

Plate 40

18th November, 1838

In ancient times, no one but the priests of nearby Philae could set foot on the Isle of Biggé, sacred to Hathor and Ups, the goddess of fire; this was the site of the famous Abaton, the tomb of Osiris. The sepulchre, whose name roughly signifies "pure mound," lay in the middle of a wood; all around were 365 small altars, and milk was poured onto one of them every day in rotation as a libation to the god. The vital spirit of Osiris, in the form of a bird, was thus able to feed daily. Every ten days, the effigy of Isis was carried to the island on a sacred boat from the nearby sanctuary of Philae so that the goddess could visit her consort. Once a year, on the occasion of a solemn festival, Isis was accompanied on her pilgrimage by her son Harendotes, "Horus who defends the father." A sanctuary was built during the 18th dynasty at Biggé, where total silence was observed so as not to disturb the sleep of the god, and then rebuilt around 245 BC by Ptolemy III Evergete. This building was further extended by Ptolemy XIII, who also built a large entrance portal. An arch, later added to this portal, led from the wharf on the Nile to the sanctuary via a staircase. A comparison of Roberts's lithograph with the photo of the same site shows the extent to which the waters of the Nile rose after the construction of the High Dam.

Phila, Nov 14, 1838

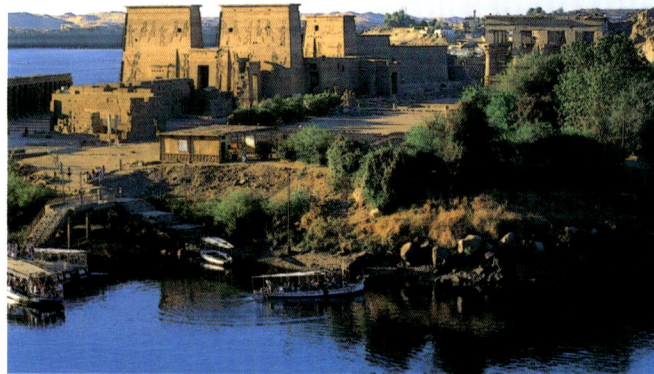

The Temples of Philae seen from the South

Plate 41

18th November 1838

From whatever angle he observed it, Roberts was enchanted by the magnificent sight of the sanctuary of Philae, which must have filled the pilgrims drawn to the spot by the esoteric popularity of Isis with even more reverential admiration. That divinity, daughter of the sun god Ra and wife and sister of Osiris, held a privileged position in the Egyptian pantheon as she was an expert in mysteries and powerful spells. She used her magic arts thaumaturgically on her divine husband after his treacherous brother Set, god of chaos, cut his body to pieces. Isis was considered the protectress of the dead, and at the same time was represented as the creating mother goddess in the region of the cataracts; when a Nubian dynasty settled in Thebes in the 7th century BC, her worship became more widely known, and eventually spread beyond the borders of Egypt. The cult of Isis became particularly popular in the Ptolemaic and Roman period, when the sanctuary of Philae reached the heights of its glory; the sick and lame flocked there from all parts of the country and the various provinces of the Empire, trusting in the favors of the goddess. The Christian repression was proportional to the fame gained by Isis; the followers of the new religion attacked the reliefs decorating the temple, which was transformed into a church, with blind fury. However, the petitions and prayers carved in numerous parts of the sanctuary demonstrate that the island was still for some time the last stronghold in Egypt of the thousand-year-old religious tradition.

The Great Colonnade in front of the Temple of Isis on Philae

Plate 42

19th November 1838

The pilgrims who flocked to the sanctuary, like modern visitors, disembarked at the southernmost tip of the island, where they were welcomed to the "kiosk of Nectanebo" not by Isis but another goddess, the benevolent cow-eared Hathor. The effigy of the mysterious goddess of beauty and pleasure appears above the capitals of six columns, the only ones left out of the 14 that were part of the restoration work on the building ordered by Ptolemy II Philadelphus; the two sovereigns are immortalized in the reliefs on the intercolumnar walls as they present their offerings to the gods. Beyond the pavilion stands the great colonnade, of exceptional scenic effect. The west side, parallel to the coastline, stretches for some 330 feet, with a row of 32 columns supporting capitals with complex shapes inspired by the plant kingdom. Stars and vultures are portrayed on the ceiling, which represents the sky. The reliefs decorating the end wall portray Octavian and Nero, whose stylized features were intended to emphasize the divine origin of the new sovereigns of Egypt. On the columns, the Emperor Tiberius brings his own offerings to the local divinities. The east colonnade on the opposite side of the courtyard was never completed; some of the 17 columns are bare of decoration, and 11 are surmounted by unfinished capitals. A third of the way along the flat area near the longer side, an underground staircase leads to the Nilometer. Nearly every temple in Egypt had a well of this kind with a gauge on the wall so that the river level could be read. Knowledge of the pattern of floods of the Nile was of great economic and social importance, as it enabled the size of the harvest and consequently the amount of the taxes to be forecasted. Only the priests held the privilege of announcing the readings of the Nilometer. The complex perspective design, admirably reproduced by Roberts, concludes at the end with the great pylon of the Temple of Isis, 60 feet tall and 150 feet wide. Begun by Ptolemy II, it was completed by his successor Ptolemy III, but the decoration work continued in subsequent eras. On the two towers Ptolemy XII Neos Dionysus is portrayed as he offers the submission of his prisoners to Isis; on the upper parts the pharaoh is received by Isis, who is accompanied by her son Horus and sister Neftis. The winged solar disk appears above the portal.

Grand Approach to the Temple of Philae – Nubia.

THE INTERIOR OF THE TEMPLE OF ISIS ON PHILAE

Plate 43

19th November 1838

During his first visit, Roberts had marveled at the exquisite proportions and magnificent bas-reliefs of the interior of the temple. He also found the paintings to be in an exceptional state of preservation. In his journal, the entry for the 30th of October states, "I was entranced by the splendid composition of its colours; they seem to be freshly painted, and even in the places where they are most exposed to the implacable sunlight, they have retained their radiant freshness." We are fortunate that the artist decided to spend the 19th of November drawing the interior of the sanctuary, because the long period spent in the waters of the reservoir has almost wiped out all traces of these elegant colors. Roberts's illustration shows the hypostyle room of the temple proper, situated immediately after the second pylon, which is smaller than the first. This room, in which eight columns support the ceiling, is preceded by an unroofed courtyard, along the shorter sides of which run two short porticoes, each supported by a central column, which constitute two extensions to the hypostyle room.

That room is followed by some vestibules and the naos, surrounded by various minor rooms. The initial sequence of these rooms can be seen in the lithograph. The walls and columns are covered with inscriptions and reliefs that show the pharaohs of the Ptolemaic dynasty and the Roman emperors Augustus, Tiberius and Antoninus Pius making offerings to Isis or performing religious rites. The courtyard could be covered with a velarium (canopy) operated by ropes; the holes through which the ropes ran can still be seen in the molding facing the pylon.

From David Roberts's journal:

19th November - Today I made some drawings of the interior of the temple and copied many of the figures covering the walls, all in excellent condition, with brilliant colours.

THE HYPOSTYLE ROOM IN THE
TEMPLE OF ISIS ON PHILAE

Plate 44

19th November 1838

This lithograph repeats the same subject as the previous one, but from a different angle. The hypostyle room was originally separated from the small inner courtyard by the usual intercolumnar walls, typical of the sacred architecture of the Ptolemaic period, which framed a central portal. This is one of the most attractive of all the lithographs because of its very effective composition and the meticulous care lavished on the decorative details. Pharaohs and divinities repeat their hieratic gestures endlessly, while the great columns almost seem to blossom into the glorious array of shapes and colors in the capitals, which, apparently effortlessly, support the mighty trabeations along which sacred ships sail. The figures of great vultures with outspread wings, repeated in long rows, stand out on the ceilings, painted like starry skies. Some Coptic crosses carved on the shaft of the columns and the remains of an altar, which demonstrate the conversion of the temple into a Christian church, can be clearly seen in the illustration. As an inscription explains, this "good work" was performed under Bishop Theodore, at the time of the Emperor Justinian and Empress Theodora in the 6th century. Another inscription still visible today commemorates the "archaeological expedition" sent here by Pope Gregory XVI in 1841. Sadly, this interference inflicted great damage on the magnificent sanctuary, although its charm still remains intact, just as it was at the height of Isis' glory.

THE ISLAND OF PHILAE
AT SUNSET

Plate 45

19th November 1838

An interesting feature of Roberts's lithographs is that they show the age-old appearance of the Island of Philae and its monuments, which remained unchanged until the construction of the First Aswan Dam. The dam brought undeniable financial advantages to Egypt, but also meant the beginning of a terrible ordeal for its monuments. Already half-flooded by the waters of the new reservoir, the temple suffered a far worse affront in 1934, when the dam was raised by several feet, causing the almost total flooding of the complex.
Its agony was only alleviated for three months a year, sometime between August and December, when the crest gates were raised, revealing the mud-covered structures as in an apparition. The soil of what was once the "garden island" then reawoke, producing lush vegetation to welcome the rare visitors to the dying archaeological site. It seemed that the destiny of Philae was to become even more tragic when the mammoth task of building the High Dam began in 1960. The monuments that had resisted only thanks to the strengthening of the foundations could not have borne the daily variations in the water level. Fortunately, during the campaign to save the Nubian monuments promoted by the United Nations, the drastic decision to move the sanctuary of the goddess Isis was taken. The choice of the new site fell on the higher nearby island of Agilkia, but considerable extension work was needed to orient the monuments correctly. The dismantling and reconstruction of all the architectural structures was put out to international tender in 1969, and the successful bidder was an Italian company. Work began in 1972, when pile-driving boats began to drive 3,000 steel piles into the bottom of the reservoir. These piles enclosed the island in two concentric dams that were to form the base of a mighty ring-shaped dam. The water was than pumped out and the mud removed by hundreds of workmen. In the meantime, the ground was leveled at Agilkia by 100 feet, and the coastline was extended.
On the 9th of September 1975, the first of the 37,363 blocks of the complex were removed, and reassembly work began on the nearby island on the 29th of May 1977. Three years later, on the 10th of March, New Philae was inaugurated. The only remaining sign of the long decades during which the complex was underwater is the grayish color of the lower parts of the structures.

Kom Ombo
Nov. 21st 1838.

From David Roberts's journal:

*21st November - I made two drawings
of these magnificent ruins, and at sunset
I painted a complete view of the place in
oils.*

THE TEMPLE OF KOM OMBO

Plate 46

20th-21st November 1838

At daybreak on the 20th of November, the crew began the complex maneuvers required for the dangerous descent of the First Cataract, which had created considerable problems on the outward journey. Towards evening the boat had finally come through the rapids safe and sound, but the captain was understandably exhausted. Until the first dam was built across the Nile between 1898 and 1912 and an annexed canal was constructed to allow even barges of very high tonnage to pass, the only way of crossing the cataract was for the boats to be harnessed and hauled across by men and animals; the effort required was enormous, and accidents were commonplace. After spending the night at Aswan, the next day Roberts and his men came in sight of the ruins of Kom Ombo, where they pitched their tents. Now a flourishing agricultural town on the right bank of the Nile, before the 4th century BC Kom Ombo was a powerful stronghold erected to defend the lower reaches of the Nile. Although no monumental ruins prior to the 18th dynasty survive, it is known that a fairly important sanctuary must have stood there during the Middle Kingdom (2100-1750 BC), and that it was later extended by Rameses II.

The area only acquired great political and religious importance under the reign of the Ptolemies, when it became the capital of a nome (province) and the construction of the second temple, whose remains are still visible, was commenced. Work began during the reign of Ptolemy V, around 204 BC, and continued for some 90 years, but the wall structures were not finished until the time of Ptolemy XIII Neos Dionysus, one century and a half after the foundation. The porticoed courtyard was completed by Roman Emperor Tiberius, and some other additions and decorations were ordered by Domitian towards the end of the 1st century AD. However, inscriptions bearing the names of the emperors Geta, Caracalla and Macrinus have also been found, and the bas-reliefs referring to the latter are the latest to survive from pagan Egypt. The word kom means "hill" in Arabic, and in fact the temple (very unusually for this region) stands on a kind of low acropolis overlooking a large loop of the river. The position of the site, which was subject to continual erosion by the river, caused the ruin of much of the complex, now protected by a large embankment.

123

THE RUINS OF THE TEMPLE OF KOM OMBO

Plate 47

21st November 1838

When Roberts visited the ruins of Kom Ombo, much of the sanctuary was still buried under the sand. Systematic excavation work did not begin until 1893, revealing the most unusual detail of the building, namely that it was a double temple, the only one of its kind in Egypt. Nearly all the Egyptian sanctuaries were consecrated to more than one god, as in the case of Karnak, where the Theban Triad was worshipped, but the effigy of the main deity usually occupied the central naos, while those of the secondary deities were placed in the side chapels.

Only at Kom Ombo was the building divided into two parts, separated by an imaginary longitudinal line; the right-hand part was dedicated to Sobek, associated in the triad with Hathor and Khonsu, and the left-hand part to Horus, accompanied by Senetnofret and Penebtaui. The structure thus consisted of two identical adjacent sectors, each of which was independent of the other for the purpose of worship. There were two entrances in the pylon and the same number in the pronaos, the hypostyle room and the chambers preceding the two cellae. The building did not appear to be formed by two separate, adjacent temples, because there were no tangible internal boundaries except in the naos. Equally, the unusual duality of Kom Ombo never gave it the appearance of a twinship, still less of inviting competition between the two deities. The design of the temple was in fact due to the policy of the Ptolemies who, wishing to confirm their sovereignty over Upper and Lower Egypt, were first crowned in Alexandria, and then crowned again at Kom Ombo.

To emphasize and at the same time sanction this double supremacy, the temple was consecrated to Haroeris, traditional patron of the pharaohs who unified the country, and to the crocodile-headed Sobek, worshipped and feared since time immemorial by the inhabitants of Nubia. In Roberts's time, and until the construction of the First Dam, the great reptile was a very common and disquieting sight along the banks of the river.

THE NILE IN THE VICINITY OF GEBEL SILSILA

Plate 48

22nd November 1838

After leaving behind the glorious ruins of Kom Ombo on the evening of the 21st of November, Roberts and his men spent the whole night on board, sailing north. What they saw the next day at dawn near Gebel Silsila surprised them: a steep ridge also known as the Chain Mountains. Here the Nile forms a gorge in which the waters become ever more restless until they form rapids and whirlpools, which, in ancient times gained it the name of Khenu, "The place where you have to row." Not far from the point where the river narrows, the ancient sandstone quarries, which were exploited during the New Kingdom to build the Ramesseum, can still be seen on the east bank.

All around stand the remains of the town of Kheni and the village where the quarrymen lived with their families, together with some commemorative rock inscriptions bearing the names of Amenhotep IV and Seti I.

However, the most important monuments are situated on the west bank, where votive shrines and inscriptions are far more numerous. The most interesting monument is the great rock chapel of Horemheb, covered with decorations. Though his curiosity was aroused by the singular shapes of the surrounding rocks, probably due to ancient mining activity, Roberts decided not to stop, partly so as not to overtire the oarsmen who had found the right pace.

He therefore merely completed the drawing he had begun on the outward journey, and spent the rest of the day spreading fixative on the finished works. A shaduf, one of the numerous lever-operated wells with which Egyptian peasants drew water from the Nile for irrigation purposes, is shown in the foreground of the lithograph. This ancient device, consisting of a long arm to which a bucket and a counterweight are fixed, is still in common use today.

THE TEMPLE OF EDFU

Plate 49

22nd November 1838

On the evening of the 22nd Roberts reached Edfu, whose temple seemed to him even more beautiful than anything he had seen so far. At sunset the sun flooded the sanctuary with a particularly warm light, and he had all the time he needed to draw a general view of the building. As he had noted on the outward journey, the building, though impressive, was not excessively large and appeared well proportioned from every point of view; the pylon in particular was a masterpiece of balance and architectural elegance.

The temple, which was excavated and restored in 1860 by French archaeologist Auguste Mariette, was consecrated to "Horus of the variegated feathers," the patron god of the district, represented alternatively in the form of a hawk, a person with a hawk's head or a winged solar disk. Despite Roberts's comments, Edfu, which is 450 feet long, 260 feet wide and 86 feet high at the top of the portal, is the largest religious complex in Egypt apart from the great temple of Amun at Karnak. It is also the least damaged. The perfect state of preservation of this huge monument means that it provides a great deal

of information about the architectural organization of the other Egyptian temples, often ruined or incomplete because of collapses and destruction. Begun in 237 BC by Ptolemy III Evergete and concluded 180 years later by Ptolemy XIII, the temple follows the distribution pattern developed towards the end of the New Kingdom, with a further addition of antechambers and stricter distribution of the interior space, especially around the saccellum. The sanctuary is entered through the great portal, which, flanked by two massive trapezoidal towers, forms the pylon. It is still impressive, although even when Roberts drew the temple it lacked the great molding that once crowned the summit. Its present height is nearly 124 feet.

The pylon is followed by the great porticoed courtyard enclosed by 32 columns and overlooked by the hypostyle pronaos. This huge room leads to what is known as the "banqueting hall," a second pronaos whose ceiling is also supported by columns.

Finally, two successive vestibules lead to the naos, the actual sacrarium, around which ten chapels consecrated to minor divinities are distributed.

THE PRONAOS OF THE TEMPLE OF EDFU

Plate 50

23rd November 1838

*R*oberts was fascinated by the perfect proportions of the Temple of Edfu, and by the magnificent polychrome bas-reliefs that decorated every surface. Braving the unbearable heat, the day after his arrival he drew two views of the superb colonnaded courtyard, the sight of which irresistibly attracted him. In fact, the sanctuary of Edfu almost gives the impression that Egypt itself, as it began its slow decline after the most glorious period of its history, wished to demonstrate its artistic skills for the very last time. In 30 BC, only 27 years after the work was finished, Augustus suppressed the last vestiges of the power of the Ptolemies, and brought Egypt firmly under the Roman yoke.

The Caesars were also fascinated by the majesty of the sanctuary, however, and took steps to ensure that it did not fall into ruin. The pronaos, with six columns facing onto the great courtyard, is perhaps the most spectacular part of the temple. It clearly demonstrates the preference of Ptolemaic taste for capitals of highly complex forms, quite different from the classical designs; the two nearest to the portal are shaped like lotus flowers, the ones in the middle are decorated with date-palm leaves, and the outer ones are inspired by the fronds of Hyphaene thebaica, *a palm tree typical of the region. Inside, 12 more columns arranged in pairs support the ceiling; here again, the capitals present a very wide variety of shapes.*

From David Roberts's journal:

23rd November - Today I made two large drawings, one of the pronaos *and one from under it, towards the pylon. To draw the former I was obliged to sit in the sun protected only by a sunshade, and the temperature reached 98°F in the shade today. I fear I did not make a very good job of it, but this colonnade is so lovely I could not resist it. From now on I will avoid exposing myself excessively to the sun, although by so doing I risk missing some interesting subjects.*

THE PYLON OF THE TEMPLE OF EDFU SEEN FROM THE PRONAOS

Plate 51

23rd November 1838

Whe looking at lithographs like this one, it should not be forgotten that before taking up painting Roberts was a talented decorator, and had painted sets for the most famous theaters in Scotland for many years. The pronaos and the great colonnaded courtyard of the sanctuary of Edfu, with their admirable perspective and the rigid symmetry of the architectural modules tempered by a profusion of ornamental elements, could not fail to galvanize Roberts's attention. This explains his evident, repeated preference for the same subject, interpreted from three different angles. From the standpoint of composition, this plate is probably one of the most successful in the entire collection; the bold insertion of the architrave in the foreground achieves the result of expanding the exterior space to the full, while the clever play of chiaroscuro suggests an almost instinctive perception of the contrast between the burning sand flooded by sunlight and the coolness offered by the shade.

The great bas-reliefs that decorate the inner walls of the pylon (perfectly reproduced by Roberts) show Ptolemy XIII Neos Dionysus making offerings to the local divinities Horus, Hathor and their son Ihy. The winged solar disk, symbol of the patron god of Edfu, is clearly visible on the jamb of the portal; a polychrome version of this symbol also appears on the architrave of the pronaos. The great courtyard, to which the faithful flocked on feast days, is surrounded by a portico whose columns end in elaborate capitals of floral inspiration. At the sight of such magnificence, Roberts greatly regretted that the interior of the temple was wholly inaccessible.

from under the Portico of Temple of Edfou. Upper Egypt

THE FAÇADE OF THE PRONAOS IN THE TEMPLE OF EDFU

Plate 52

24th November 1838

During his first visit to Edfu on the 26th of October, Roberts had described the temple as the loveliest in Egypt, so well proportioned in every part that it appeared perfect from every point of view. With a taste wholly in keeping with the romanticism of his age, he added that the fact that it was half-buried in the sand made it look even more delightful, as it reminded him of the views of the Roman forums drawn by Piranesi.

This time the artist drew the façade of the pronaos *from the southeast, focusing all his attention on the huge capitals that surmount the columns and on the complex hieroglyphics that cover nearly all the available space. Unfortunately, because of the sand that obstructed much of the building, the Scottish artist was unable to see the wall built to halfway up the lateral intercolumniations, which has no openings except at the portal in the center, another element typical of Ptolemaic architecture.*

Much interested in the details of local life, Roberts painted a portrait of a weaver at work under the portico in the background. As in the three previous illustrations, some of the miserable wattle and daub huts that had sprung up like birds' nests all over the building, ruining its magnificent proportions, can be seen above the huge trabeation of the pronaos. *These hovels were later demolished by Mariette.*

Unusually, this lithograph is correctly dated - almost a tangible sign of the vivid impression that the Temple of Edfu left in Roberts's memory.

From David Roberts's journal:

24th November - Today the thermometer read over 98°F in the shade, and even with the aid of a sunshade and a tent, drawing was extremely tiring.

THE INTERIOR OF THE TEMPLE OF ESNA

Plate 53

25th November 1838

*I*ncessantly urged on by Hassan Amoris, the crew spent the whole night manning the oars, and as day broke the boat reached Esna, 30 miles north of Edfu. Although the remains of the temple of Knhum could not bear comparison with the size of the splendid sanctuary he had visited in the past few days, Roberts did not have the heart to pass it by without drawing it; its decorations were in no way inferior to those of any other temple in terms of quality and wealth of details. In fact, the monument remains to this day the greatest pride of this ancient city, whose economy is still largely based on trade in high-quality fabrics and the camel market. The sovereigns of the 18th dynasty, who governed the country around 1500 BC, built the first temple dedicated to the ram's-head god, considered by the local people to be the creator of the human race, who modeled on his potter's wheel the egg that generated every form of life. Under the rule of the Saites the temple was partly renovated, but it was not until 181 BC that Ptolemy VI Philometor began total reconstruction work. The sanctuary was later extended under Roman rule. The building, which may have been surrounded by an outer wall, consisted of the pronaos or hypostyle room, two vestibules, the cella, and two antechambers connected by corridors. The hypostyle room is the only structure that has survived intact through the centuries. The façade, with six columns whose intercolumniations are occupied by partition walls built to halfway up, fully reflects the Ptolemaic building styles, whereas the main body of the building was completed in the second half of the 1st century AD during the rule of the emperors Tiberius, Claudius and Vespasian. The latter is described in a dedicatory inscription as "the lord of capital Rome." The uniqueness of the Temple of Esna lies in the fact that it is entirely covered with reliefs. The walls and columns are decorated with religious texts covering an unusual variety of subjects; they recount the origin of the world, life and its transmission, the creation of man and the theological bases of royal power. The most important parts were carved during the reigns of Trajan and Hadrian (2nd century AD), while the most recent are attributed to Decius (AD 250), and constitute the last known collection of hieroglyphic inscriptions. The ceiling of the hypostyle room, supported by 18 columns whose capitals are finely carved with nature motifs, is decorated with some splendid astronomical scenes.

Because of the accumulation of debris all around it, the temple now lies 30 feet below road level. When Roberts visited the site it was accessible by climbing down a ladder.
At that time the room was used as a powder magazine; it was later converted into a corn and cotton store for a few years.

From David Roberts's journal:

25th November - While I was at work, I was surrounded by a group of very friendly Coptic Christians, who seemed to consider me as one of them. I portrayed some of them in my drawing, which they very much enjoyed. Esna is the last Christian town on the Nile before Abyssinia. When I went back on board, I found Hassan Amoris suffering from terrible pains; thinking that he had cholera, I administered 30 drops of laudanum. To my great relief, he recovered in a few hours.

THE RUINS OF THE TEMPLE OF HERMONTHIS

Plate 54

26th November 1838

When Hassan Amoris recovered from a bout of fever that caused serious concern to Roberts and the crew for some hours, the boat set sail from Esna, reaching Erment during the night.

The Scotsman went ashore in the early morning and spent several hours drawing the temple of Montu, which he had considered very picturesque on the outward journey.

The town, situated around 12 miles from Luxor, was probably the birthplace of it became the capital of a fairly flourishing nome. The temple, which was rebuilt first by order of Nectanebo II and later by two sovereigns of the Ptolemy dynasty, Cleopatra VII and Ptolemy XV Caesarion, remained open for worship during Roman rule.

This plate is of great historical and archaeological value because the building, which was already very dilapidated and partly occupied by the sheik's residence when Roberts saw it, was razed to the ground a few years after Roberts's visit so that its stones could be used to

the sovereigns of the 11th dynasty, who founded the important sanctuary there; known by the name of Iuni, it was also called Per-Montu (Dominion of Montu) because the hawk-headed god of war was worshipped there. In the Roman period, when it was known by the Greek name of Hermonthis, build a great sugar refinery and wharves on the Nile.

During excavations conducted on several occasions this century, the necropolises where the bulls consecrated to Montu and the cows that gave birth to them were buried were uncovered a few miles north of the town.

View of the Temples of Karnak from the South

Plate 55

27th November 1838

Roberts left Erment at 11 a.m. on the 26th of November. He came in sight of Karnak two hours later, and landed near the great sanctuary after a few minutes. The next day he began to draw the ruins that had so impressed him a few weeks earlier. Although he was getting used to similar sights after having seen the Temple of Edfu, the Isle of Philae and the colossi of Rameses the Great at Abu Simbel, the ruins of ancient Thebes still filled him with awe. The impressions recorded in his journal on the 23rd of October give an insight into his feelings, which were shared by all the intrepid travelers who sailed up the Nile to discover pharaonic Egypt in the 19th century. "Karnak is even more astonishing than Luxor. Its magnificence is unimaginable. Trying to describe rationally what I have seen would be ridiculous. The temple is so far removed from any previous experience of mine that I have nothing to compare it with. Like other Egyptian temples, at first sight it is actually a little disappointing, as the sanctuary stands in a huge plain which gives a misleading impression of its size; only as you draw closer to it are you astonished, indeed overcome by amazement. "You have to stand in their shadow, look up, and walk among these gigantic structures to understand; this frightens me, and my hand trembles at the thought that my drawings are unlikely to convey exactly what I mean. The columns are over 30 feet in circumference, so that a man looks like a pigmy beside them. The blocks that lie scattered all around are so huge that, even without considering how they were cut, it is impossible to imagine how they were brought here and put in their places."

THE COLONNADE OF THE GREAT HYPOSTYLE ROOM IN THE TEMPLE OF KARNAK

Plate 56

27th November 1838

*A*s already mentioned, Karnak and Luxor, with their famous temples, stand on the site of the ancient city of Thebes, several times the magnificent capital of the Egyptian empire and famous for its huge wealth. Homer described it in the ninth canto of the Iliad as the "city of a hundred gates" because of the countless caravans that arrived there every day, helping to increase the great economic and political power that came to dominate the area between the Sudan and the shores of the Mediterranean, Libya and Palestine. Founded as a modest fishing village in the Memphis period, Thebes grew enormously after the second unification of Upper and Lower Egypt; it reached the height of its glory between 1580 and 1085 BC. The great metropolis was dominated by the temple dedicated to the Theban Triad, which was extended and embellished by the pharaohs after each new victory against ever more distant enemies. Then, inexorably but unexpectedly, it fell into decline; the very geographical location that a thousand years earlier had led to its foundation and enhanced its power became the primary factor in its fall. Situated deep in the interior of the country, too far from the Mediterranean, which by then was becoming the center of the world, and from the Delta area, where the sovereigns of Rameses' dynasty had founded new military outposts against foreign invaders, Thebes rapidly lost its political and spiritual supremacy. Sais, Tanis and, finally, Bubastis, replaced Thebes as the imperial residence, beginning its decay. The Assyrian invasion, with the sack of Thebes by Assurbanipal in 672 BC, followed by the rule of the Ptolemies, finally condemned the city, so that by the time the Roman legions arrived, much of it had already fallen into ruin. During the Christian period many of the city's monuments were converted into churches and monasteries, while its works of art were scattered, or destroyed by those who viewed them as hideous symbols of paganism. Uaset (the Egyptian name of Thebes) was divided in half by a canal; the town of Luxor was founded to the south, while Karnak developed to the north. Despite the destruction and pillaging it has suffered, the Temple of Amun is still astonishing today for its extraordinary size, clearly depicted in the magnificent lithograph drawn by Roberts.

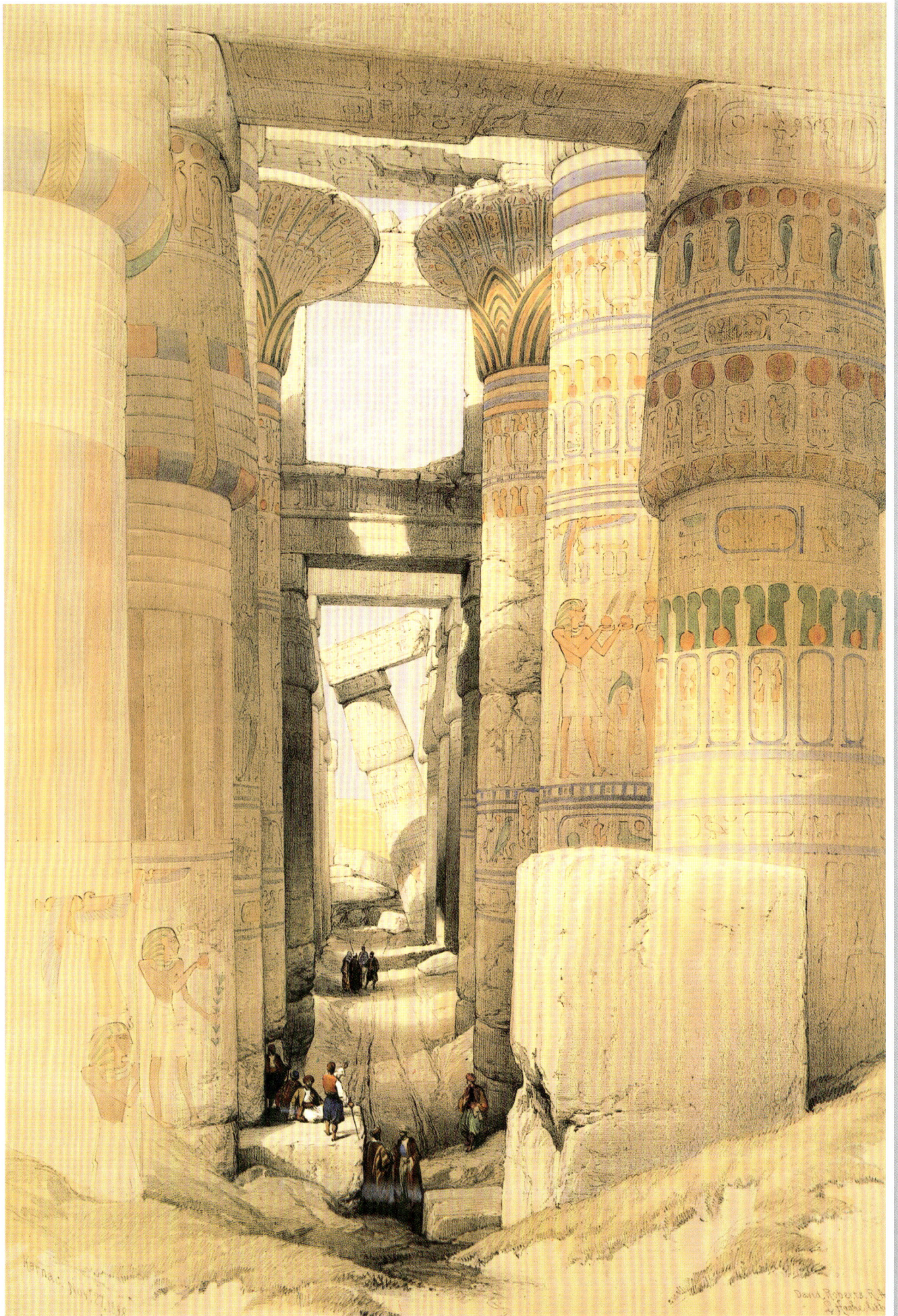

THE NAVE OF THE GREAT HYPOSTYLE ROOM AT KARNAK

Plate 57

28th November 1838

This lithograph, like the previous one, shows a view of the hypostyle room in the Temple of Amun; this room, more than any other, left an indelible impression on Roberts's mind, and he drew it from various angles.

The great room, built by Seti I and Rameses II, can rightly be considered one of the wonders of the ancient world. In a total area of 6,000 square yards, 134 sandstone columns are aligned in 16 rows; the 12 that line the nave, shown in this lithograph, are over 80 feet tall, and are surmounted by capitals whose maximum circumference exceeds 50 feet. It is therefore not surprising that this room, the largest in the world to have a stone roof, was described by early archaeologists as a "forest of columns."

The considerable difference in height between the central columns and those in the aisles enabled numerous windows to be inserted between the architraves and the ceiling, thus ensuring that the room, enclosed by high walls on all sides, was adequately lit. One of these windows is clearly visible in the lithograph, at the top left. The slender obelisk of Thutmoses I, the only survivor of the four that the powerful pharaoh erected in the courtyard between the third and fourth pylons, can be seen in the background. Every surface is extensively decorated with bas-reliefs and inscriptions explaining the complex liturgical rites and the relationships between the sovereigns and the gods; sadly, the bright colors reproduced by Roberts have now faded in many places, or even disappeared.

Although Roberts usually portrayed his subjects faithfully, he made an exception in this lithograph. Probably fearing that he might embarrass some of the subscribers of the work, and even offend against the moral code of the period, he decided to censor the bas-reliefs portraying the immodest god Min, protector of fertility, who was represented by the ancient Egyptians as ithyphallic.

THE GREAT HYPOSTYLE ROOM AT KARNAK SEEN FROM THE EXTERIOR

Plate 58

28th November 1838

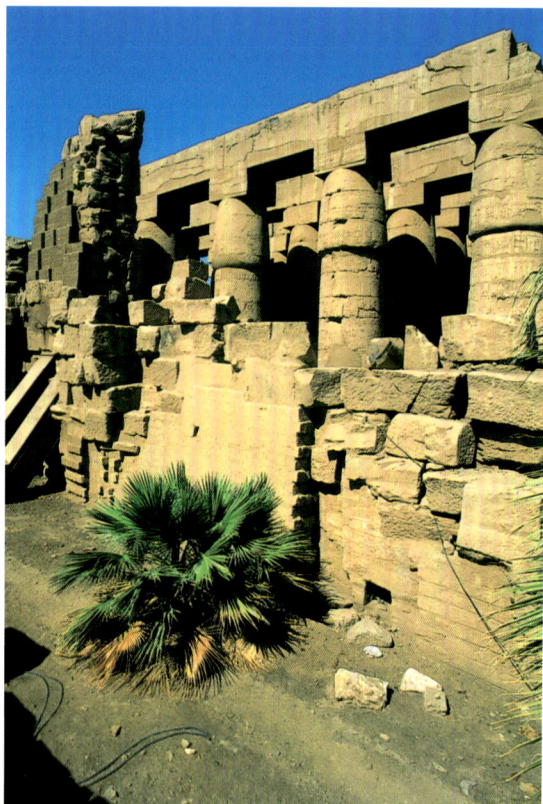

*R*oberts spent four days at Karnak, working feverishly, as if obsessed by the idea that he would be unable to do justice to the magnificence of what was once the earthly dwelling of Amun, lord of the gods. He rose at dawn, and braving the heat and the tiresome bites of the ever-present mosquitos, continued drawing and taking measurements until twilight. Then he finally took a well-deserved rest, dining with two British travelers, Woolner Corry and William Hurnard, whom he had met earlier on his way to the Second Cataract.
On the return journey the two had stopped at Karnak and, hearing that Roberts was there, decided to stay for a few days to visit ancient Thebes together with him. In his journal the Scotsman describes them as affable and good company.
The pair set off for Cairo on the evening of the 4th of December. Corry's signature can still be seen carved in the stone of various Egyptian monuments, according to a deplorable custom that knows no limits of time or place.
The lithograph shows another view of the hypostyle room, this time seen from the outside. Roberts's evident fondness for this room, which in our eyes may appear excessive, is justified by the fact that at the time, the remains of the sacred building appeared as a jumble of very badly damaged structures, partly buried in the sand, which were difficult to interpret as a whole.
Nearly all the pharaohs decided to extend the sanctuary, sometimes demolishing and re-using the previous constructions, with the result that the architecture of the building is highly complex, even after extensive restoration work, which began in the last century and has not yet been completed. The temple, which was called Ipet-isut, can be described as a theological treatise in stone, as it develops along two axes running from east to west and north to south, constituting mystical representations of sky and earth, divine power and royal power.
It comprised four courtyards, ten pylons, a sacred lake and numerous associated buildings, including the Temple of Khonsu and a small sanctuary consecrated to Opet, the mother of Isis.

VIEW OF THE RUINS OF KARNAK
AT SUNRISE

Plate 59

29th November 1838

This large view of the Temple of Karnak, drawn at dawn on the 29th of November, is one of the most successful in the entire collection both in its composition and in purely emotional terms; the ruins are bathed in the warm morning sunlight, while the group of local people portrayed in the foreground gives the scene a touch of romantic exoticism. In the background, from left to right, can be seen the first pylon of the huge religious complex, the column of Taharqa, the remains of the second pylon, the colonnade of the great column-supported temple in the world. Begun under the sovereigns of the 12th dynasty, the huge building represents the result of over 16 centuries of work and extensions, which make it a kind of compendium of Egyptian art. As this was the largest center for the worship of Amun, it was very important for every sovereign to make improvements to it.

Soon, because of the logic of its general proportions, extension required the erection of ever more colossal buildings; the result is this gigantic structure, full of repetitions and some degree of architectural

hypostyle room, the obelisks of Thutmoses I and Queen Hatshepsut, the banqueting hall of Thutmoses III and the portal of Nectanebo I.

The view is expressly designed to highlight the immense size of the sanctuary which, with its area of 75 acres, is the largest confusion, but undoubtedly unique. The Temple of Amun is the monument that, more than any other, represents the magnificence of the triumphal buildings erected by the pharaohs for religious reasons and to enhance their political prestige.

149

THE GREAT COURTYARD OF KARNAK AND THE COLUMN OF TAHARQA

Plate 60

29th November 1838

The sacred complex of Karnak consists of three areas separated by enclosure walls made of air-dried bricks. In the main enclosure stand the great Temple of Amun and the smaller Temple of Khonsu, the moon god, who was considered the son of Amun and Mut in Thebes; on the left is the Sanctuary of Montu, the god of war, while on the opposite side, still largely unexplored, is the temple of the goddess Mut. Access to the Temple of Amun was originally obtained via two different routes, depending on whether visitors arrived from the Nile or overland. In both cases the entrance was announced by a row of tall pylons, each of which resembled two large trapezoidal towers framing a portal, probably inspired by military architecture. These characteristic structural elements are almost certainly the reason for the present name of Karnak, which in Arabic designates a fortified place. Worshippers arriving from the south walked down a long sphinx-lined avenue and entered through the south propylaea, which led to the courtyard enclosed between the third and fourth pylons, onto which the actual temple opened. The main route, from the river, was perpendicular to the cella. After passing the first pylon, visitors entered the great courtyard, the largest in any of the Egyptian temples: built during the 22nd dynasty (945-745 BC), it is lined with 18 columns on the left and 9 on the right, all in the shape of closed scrolls. At the center of the huge area stands a column 70 feet tall, the only one surviving from a kiosk built by Ethiopian King Taharqa around 680 BC.

When Roberts explored the temple, the great courtyard was blocked by ruins, and only half of the huge column was above the surface, the rest being buried in the sand.

The courtyard leads to the great hypostyle room, which is followed, after the third and fourth pylons, by a room called the "small vestibule"; two more pylons precede the sacrarium, which is followed by the "banqueting hall."

TRANSVERSE VIEW OF THE GREAT HYPOSTYLE ROOM AT KARNAK

Plate 61

29th November 1838

*T*his umpteenth view of the hypostyle room shows not only the gigantic proportions of the columns by comparison with the Lilliputian figures that appear at the foot of one of them, but also the badly damaged condition of the building. Roberts also emphasized the extraordinary complexity of the bright, polychrome decorations of the temple. During the thousand-year history of the sanctuary, whole generations of sovereigns left their mark by covering every available surface with hieroglyphics and figures. These bas-reliefs not only illustrate the religious beliefs of the ancient Egyptians in great detail, but also contain a wealth of invaluable references to historical events in the country. The information provided by the Temple of Karnak has enabled the exact chronology of the events that took place during the New Kingdom to be reconstructed, and a complete list of the successive sovereigns who built the sanctuary to be drawn up. None of them spared any expense: an inscription recalls that Queen Hatshepsut lavished on the temple "as many bushels of gold as sacks of corn." During the 19th dynasty (1335-1205 BC) over 80,000 men worked at the temple, including manual workers, peasants, slaves, watchmen and priests. In order to understand the enthusiasm for construction work of these followers of Amun, it should be remembered that the worship of the lord of the gods had received its official consecration at Karnak, supported by a magnificent liturgy far removed from the simple, spontaneous faith of the people.

Around 2000 BC Amun was beginning to be considered the supreme being by all those who recognized the authority of the pharaoh, often associated with the image of the god.

The development of the sanctuary into the greatest religious center in Egypt, which involved countless renovations, completely changed the original appearance of the sacred complex, although it still retained the basic characteristics of the Egyptian temple, considered the "palace" of the god on earth.

The ruins of the Temple of Medamout near Karnak

Plate 62

30th November 1838

The inclusion of this lithograph in our book presented a real puzzle, because Roberts never made any explicit mention of the Temple of Medamout during either the outward or the return journey. However, on the basis of some practical considerations, it is reasonable to assume that the artist visited the site on the 30th of November. His journal shows that during the previous three days he was engaged in drawing the Temple of Karnak, of which he notes that he made seven drawings, probably the same ones that appear in the previous pages (including the frontispiece of this chapter, portaying the great portal erected by Ptolemy III). On Saturday, the 1st of December, he wrote that he had "started and finished at Luxor," and on Sunday, in observance of Biblical precepts, he did no work, but merely visited Medinet Abu. From that time until his departure for Dendera on the evening of the 6th he stayed on the left bank of the Nile where the funeral temples, the Colossi of Memnon and the Valley of the Kings are situated. That only leaves the 30th of November, about which he vaguely wrote that he had drawn some sketches and made two studies in oils.

The Temple of Medamout is situated just under four miles north of Karnak, on the same bank; at the time the area was not encumbered by modern buildings, and the ruins must have been easily visible, representing a great attraction for the untiring Roberts. We therefore hope that we are not mistaken in our supposition, but if we are, we trust that readers will excuse our long digression.

The remains of the Temple of Montu, still visible today at Medamout, date back to the Ptolemaic and Roman age, although the origins of the sanctuary are far more remote. In ancient Madu (the original name of the place) the worship of the war god began during the Old Kingdom, when the first temple was founded. This temple was later extended by Sesostris III and, when the importance of the war god increased, by the sovereigns of the New Kingdom. During the three centuries of Ptolemaic rule in Egypt, a large number of existing sanctuaries were restored and new ones consecrated to the ancient lords of the Egyptian pantheon, and it was in this context that the temple was renovated.

All that now remains of the building are the five columns drawn by Roberts; the two flanking the great portal are surmounted by richly decorated capitals with floral motifs, while the others are the fascicular papyrus type with closed capitals.

THE FAÇADE OF THE GREAT TEMPLE OF AMUN AT LUXOR

Plate 63

1st December 1838

Roberts stayed only one day, the 1st of December, at Luxor; this suggests that he had already made various sketches during the outward journey, which he then completed on the basis of new observations.

While he was working on the preparatory drawing for this lithograph, a falcon perched on the top of the obelisk facing the great pylon of the temple. Every so often the bird took off and swooped on the intrusive pigeons surrounding the artist, who scattered in terror.

As if to express his thanks, Roberts included the bird in his view. The great sanctuary, half buried by debris, was suffocated by a myriad of shacks, with hundreds of earthenware pots used as dovecotes on their roofs. A building surmounted by a dome can be seen in the first courtyard, while the summit of the minaret of the Mosque of Abu el-Haggag, which still stands inside the archaeological site, appears behind the left-hand tower. The temple was only dug out in 1885 by French archaeologist Gaston Maspéro, who began the large-scale excavations that are still continuing.

THE OBELISK OF RAMESES II AT LUXOR

Plate 64

1st December 1838

The temple of Luxor was the main satellite of the huge sacred complex of Karnak, to which it was connected under Nectanebo I by a majestic avenue of human-headed sphinxes almost two miles long. A monumental site already existed in this part of Thebes in the Middle Kingdom, as confirmed by the reuse of older materials; however, the architectural history of the Luxor sanctuary is far more unified than that of Karnak. The present building was erected under only three pharaohs: Amenhotep III, Tutankhamen and Rameses II. The first, in the 14th century BC, commissioned the design from Amenhotep son of Hapu, famous for his wisdom and worshipped as a god after his death, who unusually oriented the temple from north to south so as to connect it directly with Amun's dwelling at Karnak. As was the usual practice, his two successors extended the temple and repeated the same structural elements. The original layout included the naos preceded by the hypostyle room, while the courtyard surrounded by porticoes and the great colonnade were added later by the Amenhotep III. On his death, his son Akhenaton the

Heretic (Amenhotep IV) abandoned the project and left the capital to found a new cult of Aton and a new imperial city, the present Tell el-Amarna; the monument was later completed by his son-in-law Tutankhamen who, after returning to Thebes and the religion of his ancestors, wished to prove his faith by making numerous embellishments. During the 19th dynasty Rameses II completed the temple by adding the great colonnaded courtyard with the axis towards the east, preceded by the huge front pylon decorated with reliefs portraying his victory against the Hittites at the battle of Kadesh. In front of it he erected two obelisks, covered with propitiatory inscriptions and scenes of offerings to Amun, which were donated to France by the Pasha of Egypt Mohammed Ali. The western obelisk, standing over 70 feet tall and weighing 240 tons, was taken to Paris and erected by engineer Jean Baptiste Lebas in the middle of Place de la Concorde on the 25th of October 1836. Roberts, who strongly disapproved of this pillage, would probably have been pleased to hear that the French government officially renounced its right to ownership of the second obelisk in 1980.

One of the Colossi of Rameses II in front of the Temple of Luxor

1st December 1838

Plate 65

*I*n addition to the two obelisks, six huge statues, half of which have been lost, originally faced the pylon of the temple. Roberts was only able to see the busts of the two dark granite colossi guarding the entrance, which emerged from the debris. The 50-foot-tall colossi both portrayed Rameses II seated on the throne, but the faces were already disfigured. The third huge statue, which can now be seen in front of the right-hand tower, was at that time buried under the sand; carved in red granite, it also portrays the pharaoh, but in a standing position. A cartouche containing some hieroglyphics can be seen on the right shoulder of the colossus. It is interesting in this respect to see that on a number of occasions Roberts expressed some doubt in his journal as to whether the ancient Egyptian language could really be deciphered. For example, on the 22nd of October, during his first visit to the Valley of the Kings, he wrote, "If it is true that hieroglyphics can be read, in this tomb it will certainly be possible to discover the entire pantheon of Egyptian mythology." Yet Jean François Champollion had published his Précis du système hiéroglyphique *in 1824, and by 1838 his method was universally recognized despite harsh criticism from English scientist Thomas Young, who also tried to solve the enigma but with no valid result.*

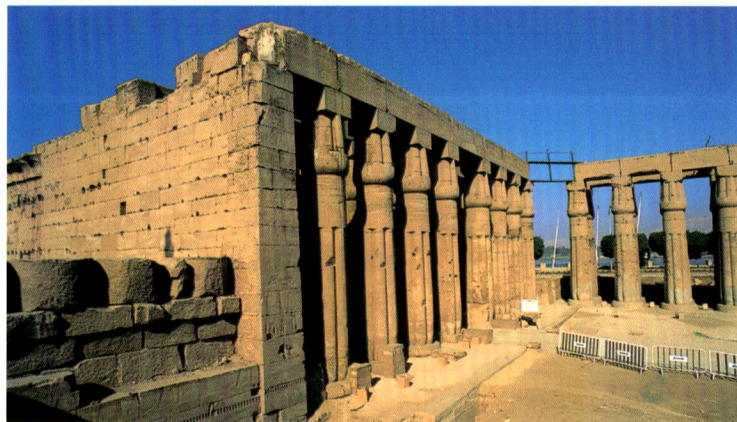

THE COLONNADE OF THE COURTYARD OF AMENHOTEP III AT LUXOR

Plate 66

1st December 1838

This lithograph shows a view of the colonnaded courtyard of Amenhotep III, a huge open space measuring 168 feet wide by 149 feet long, surrounded on three sides by two rows of closed-capital fascicular columns. At the time when Roberts made the drawing, this part of the temple was also half-buried, and many of the columns had fallen to the ground and were totally covered with sand. The temple of Luxor, which was called Ipet-resit (southern harem of Amun) had a very complex function. Every year during the Lovely Festival of Opet, celebrated in the second or third month of the flood season, the effigy of Amun was removed from the great temple of Karnak and placed on the sacred boat in a magnificent ceremony. Following a rigid hierarchy, the craft was followed by three other sacred boats; the first carried the statue of Mut, wife of Amun, the second the statue of their son Khonsu, and the third the pharaoh in person. The procession sailed slowly up the Nile as far as the temple of Luxor, which was situated on such high ground that it was never underwater even during the greatest floods. The statues were taken from the vessels and placed on symbolic boats shouldered by the priests; they passed the entrance pylon, advanced between the columns of the sanctuary, and were finally placed in the naos. The ritual boats, each placed in a different cella, were only removed ten days later; in the meantime Amun, by consecrating his mystic and carnal union with Mut, once again fertilized the world. At the same time, in the twilight of the most secret chambers of the temple, the pharaoh met the queen. During the festival the people, invited to manifest their joy, flocked from all over the region, while votive offerings poured incessantly into the temple, and were all the more plentiful if the harvest had been good. Women desiring children made pilgrimages to the sanctuary to invoke the aid and protection of Amun, honored in the guise of Min, whose erect phallus promised fertility. On the tenth day the statues were again placed in the boats, and the procession returned to Karnak. The pharaoh, regenerated and confirmed in his royal role, could then guarantee the prosperity of his people for another year, certain that the next harvest would be plentiful thanks to the benevolent influence of Amun.

THE WEST BANK OF THE NILE
SEEN FROM LUXOR

Plate 67

1st December 1838

*I*n order to make this drawing, Roberts had to scale one of the architraves of the colonnade surrounding the courtyard of Rameses II in the Temple of Luxor. From that privileged position the eye could range freely over the verdant plain that occupies the west bank of the Nile, where the pharaohs of the New Kingdom built their funeral temples. From left to right can be seen the temple of Rameses III at Medinet Habu, the solitary figures of the colossi of Memnon, the Ramesseum and the temple of Sethi I, near which stood the village of Goorna, now known as Qurnah. Behind the village lies the Valley of the Kings, where 62 royal tombs have so far been rescued from centuries of oblivion.
The powerful sovereigns of the Memphis period revolutionized Egyptian architecture by building pyramids to house their eternal dwelling-places, while Theban Pharaoh Thutmoses I (who reigned from 1525 to 1512 BC, at the beginning of the 18th dynasty)

made the equally innovative decision to separate the mortuary temple from the actual sepulchre. This design greatly interested his successors, who trusted in the inviolability of their tombs to ensure that their journey to the afterlife would not be disturbed by grave robbers. Aligned along the Nile, not far from the entrance to the valley, stood the temples in honor of Amenhotep I, II and III, Merneptah and Merneptah-Sipta, Rameses I, II, III and IV, Sethi I and Thutmoses II, III and IV. The only survivors of these splendid buildings, which the pharaohs of three dynasties consecrated to the Theban Triad and their own worship, are those made of stone, while all the others, made of air-dried brick, have practically disappeared. Roberts did not include the temple of Queen Hatshepsut in the valley of Deir el-Bahari in the view; in fact, reconstruction work on the magnificent terraced complex, which can now easily be seen even from Luxor, was only commenced in 1967.

A GROUP OF EGYPTIANS IN THE TEMPLE OF SETI I AT THEBES

Plate 68

3rd December 1838

Roberts spent the first Sunday in December visiting the neighborhood of the village of Qurnah, probably with Hurnard and Corry, abstaining from work on the Sabbath. The next day he started work again with a will, and was already on his way to the Valley of the Kings in the early hours of the morning. During the journey he stopped briefly at the ruins of the mortuary temple of Seti I, which stands in the plain of Thebes on the edge of the fertile area. Built on the foundations of a previous building, the impressive structure was dedicated by the pharaoh to the god Amun with the intention of perpetuating his own memory and honoring that of his father, Rameses I. The sovereign, who reigned from 1306 to 1290 BC, did not live to see the temple completed; it was finished by his successor Rameses II.

The great complex is now badly damaged; little remains of the first and second pylons, or of the two huge courtyards. All that remains of the long processional avenue that led to the temple are two sphinxes, while the portico that closed the second courtyard to the east, behind the smaller pylon, still has nine of the ten original fascicular columns. Three portals connect the portico to the corresponding sectors of the temple dedicated to the three sovereigns, in accordance with a very unusual layout. The central hypostyle room, surrounded by numerous secondary rooms used as stores for boats and sacred articles, leads to the actual naos, the ceiling of which rested on four pillars. The chapels of Rameses I and Rameses II and their ancillary rooms have unfortunately been badly damaged.

The background to the scene portrayed by Roberts in this lithograph is a section of the portico, which provided refreshing shade for some very picturesque characters. In front of the water pipe in the center sits one of the pasha's officials, who had come to Qurnah to collect taxes and adjudicate on any disputes relating to the actions of local administrators; on his right is the village sheik, accompanied by an attendant. Some local dignitaries are waiting their turn, probably to buy the official's favors with gifts and offerings, as corruption was rife at this period. Fascinated by exotic scenes as always, Roberts also included the figure of a veiled woman and two children, whose clothes indicated that they belonged to different classes.

THE VALLEY OF THE KINGS

Plate 69

3rd December 1838

*A*fter leaving the Temple of Seti I, Roberts went on to the Valley of the Kings. When the artist paid his first visit to the valley on the 22nd of October, he made no drawings but merely took notes on the most interesting tombs, especially that of Seti I, discovered by Belzoni 21 years earlier. The undulating Valley of the Kings, surrounded by overhanging rocks, stretches sinuously along the foot of Mount el-Qurn, also known as the Theban Heights, whose triangular shape is reminiscent of a pyramid. Here lie the tombs of the pharaohs of the 18th, 19th and 20th dynasties. The Arabic name of the place, Biban el-Moluk (The Kings' Doors) alludes to the entrances of these sepulchres, which were excavated in the calcareous rock. As already mentioned, the Valley of the Kings was destined to become one of the most famous archaeological sites in the world as a result of an original decision by Thutmoses I who, breaking with a tradition 17 centuries old, decided to separate his eternal resting place from the funeral temple and conceal it in a well-protected place.
The pharaoh's architect Ineni excavated a well-type tomb in the inaccessible rock wall of the valley, and placed a burial chamber at the end of it to receive the sarcophagus of the deceased and his burial objects. This inaugurated the typical design of the royal tomb, which was gradually developed by his successors with the addition of corridors, hypostyle rooms and secondary rooms. After the mortal remains of the pharaoh had been buried, the tomb was never visited again, as the royal cult continued in the funeral temples situated in the plain on the edge of the cultivated areas. Contrary to common belief, the accesses to the tombs were not secret; in fact, the guardians of the valley periodically checked the seals affixed at the time of burial. Sadly, this precaution was insufficient to protect the luxurious burial objects from tomb robbers, who often acted in partnership with the guards. Two papyrus scrolls and other written documents record violations of the tombs as early as the 20th dynasty; later, nearly all the tombs were pillaged, and the Theban priests had to conceal the mummies of many pharaohs in a secret hiding place, which was not discovered until 1881.
The only tomb that was not violated was that of Tutankhamen with its fabulous treasure, discovered by Howard Carter and Lord Carnarvon in 1922. Oddly, Roberts only drew a panoramic view of the valley, with the entrances to the tombs that could then be seen, neglecting the spectacular interior decorations he had been so excited about. However, the lithograph is of some interest because it shows the artist himself together with Hurnard, Corry, Ismail and Hassan Amoris.

The Temple of Ptolemy iv at Deir el-Medina

Plate 70

3rd December 1838

*T*he road that now winds through the Valley of the Kings follows the route used in ancient times to take the royal sarcophagi from Thebes to their last abode. The men who worked on the construction of the tombs and lived in the village of Deir el-Medina went to work by a much shorter route, still easily followed, which crosses the ridge between the two parallel valleys. After exploring the tombs Roberts preferred to take this shorter footpath back to Qurnah, and it soon led him to the place where the builders of the royal necropolis had lived. Nearby stood a very well preserved small temple, built by Ptolemy IV Philopator in honor of Hathor and Maat, the patron deities of Theban sepulchres; the small sanctuary was also consecrated to architects Imhotep and Amenhotep. The former had designed the first pyramid in Egypt, at Djoser, while the latter built the temple of Luxor under Amenhotep III; in accordance with the complicated syncretism of the Egyptian religion, both of these historical figures were later deified, thus entering the huge pantheon presided over by Amun-Ra. The building, completed by Ptolemy VII Evergete II, has a regular plan; the hypostyle atrium, whose ceiling is now missing, is followed by a small vestibule onto which the doors of three adjacent chapels open. The architrave of the vestibule is supported by two columns with magnificent floral patterns and two attractive Hathor pillars; the window seen in the lithograph shed light on a staircase leading to the terraced roof. The building is very small: less than 30 feet wide by 45 feet long. The very well balanced proportions of the whole and the exquisite workmanship of the decorations justify the attention devoted to it by Roberts, who in this illustration portrayed himself at work, exotically dressed in the Turkish style, as was then customary in Egypt.

THE COLOSSI OF MEMNON
IN THE PLAIN OF THEBES

Plate 71

4th December 1838

*R*oberts spent the whole of the 4th of December, drawing the Colossi of Memnon from three different angles. These huge twin statues, already famous in ancient times, are all that remains of the funeral temple of Amenhotep III, the largest in western Thebes, designed by the architect Amenhotep. The building, situated in the easternmost part of the alluvial plain of the Nile, was largely made of air-dried bricks and almost certainly undermined by the annual floods of the river. It was eventually reduced to a heap of rubble, and used by the pharaoh's successors as a source of building material. A similar fate was suffered by the pharaoh's magnificent palace at Malqatta, a few miles northeast of the temple.

The great palace, protected by a massive enclosure wall inside of which there were also numerous food stores, stood opposite the huge reservoir of Birket Abu, connected to the Nile by a navigable canal. The only remaining signs of its bygone glory are the two statues portraying the deified Amenhotep III, which originally stood on either side of the entrance portal of the temple. Carved in the very hard siliceous sandstone from the Edfu quarries, they have withstood continual erosion and still survive today. The outline of the funeral temple of Rameses III at Medinet Habu can be seen in the background of the lithograph.

THE COLOSSI OF MEMNON
SEEN FROM THE SOUTHWEST

Plate 72

4th December 1838

*B*oth of the huge statues of Amenhotep III, called the Colossi of Memnon by Greek travelers because of a mistaken interpretation of the Egyptian name, were damaged by an earthquake in 27 BC that also probably inflicted the finishing blow on the temple behind them. After the earthquake, the northern statue began to emit a characteristic wailing sound when it was heated by the rays of the rising sun. This increased the popularity of the colossi and strengthened the legend, dating from the Ptolemaic period, that identified them with Homer's hero Memnon, slain by Achilles beneath the walls of Troy, whose effigy received the beneficial caresses of his mother Aurora every morning with a gentle moan. The Colossi of Memnon became the most popular monuments in Egypt, and in Roman times attracted hordes of travelers, who also admired their huge size. Including the bases, the two statues are just under 65 feet tall. The bas-reliefs that can still be seen on the sides of the thrones depict the two Nile divinities entwining a lotus and a papyrus, the heraldic plants of Upper and Lower Egypt, symbolizing the union of the two kingdoms. Statues of Amenhotep's mother, Mutemuia, stand on the left-hand side of the legs of each colossus, and those of his wife, Teie, on the right. In the scene portrayed by Roberts, Hurnard, Corry and Hassan Amoris, who accompanied him on his excursion, are scaling the "wailing" colossus with the aid of a rope.

175

The Colossi of Memnon at Sunrise

Plate 73

4th December 1838

During the first two centuries AD, visiting the Colossi of Memnon at Thebes became fashionable among Greek and Roman travelers. Already mentioned by Strabo, the phenomenon of the wailing statue was confirmed by Pausania and Juvenal in the 2nd century AD. Numerous Greek and Latin inscriptions can still be read on the lower part of the northern statue, demonstrating that it was only this one that produced the strange lament; they include inscriptions by poet Julia Balbilla, who accompanied the Emperor Hadrian and his wife, Sabina, on their trip to Egypt, and by the Greek poet Asklepiodotos. Unfortunately, the sound entirely ceased when Septimius Severus, perhaps to alleviate the anguish of Memnon, restored the colossus and rebuilt the upper part. This lithograph, in which the colossi are bathed in the light of the rising sun reflected on the flooded plain, represents a good example of the virtuoso technique and romantic spirit of the artist, who reached heights of true lyricism, although the scene was artificially constructed. In fact, the floods of the Nile began between May and June and increased until early October, after which they decreased rapidly; Roberts could not, therefore, have witnessed this event.

Statues of Memnon at Thebes, during The Inundations.

From David Roberts's journal:

5th December - Today I was particularly busy, mainly because of a furious storm, a very rare event in these parts. I made two large drawings of the Memnonium and two of the Temple of Medinet Abou.

The Ramesseum at Thebes during a Storm

Plate 74

5th December 1838

On the 5th of December, a violent thunderstorm broke unexpectedly. The ancient ruins stood out clearly against the Theban plain like apparitions, illuminated by spectral flashes of lightning as the sky grew darker and darker. Fascinated by this scene of wild beauty, Roberts decided to take advantage of the rare opportunity of drawing the funeral temple of Rameses II in the storm. Although it has suffered ill treatment at the hands of man and the elements, the great building, which Champollion baptized the Ramesseum, is one of the most perfect and elegant examples of this architectural style. The temple was already famous in classical antiquity; historian Diodorus Siculus wrote a marvelling description of it, and it was also mentioned by Greek geographer Strabo, although he called it the Memnonium because Rameses was incorrectly identified with the legendary Ethiopian King Memnon, son of Eos (Aurora) and Tithonos, slain during the Trojan War. The Ramesseum originally consisted of a number of buildings surrounded by an outer wall of sun-dried bricks, namely the temple for royal worship where the glories of the pharaoh were celebrated with great pomp, a minor sanctuary dedicated to his mother and wife, the great stores containing the provisions required for the liturgy and the sustenance of the priests, and the royal palace where Rameses himself resided during the ceremonies. Although the term "funeral temple" is now in common use, this variety of functions suggests that it is incorrect; in fact, these magnificent buildings were used by the pharaohs while they were still alive. Associated with the worship of the deified sovereign and with the god Amun, the chief Theban deity, they were called Million-Year Castles by the ancient Egyptians. The pharaohs celebrated there a festival of very ancient origin that, formally, was held during the thirtieth year of their reign in order to regenerate their strength and that of the whole country. The elaborate purification rites and offerings needed to aid the reunion of the deceased with the supreme deity only began on the death of the sovereign, in the silence of these temples.

THE COLOSSUS OF RAMESES II IN THE RAMESSEUM

Plate 75

5th December 1838

Like all travelers who visited the ruins of the Ramesseum, Roberts was astonished by the fragments of the colossus of Rameses the Great. The huge statue, made by order of the pharaoh in his own likeness and placed in front of the second pylon of the temple, was originally just under 60 feet tall. Made of a single block of red Aswan granite weighing over 1100 tons, it portrayed the sovereign seated on his throne, with the double crown of Upper and Lower Egypt on his head. The pharaoh's name is still easily visible on the cartouches carved on the forearms and seat. The colossus inspired Shelley's famous sonnet Ozymandias; this name derives from the Greek translation of Rameses II's forename, Usermaatra (Powerful is the Truth of Ra). Many theories have been postulated to explain the destruction of this wonder of the ancient world, including the earthquake that devastated the region in 27 BC, but the responsibility for the damage probably lies with the Coptic Christians, who considered any image associated with the ancient Egyptian religion to be blasphemous. On the left of the huge fragmentary bust stand four Osiris pillars surviving from the portico that ran around the second courtyard of the temple; behind them can be seen the few remains of the second pylon.

The ruins of the first pylon, decorated on the right-hand side with a bas-relief depicting Rameses II on his battle chariot as he stops the advance of the Hittites, can be seen in the background. In the left foreground lie fragments of the two impressive statues of the pharaoh that stood guard over the large hypostyle room; the splendid head of one of them, called the Young Memnon, was recovered by Giovanni Battista Belzoni in 1816 and conveyed to the British Museum. The Ramesseum was one of the most monumental works ordered by Rameses the Great, an enterprising, determined sovereign sometimes identified with the pharaoh of the Exodus, who left signs of frenetic construction work all over Egypt and Nubia. Abandoned at the end of the 20th dynasty, the temple was later used as a burial place for Theban priests, then as a source of building materials, and finally as a Coptic church; it has undergone extensive restoration work in recent years.

THE TEMPLE OF MEDINET HABU AT THEBES

Plate 76

5th December 1838

Not far from the Ramesseum, at Medinet Habu, stand the spectacular ruins of the mortuary temple built by Rameses III in an area occupied by some older sacred buildings. Roberts had already admired the great complex during his previous visit on the 21st of October. "We then visited the temple of Medinet Habu, which of all those standing on the west bank of Thebes is the most extraordinary, beyond description."

The sanctuary area is bounded by a mighty enclosure wall of sun-dried bricks, in the south side of which opens the lovely South Gate, set between two tall towers, which the archaeologists in Napoleon's entourage renamed The Pavilion. This unusual structure (the tallest part of the building visible in the lithograph) is entirely covered with bas-reliefs, mainly of a military nature, glorifying the figure of the pharaoh. On the right-hand side of the pavilion stands the temple of Thutmoses II: two slender columns surmounted by capitals in the shape of open scrolls precede an elegant portal dominated by a winged solar disk. The mortuary temple of Rameses III, which stood inside a second enclosure wall that has now practically disappeared, is one of the most stylistically perfect surviving specimens of Egyptian architecture.

Two courtyards, each preceded by a tall pylon, follow one after another along the southwest northeast axis; these are followed, again in a straight line, by a roofed part constituted by three hypostyle rooms, and finally the naos. The ruins of the royal palace, consisting of a hypostyle audience chamber, the throne room and numerous service rooms, can still be seen on the left-hand side of the temple.

Archaeological excavations have also uncovered traces of a town built around the palace, but only the home of an inspector of the Theban necropolises has remained sufficiently intact to be recognizable. The openings of what are known as the Tombs of the Nobility, excavated in spurs of rock bounding the Theban plain, are recognizable on the right side of the lithograph. Here, as in two other similar necropolises, court dignitaries, priests and high-ranking soldiers were buried during the Middle Kingdom.

RUINS OF A COPTIC CHURCH IN THE TEMPLE OF MEDINET HABU

Plate 77

5th December 1838

*F*ollowing the edict issued in 383 AD by the Emperor Theodosius which proclaimed Christianity to be the sole religion allowed in the Roman Empire, many Egyptian temples were converted into churches. At Medinet Habu, the sanctuary of Rameses III actually became the center of a large Coptic village that prospered until the Arab conquest of Egypt in the 7th century. The remains of this village, demolished from 1858 onwards during excavations begun by Auguste supported by porphyry columns surmounted by Corinthian capitals, which Roberts saw still standing and portrayed in his view. As these remains were removed during the excavation and restoration of the mortuary temple, the lithograph is now of great historical value.

The second courtyard has been restored to its original appearance, and is now surrounded by porticoes on all sides; to the north and south are the traditional Osiris pillars, badly damaged by the Christian monks, and to the east and west

Mariette, can be seen in the previous lithograph.

Inside the temple, in the second courtyard, the Coptic monks erected a great basilica after plastering over the ancient structures to eliminate all traces of the pagan religion.

This proved fortunate, because the bas-reliefs were thus perfectly preserved. The nave and aisles of the basilica were ten columns in the shape of closed scrolls. The reliefs decorating the end walls show battle scenes, clearly for propaganda purposes, or scenes of ostentatious religious devotion depicting the procession following the sacred boat, the apparition of the god Min, the exit of the pharaoh from the palace and his entry into the temple.

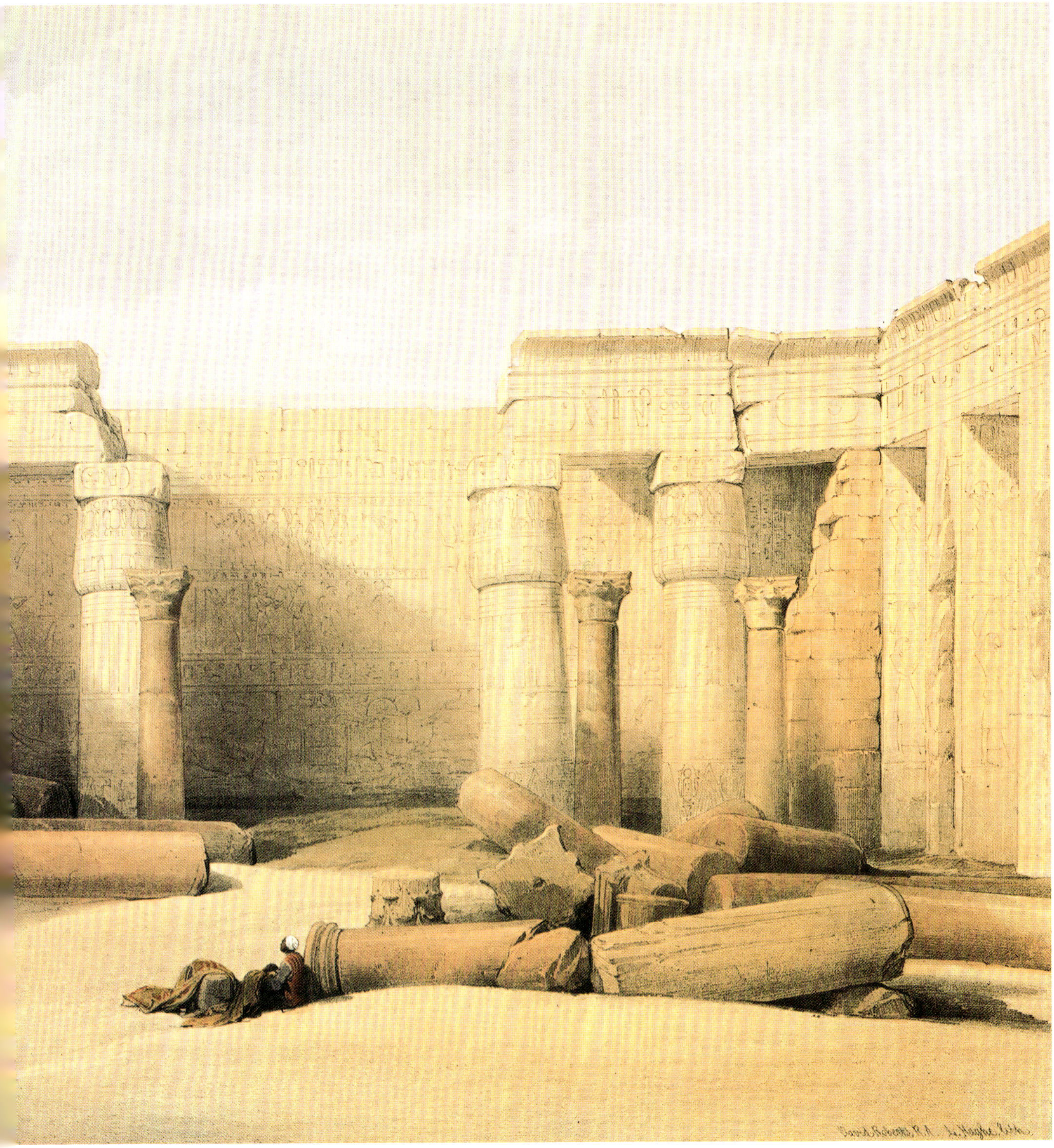
David Roberts R.A. L. Haghe Lith.

THE INTERIOR OF THE TEMPLE OF DENDERA

Plate 78

6th December 1838

Roberts took his leave of ancient Thebes on the afternoon of the 5th of December, and thanks to the favorable wind that enabled the crew to unfurl the sails for the first time since Abu Simbel, was in Dendera by 11 o'clock the next morning. He set to work enthusiastically, enraptured by the majesty of the Temple of Hathor. The great sanctuary exercised an indelible fascination on his mind, almost amounting to a spell, as demonstrated by the huge canvas now in the Bristol City Art Gallery, painted in oils in 1841 from sketches made locally. Dendera, originally called Tentyris, was one of the most important religious centers in ancient Egypt. The city was rendered sacred by three sanctuaries: the Sanctuary of Horus, god of the sky and protector of the pharaohs, the Sanctuary of Ihy, the young sistrum-playing son of Horus, and the Sanctuary of Hathor. Only the latter has survived practically intact, while no more than a few traces remain of the other two. Like Roberts, all the European travelers and archaeologists who made their way to the heart of Upper Egypt in the last century were deeply enchanted by the temple consecrated to the goddess of love and pleasure; at the time of Roberts's visit the building was half-buried in the sand, but it already emanated the charm that is now manifested in all its splendor as a result of extensive excavation and restoration work. When researchers and draftsmen began systematic exploration of the ruins, it soon became clear that the southern orientation of the temple and the great mask of Hathor on the south wall had a precise meaning; several miles lower down on the same bank of the Nile stands the temple of Edfu, dedicated to Horus, husband of the gentle goddess worshipped at Dendera. The two sites were the major centers of worship of these deities, and were linked by a mystic twinship that culminated every May in a great festival during which the effigies of Horus and Hathor were taken in procession along the Nile in sacred boats to recall their divine union. Since the most ancient times Dendera must have had a sanctuary, that was destroyed and rebuilt several times; however, the present complex dates from the late Ptolemaic and Roman period. This explains the prevalence of a magnificently scenic style, less severe than that of the oldest Egyptian temples, clearly evident in this lithograph, which shows the interior of the first hypostyle room, a magnificent chamber over 80 feet deep, featuring 18 huge columns covered with bas-reliefs.

From David Roberts's journal:

6th December - Today I drew the interior of the temple, the best preserved in all Egypt, which far surpasses all the others in the variety and quality of its reliefs. Although they are rather late, to my eyes they have all the majestic grandeur and effective simplicity of the older ones.

View under the Portico
of the Temple of Dendera

THE FAÇADE OF THE TEMPLE OF HATHOR AT DENDERA

Plate 79

7th December 1838

The temple of Dendera does not feature the pylon usually present in sacred Egyptian architecture; the front of the building is formed by a massive structure measuring 139 feet wide by 60 feet high, with six columns on the façade on which an impressive cornice rests. The intercolumniations are occupied as far as halfway up by panels covered with hieroglyphic texts and bas-reliefs, while the entrance opens in the center, forming a high, empty space wider than the adjacent ones. Inside, 18 more columns stand in three rows; all the capitals reproduced the features of the patron goddess of the place. As it is higher than the rest of the temple, this hypostyle room, added under Tiberius, to some extent acts as the missing pylon. The whole building, with its markedly trapezoidal shape and massive columns, might appear graceless and even unharmonious, but the perfect balance between solid and hollow effects and the minute details of the rich ornamentation are some of the features that make it an architectural miracle. Roberts was evidently somewhat awestruck by this miracle, as by his own admission he spent much of the 7th of December, looking for the right angle from which to make his drawing. Despite the hesitation he expressed about the success of his work, the drawing is very high quality, and gives very good insight into Roberts's outstanding technique, here splendidly enhanced by the craftsmanship of Louis Haghe. The descriptive detail of one is emphasized by the meticulous sensitivity of the other in a symbiosis rarely equaled for evocative power and the success of the aesthetic result.

As in the previous lithograph, the almost obsessive attention to reproducing even the smallest details is quite incredible. It is therefore a real tragedy that the fury of the Coptic monks, who had converted the temple into a church, was mainly unleashed against the images of Hathor, a young woman with an enigmatic smile; Roberts regretted that he could not draw the huge capitals as they once were, decorated with the lovely face of the goddess, now pathetically disfigured. Fortunately, the colors were still vivid, especially on the ceiling of the hypostyle room and the column drums.

THE KIOSK OF ISIS ON THE ROOF OF THE TEMPLE OF DENDERA

Plate 80

8th December 1838

As they were associated by the worship of Hathor and Horus and built at almost the same time, the temples of Edfu and Dendera present some very similar architectural features. Although they are both very well preserved, only the one consecrated to the goddess has the "irradiation chapel" still intact, at the southwest corner of the terraced roof. Once a year the sacred image, usually kept in the naos, was brought here and exposed to the sunlight to be regenerated. The procession of priests followed a long staircase cut in the left-hand embankment, the walls of which are decorated with figures going up one way and down the other, showing how the ceremony was performed. The kiosk where the rite of presentation to the sun god Ra was performed is an elegant peripteral building with 12 Hathor columns, connected halfway up by the usual curtain walls. In the northern part of the terrace stands a small chapel dedicated to Osiris, which was probably choked with sand and debris when Roberts saw it.

After Abydos, Dendera was the most important of the sanctuaries containing the 14 parts of the body of the god, cut to pieces by the cruel Seth. This importance was due to Hathor's associations with Osiris and Horus. In Egyptian cosmogony the goddess Hathor (whose name literally means "house of the god Horus"), daughter of Isis, at some point began to be identified with her mother, who had generated Horus by coupling with part of her husband's corpse after regenerating the phallus with her magic arts. Thus the two eventually came to be considered one and the same. Isis, daughter of Ra and mother of Horus and Ihy, goddess of nature and magic, was the wife of Osiris, the god of death and resurrection; she searched for the parts of his body scattered by Seth along the Nile Valley, and buried them in various sacred places. This explains the complex relationship and the reasons for what might be called the cross-worship between Dendera and Edfu.

THE GREAT ENTRANCE PORTAL TO THE SACRED ENCLOSURE OF DENDERA

Plate 81

8th December 1838

*T*he Temple of Dendera, built by Ptolemy IX Soter II, stands in the middle of a huge area bounded by a wall of air-dried bricks, almost entirely ruined, whose sides are between 925 and 990 feet long; on the north and east sides are two magnificent portals built during the period of Roman rule. Roberts drew the one facing east, the best preserved; as is clear from the lithograph, much of the structure was buried at the time, as were the Temple of Hathor and the other buildings surrounding it.

Apart from the great sanctuary, some outstanding monuments stand in the sacred enclosure. Not far from the rear façade of the great temple are the badly damaged remains of a small sanctuary dedicated to the birth of Isis; the surviving reliefs portray Nut, goddess of the sky, giving birth while sitting on a stool in accordance with the ancient local custom. Nearby, to the west, is a deep rectangular hollow enclosed by a boundary wall; this is all that remains of the sacred lake typical of all Egyptian sanctuaries, where the priests had to perform their ritual ablutions several times a day. The most interesting remains, including a well, a sanatorium dating from the Roman period, a Coptic church and two mammisi, one Ptolemaic and the other Roman, are scattered along the western wall and in the northwest corner of the Temple of Hathor. The Roman mammisi, incorrectly called the Typhonium, appears in the lithograph shown in Plate 9 of this volume, which was probably drawn, or at least sketched, on the 20th of October, as Roberts made no reference to it during his second visit. Mammisi, whose name literally means birth chapel, are small temples typical of the Early Period in which the pharaohs' children were honored on the pretext of worshipping the birth of the gods. Their children, considered to be on a par with living deities, could only be born within the sacred precincts of the temple. The first building of this kind was erected at Dendera by Nectanebo I between 378 and 360 BC, while the adjacent one was built by order of Augustus.

After taking leave of Henry Tattam, one of the most famous Egyptologists of the day, whom he had met on his arrival at Dendera, Roberts decided that he was satisfied with the work he had done, and recommenced his journey on the evening of the 8th of December.

The Nile near the Pyramids of Dahshur and Saqqarah

Plate 82

9th-20th December 1838

After spending three days at Dendera, Roberts felt satisfied with the work he had done, and ordered the crew to set sail for Cairo; after the temples of ancient Egypt, the time had now come to look at Islamic architecture. The nights had become very pleasant and the climate similar to the English weather towards the end of September, so the voyage promised to be very enjoyable. In the next few days Roberts spent much of his time finishing the drawings; when he counted them, he found that there were about a hundred. "Not bad for a month's work," he commented with legitimate pride. "Perhaps I did not do justice to these ancient relics, but few other artists in my circumstances could have afforded to stay longer, and I wonder how many of them could have produced more in the same time."

On the 10th he stopped for a few hours at Abydos, the main city sacred to Osiris, where he visited the few remains still visible of the temples of Seti I and Rameses II, which were to be excavated 21 years later by Auguste Mariette.

When he reached Siout on the 13th of December, Roberts realized to his horror that he had left his portfolio of drawings on the heights of Girgeh, where he had climbed two days earlier to compare some of his earlier sketches with the reliefs on the tombs in that area. As luck would have it, while he was wondering anxiously what to do, a southbound boat flying the Union Jack drew near, sailing before the wind.

On hearing of the incident the boat's owner offered to take Ismail and Hassan Amoris to Girgah to look for the drawings. Roberts was on tenterhooks until the 17th, when the pair returned triumphantly after covering the 80 miles between the two towns in only 30 hours, rowing nearly all the time in a hired rowing boat.

As if reborn after his anxious wait, Roberts decided to stop at Minieh to visit the bazaar. However, the weather was breaking and the days growing colder, so he decided to exploit the favorable wind in order to conclude the voyage as soon as possible. On the 20th the boat finally came in sight of the pyramids of Dahshur; the "Bent Pyramid" and the "Red Pyramid," both built by Snefru around 2570 BC, can be seen on the left-hand side of the lithograph, and the southern pyramids of the Saqqarah necropolis can be glimpsed on the horizon. In the foreground is a boat with a cargo of slave-girls, whose owner, an unpleasant-looking Greek, began to sing the praises of with the skill of an auctioneer.

Disgusted, Roberts regretted that he only knew a few words of Arabic and Greek, not enough to express all his disapproval and the abhorrence with which the slave trade was regarded in England.

From David Roberts's journal:

20th December - This morning we came in sight of what are called the False Pyramids. The men sang all the time, happy at the thought that they will finally be home tonight. I have grown so used to their company that I am saddened at the thought of the imminent farewell. The journey has been fascinating, and undoubtedly the most important of my entire life. I believe that my drawings are of great interest, irrespective of their artistic worth.

195

CAIRO

21st December 1838 - 6th February 1839

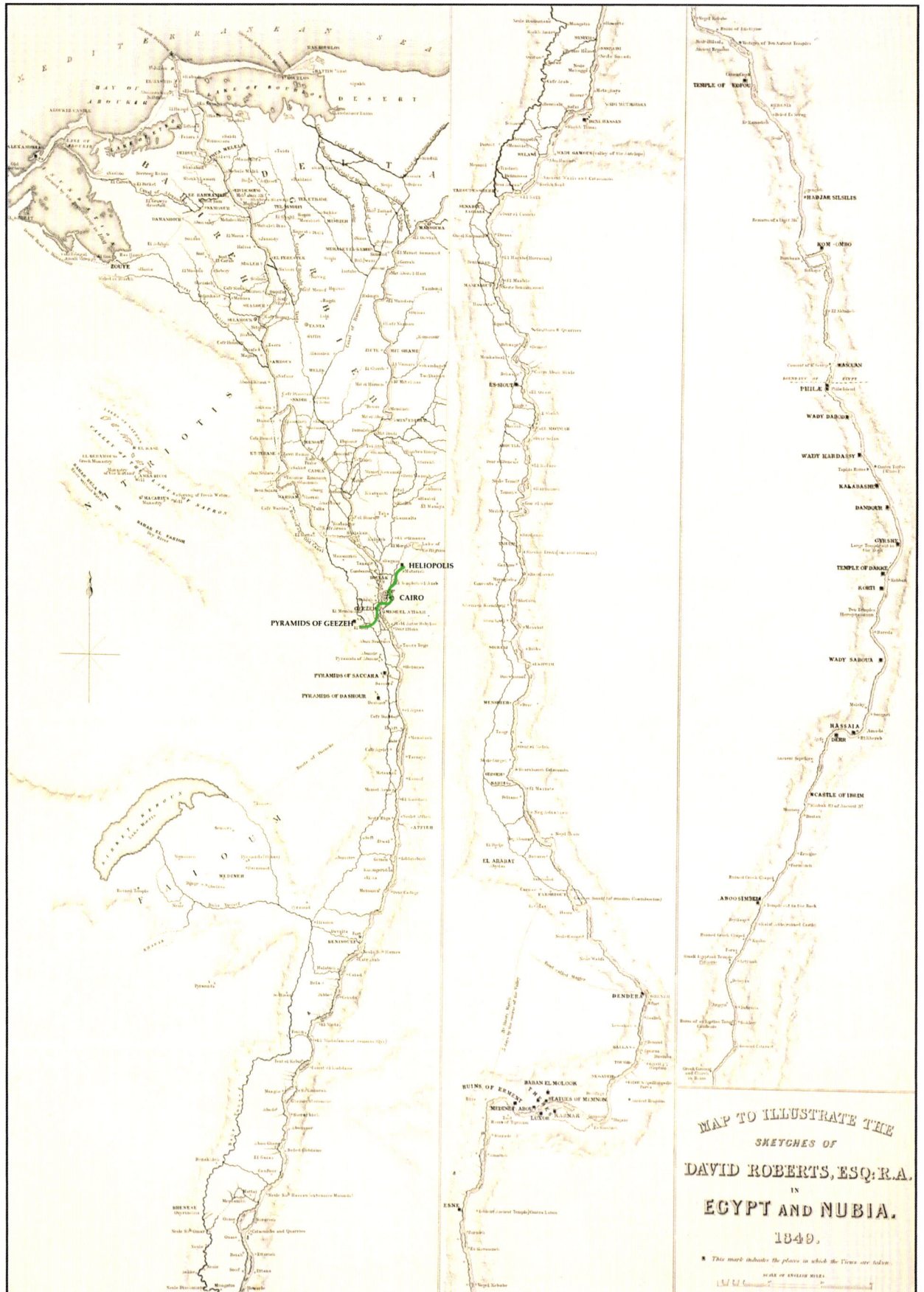

MAP TO ILLUSTRATE THE
SKETCHES OF
DAVID ROBERTS, ESQ: R.A.
IN
EGYPT AND NUBIA.
1849.

* This mark indicates the places in which the Views are taken.

SCALE OF ENGLISH MILES.

EGYPT & NUBIA.

David Roberts, R.A.

WILLIAM BROCKEDON, F.R.S.

LOUIS HAGHE.

From David Roberts's journal:

24th December - From the heights of the Citadel, the spectacle offered at nightfall was magnificent. The sky was full of clouds, between which the rays of the setting sun managed to peep every so often; the pyramids loomed on the horizon, dark as the clouds that hung over them, and the Nile reflected the last glimmers of light, while the city stretched out as far as the eye could see, studded with fantastically shaped minarets. I am enjoying this Christmas Eve alone, grateful for being in good health and having concluded the most arduous part of the journey.

THE MOSQUE OF SULTAN HASSAN

Plate 83

21st-26th December 1838

When Roberts finally reached Cairo on the morning of the 21st of December, he found a letter waiting for him from Christine, telling him of his election as an Associate of the Royal Academy. The next day he rented a house at a reasonable price and sent a letter to his daughter in which, together with his usual fatherly advice, he told her about his recent adventures and his plans for the immediate future. Above all he wished to add to his already bulky portfolio a comprehensive range of Cairo's mosques, which were unequaled throughout the world, although he was worried that the people might be hostile and almost certain that he would not be allowed to enter any of them. His only hope in this respect was Colonel Campbell, who was already making representations to the pasha. Roberts then spent a day or two writing more letters home and making his new residence as comfortable as possible. On the 23rd he made his first reconnaissance at the tombs of the Caliphs, and the next day visited the Citadel, then the magnificent residence of Mohammed Ali; he was given permission to visit the Audience Chamber and the pasha's private apartments, which he described as "all modern, and gaudily painted."

Roberts spent Christmas Day strolling around the city; after a walk through the city center he visited the Tombs of the Mamluks, followed by the great mausoleum recently built by Mohammed Ali, the reliefs of which seemed to him rather coarse compared with the delicacy of the older ones he had seen a little earlier. He was invited to lunch by Colonel Campbell, whose hospitality was as delightful as usual, and also spent a very pleasant evening.

The next morning he started work early. As his first subject he chose the majestic outline of the Mosque of Sultan Hassan, seen from the large square in front. While he was busy drawing, the guard provided for him by the pasha had difficulty keeping back the crowd of curious onlookers. The mosque is considered one of the greatest works of Islamic art; it was built by order of Sultan Hassan al-Nasir between 1356 and 1363, perhaps by a Syrian architect. The façades, featuring deep vertical niches containing two rows of windows, are surmounted by a projecting cornice made of stalactite work (muqarna) that was completed with crenellations at the turn of this century. The sultan's mausoleum, which projects from the building like a die, is surmounted by a 200-foot-tall dome rebuilt in the 18th century in a style influenced by Turkish art. The main minaret, 269 feet tall, is still the highest in Cairo.

199

VICTORY GATE

Plate 84

27th December 1838

On the morning of the 27th, Roberts made a drawing of Bab al-Nasr, the Victory Gate, one of the three surviving gates of those that opened in the city walls of Cairo built between 1087 and 1091 by the Vizier Badr el-Jamali. The mighty structure is flanked by two massive square towers, whose proportions were evidently inspired by the canons of ancient Roman *castrum* architecture. In the background, behind Bab al-Futuh (the Conquest Gate), stands the minaret of the mosque built between 990 and 1013 by the mysterious Caliph al-Hakim Bi Amrallah. In the afternoon Roberts went to Hill's Hotel, where he had stayed in September, to obtain news of England and exchange a few words with guests who had recently arrived from Europe. Later Colonel Campbell delivered the precious pass he would need during his imminent journey to the Holy Land. On his arrival in Cairo Roberts had made the acquaintance of two English gentlemen, John Pell and John Kinnear, who intended to travel to Syria after crossing the Sinai and Palestine. The pair invited him to join their expedition and the artist willingly agreed, particularly attracted by the idea of seeing the famous monastery of Saint Catherine. He immediately began the complex preparations for the journey, which seemed likely to be even more difficult than the one he had just finished.

EL-RHAMREE MOSQUE

Plate 85

27th December 1838

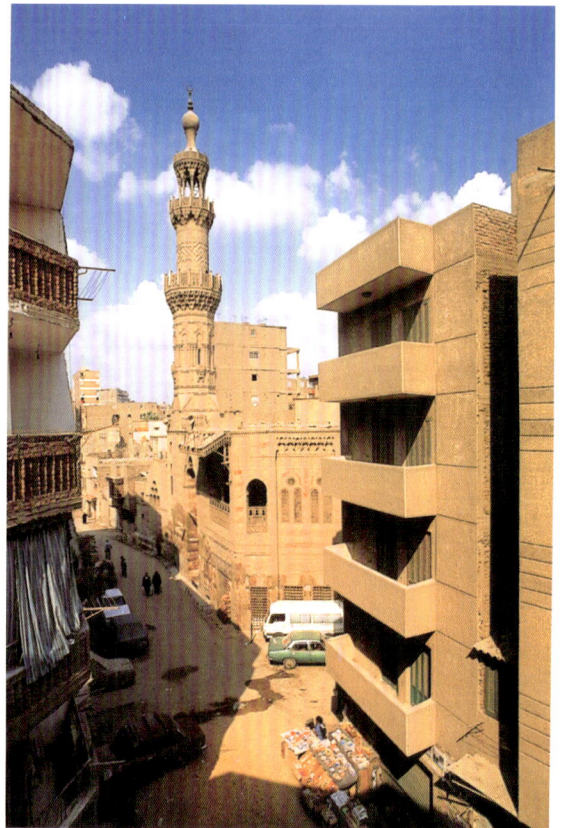

ear the Victory Gate stood El-Rhamree Mosque, whose elegant masonry with alternating rows of red and white stone betrayed its Mamluk origin; in other words, it dated from the period between 1250 and the incorporation of Egypt into the Ottoman Empire in 1517.

The Mamluks were originally bought slaves (mamluk *in Arabic*) of Turkish and Circassian descent who were trained as bodyguards or elite soldiers. This militia became increasingly powerful and overthrew the Ayubbid dynasty in a coup d'état. The regime of military feudalism they imposed was often bloodthirsty, but brought a period of economic, political and artistic glory to Egypt, largely due to the energetic personalities of sultans like Baybars, Hassan and Qalawun. Their last sovereign, Tuman Bey, was deposed by the Ottoman conquerors, but the Mamluks retained much of their power, often in open conflict with the pashas of Constantinople. During Napoleon's expedition to Egypt they offered strong resistance to the French troops, but were defeated at the Battle of the Pyramids, and their chiefs were treacherously massacred by Mohammed Ali, as they had become an obstacle to his desire for power.

In Mamluk architecture, the ornamental emphasis mainly focuses on the entrances, decorated with elaborate engravings and inlays in geometrical and floral patterns in accordance with the precept in the Koran that prohibits the portrayal of human beings or animals, and on the minarets, whose balconies are usually supported by a myriad of muqarnas. The domes, surmounted by the alam, the crescent-shaped metal ornament common to all styles of Islamic architecture, are usually so slender as to appear almost diaphanous. Although the monument was not particularly important, Roberts must have particularly liked the subject, as in both the lithograph and the watercolor displayed in Nottingham Museum the attention given to reproducing the contrast between the mysterious darkness of the alley and the soaring silhouette of the minaret is clearly evident.

David Roberts R.A.

THE ZUWAILAH GATE
FROM THE OUTSIDE

Plate 86

28th December 1838

R oberts spent much of the 28th drawing Bab Zuwailah, one of the three monumental gates that still open in the remains of the ancient Fatimid city walls. The massive structure, formed by two semicircular towers that frame the single-arch portal, was completed around 1091. The great lobed blind arches that decorate its sides were a characteristic feature of North African architecture, imported to Egypt by craftsmen in the retinue of the Fatimid conquerors who ruled the country between 969 and 1171. The Fatimids, who came from what is now Tunisia, took their name from the family of Mohammed's daughter Fatima, whose descendants they claimed to be. Despite these decorative elements the gate, like Bab al-Nasr and Bab al-Futuh, clearly reveals the influence of the Roman-Byzantine construction style. The loggia on the portal, which was bricked up when Roberts saw it and has been reopened recently, originally housed the ceremonial orchestra, whose task was to announce the arrival of the royal court with music, in accordance with a protocol that is fairly common in the East. The gate is named after a brave North African tribe whose men fought in the Fatimid army.

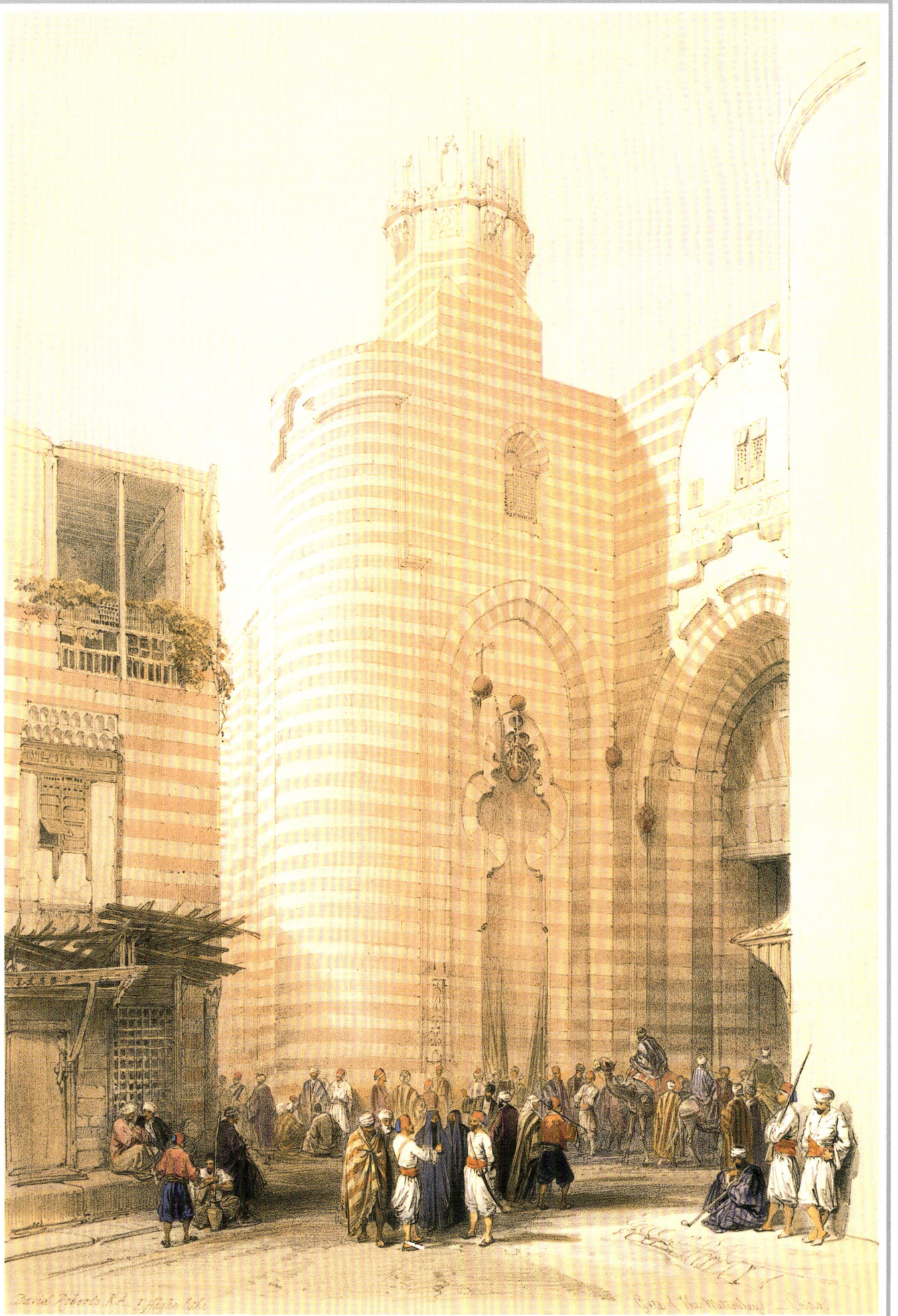

David Roberts R.A. 1 Hague lith.

205

THE ZUWAILAH GATE
FROM THE INSIDE

Plate 87

28th December 1838

O n the two mighty towers of Bab Zuwailah stand the slender minarets of the al-Muayyad mosque, one of the most magnificent dating from the Circassian Mamluk age. The mosque, also called el-Ahmar (the Red), was begun in 1416 by Sultan al-Muayyad and completed a year after his death, in 1421.

After its defensive function became unnecessary, Bab Zuwailah was long used as a prison, and sentences of capital punishment were carried out nearby. The mosque built onto the gate is the result of a curious political incident; al-Muayyad made a vow to build a sanctuary on the site of the prison into that he was thrown after a palace revolt, an incident that was by no means unusual in those days.

On regaining his freedom and his power, the sultan kept his vow. The bronze-clad doors of the entrance come from the Mosque of Sultan Hassan, and are considered some of the loveliest in Cairo; the interior, with its profusion of colored marble, stucco and gilding, is extraordinarily but not exaggeratedly luxurious. The lithograph shows a view of the street that led from the gate to the city center; thronged with incessant traffic and lined with shops of all kinds on both sides, it was the scene of indescribable bedlam. Roberts, almost buried by the human tide, had to manage as best he could, as he was resigned to doing since his first few days in the city.

Though picturesque, the narrow, crowded streets of Cairo constituted a rather difficult subject, because pedestrians continually ran the risk of being crushed by overloaded camels, which also had the unfortunate habit of shoving to the left and right with no respect for artists. The streets around Bab Zuwailah are still very busy and retain the atmosphere of bygone days, especially because of the numerous workshops specializing in the manufacture of the great canopies used to shade the streets during major ceremonies.

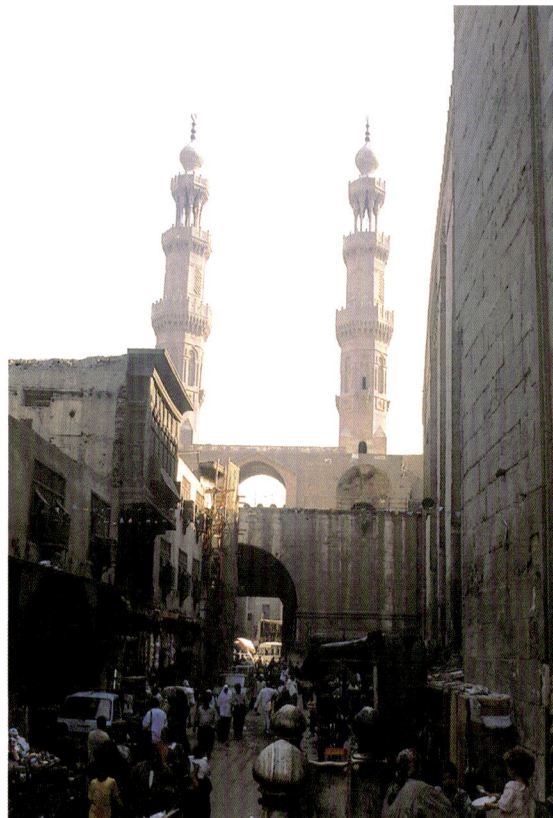

From David Roberts's journal:

28th December - Today I made two drawings of the Bab Zuweileh gate with its minarets.
I am still bewildered by the extraordinarily picturesque appearance of the streets and buildings of this most wonderful of cities.
Only the population is even more extraordinary, but a reliable description is impossible, and I will not even attempt one.

Mosque and Grand Entrance
of the Metwalys at Cairo

THE MARISTAN OF SULTAN QALAWUN

Plate 88

29th December 1838

*T*his view of the road leading to the Mosque of Sultan Qalawun shows the chaotic traffic that was one of the characteristic features of the city. For an artist dressed in the European style it was impossible to pass unnoticed, and discomfort sometimes gave way to a slight feeling of fear, though Roberts never suffered any serious incident. Although their curiosity was aroused by his appearance the people behaved very politely towards him; they usually did no more than gaze in amazement at his stock of pencils, paper and paints.

Nevertheless, in a letter to his friend David Hay, the artist had to admit that his irritation was sometimes hard to control. However, Cairo had some 300,000 inhabitants, a sixth more than Edinburgh, and it was unreasonable to expect to be able to wander around freely with no inconvenience, drawing undisturbed as if in the grounds of a Scottish castle. The complex, built in 1285 by Sultan al-Mansur Qalawun and consisting of a madrasa, the sultan's mausoleum and a hospital, is one of the most magnificent monuments in Cairo. The most interesting and in many ways innovatory feature of this group of buildings (to which a madrasa was added by the sultan's son in the late 13th century) is certainly the hospital. It was not the first to be built in Cairo, as Ibn Tulun had already founded a similar charitable institution in the 9th century, imitated by the Fatimid sultans and by the great Saladin, but it was the best known, as it retained its function as a shelter for the sick and a center for the study of medicine until the 19th century. The sultan built the hospital on the basis of personal experience, as he had been successfully treated at the hospital of Nur al-Din in Damascus years earlier. The hospital, called maristan (place of illness), was far ahead of its time, as was Arab medical science, which was still taught in Europe at the beginning of the last century. The hospital was divided into two sections, for male and female patients, and received needy patients of all ages and social classes from all over the Arab world; a bed, food and appropriate treatment was guaranteed for all.

The Tombs of Mamluks

Plate 89

30th December 1838

By contrast with the pharaonic custom of locating necropolises on the west bank of the Nile, the Mamluks built their sepulchres to the east, not far from the Citadel. Roberts visited the site on the 30th, a clear but very cold day. The huge depression contained a succession of minarets and domes of all shapes and sizes, even then in a dilapidated state; these monumental buildings housed the tombs of sultans, princesses and court dignitaries who lived during the great age of the Bahrite Mamluks and the Circassian Mamluks, between the 13th and 15th centuries. In time, a large number of smaller tombs were erected around the monumental buildings.

As it was the custom to go there to honor the dead on Fridays, closed courtyards and roofed areas were added to the tombs of the wealthier citizens for the use of visiting relatives, with the result that the cemeteries came to resemble towns. Nowadays, some 600,000 Cairo residents live in the huge necropolises outside the walls of the Fatimid city.

The tentacular capital city, which has grown beyond all recognition in the past few decades, has around 15 million inhabitants, many of whom live in dreadful conditions; it is therefore easy to understand the choice of those who prefer the vaguely supernatural peace of the city of the dead to the chaos of the new districts or the slums of the shanty towns.

The Tombs of Mamluks,
WITH A FUNERAL PROCESSION

Plate 90

30th December 1838

The building reproduced by Roberts, which stands in the cemetery to the south of the Citadel, is known as the Sultan's Mausoleum. However, this name only indicates that it belonged to a person of high rank, as the mysterious monument has not yet been attributed, and is roughly dated at around 1360.

The main structure, which has a rectangular plan, is surmounted by twin fluted domes resting on very tall drums and connected by a barrel-vaulted iwan; a few yards away, situated in a corner of the enclosure wall that has now been destroyed, stands a soaring octagonal minaret that was probably part of the complex. The construction style

of the mausoleum is out of the ordinary in many respects and presents some unusual analogies with the Central Asian architecture of Samarkand. The minaret that stands on the left of the building is part of the funerary complex of Emir Qusun, while the one silhouetted in the background dates from the Ottoman period. While Roberts was busy drawing, he suddenly heard loud shouts and laments. A few moments later he saw a funeral procession approaching, followed by veiled women weeping piteously; judging by the small size of the coffin, it must have been a child's funeral. The Scotsman was sincerely moved by this tragic scene, and included it in his view.

THE COPPERSMITHS' BAZAAR

Plate 91

31st December 1838

Cairo's bazaars were too fascinating a subject for Roberts to resist, so on New Year's Eve he decided to visit the great market, which he portrayed in this magnificent view. With its colors and the groups of purchasers who lingered around one merchant or another to examine goods or haggle at length over prices, the bazaar provided an exciting spectacle, quite new to European eyes. Where the ancient city of the Fatimid dynasty once stood, the streets were now cluttered with goods of every kind. Scale makers vied for the little available space with fabric sellers, whose caverns were jam-packed with rolls of brightly colored silk and cotton. Not far away was a small jewelers' shop where jewelery could be valued or the price of some trinket bargained over. Each neighborhood specialized in a different type of goods; in one, perfumes and essences were sold, in another, spices and tea, and around the corner, carpets and haberdashery. Near the ancient religious complex of Sultan al-Salih Najm al-Din Ayyub, dating from 1243, coppersmiths and cauldron makers displayed embossed plates, bowls and cauldrons. In the midst of this bedlam pedestrians continually had to dodge carts laden with fruit, and freshwater sellers who staggered under the weight of the great jars they carried on their shoulders. Now as then, in the districts between the Citadel and Bab al-Futuh, craftsmen and shopkeepers with their baskets full of all sorts of products keep alive a tradition that seems eternal.

Drawing in the great bazaar involved no problems, but Roberts had a very different experience in a market in one of the poor districts of Cairo. While he was working with some difficulty in the midst of a curious crowd that continually interrupted him and even bumped into him by standing too close, he suddenly had his sketch pad torn out of his hands by a missile that appeared out of nowhere. It was a half-eaten orange, thrown from one of the galleries jutting out over the square, which must have been designed for that very purpose. Roberts decided that a change of scenery might be the wisest course of action but, irritated and perhaps rather ashamed of his inglorious retreat, he wondered whether an Arab artist would have taken to his heels quite as fast as he did.

The time had really come to wear more suitable clothing.

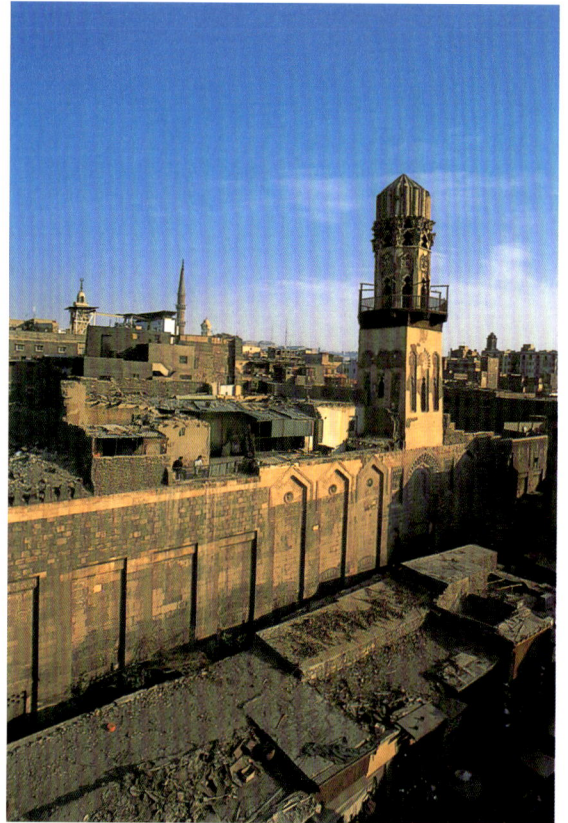

From David Roberts's journal:

31st December - It's New Year's Eve, but how different from those spent in London. The days are so bright, and I can eat fresh vegetables in abundance. I am in excellent health, and living in a city which surpasses the fantasy of any artist. I received a letter from my dearest Christine today; thank God all are well at home... This is the last night of the old year, and my thoughts turn to all the happy New Years I have spent so far. I send my heartfelt good wishes to all my nearest and dearest in my beloved Scotland.

The entrance to the Mosque of Sultan Hassan

Plate 92

1st January 1839

On New Year's Day, Roberts was busy as usual in the streets of Cairo, looking for more picturesque subjects. Drawing in the midst of such a crowd was very tiring, so that by the time he got home in the evening he was worn out.

As he wrote in his journal, no-one in England, seeing those sketches, could possibly imagine how much labor they had cost him. In any event, his work would increase knowledge of the various architectural styles that had developed in Egypt over the centuries, and this was sufficient reward to justify all the effort he had put into it.

He spent that day drawing the magnificent entrance to the Mosque of Sultan Hassan, considered by many to be the loveliest in the whole of Cairo, although it was never completed.

The great structure was designed as a madrasa dedicated to the four orthodox law schools of Sunnite Islam (Maliki, Shafii, Hanbali and Hanafi), and also as a congregational mosque for the Friday sermon.

In the Islamic world, a madrasa was an institute in which students could study the legal/religious sciences, theology, grammar, literature and rhetoric free of charge. Founded towards the mid-11th century to strengthen Sunnite orthodoxy and combat Shiite propaganda, the madrasas are far less widely attended now than they once were, but still combine the functions of mosque and theological seminary.

Sultan Hassan had the magnificent building erected in one of the most privileged positions in Cairo and lavished huge resources on it; however, near bankrupted by the increasing costs, he admitted that he would have abandoned the project if he had not been ashamed at the thought that someone might say an Egyptian sultan was incapable of finishing the mosque he had started. His death as a result of a court conspiracy put an end to all but part of his ambitious project.

THE SCRIBE

Plate 93

2nd-5th January 1839

On the 2nd of January, Roberts received a visit from the vice-consul Mr. Walne, who told him what he needed to do to in order to obtain permission to enter the mosques. First of all, he would have to obtain suitable clothes, and secondly he would have to shave off his rather flashy sideburns. While the idea of dressing Turkish-style appealed to him, he was very sorry to lose the facial ornaments he was so proud of, but realized the concession was worth it. After all, he was the first European to be given such an opportunity, and there was no point worrying about such silly little details. Finally, he had to promise that he would not use brushes made of pig's bristles, as the pig is considered impure in the Islamic world.

He spent the same day making the necessary purchases, although he did not feel quite well. As he strolled around the maze of alleys he was amazed at everything he saw: superb relics of a legendary past, extraordinary people and customs, indescribable lights and colors.

Cairo was so picturesque that it seemed to him to have no equal anywhere in the world. The only drawback was the evident poverty of much of the population, which particularly upset him. Among the many scenes of everyday life, he was particularly struck by the sight of a young woman, evidently illiterate, who was dictating a letter to a public scribe with a sorrowful expression; this lithograph betrays the human compassion Roberts felt for those poor people.

When he got home he tried on the new clothes and was pleased with the result; with his now sunburned skin and dark eyes he could reasonably pass for a Turk. He had not shaved his head, but his hair was well concealed under the turban, and to complete the effect he would grow a mustache in accordance with the local fashion.

Despite his enthusiasm, he had to delay the long-awaited experience for a few days because an unpleasant gastrointestinal disorder confined him to bed until the 5th, when he was able to take a walk through the town to regain his strength.

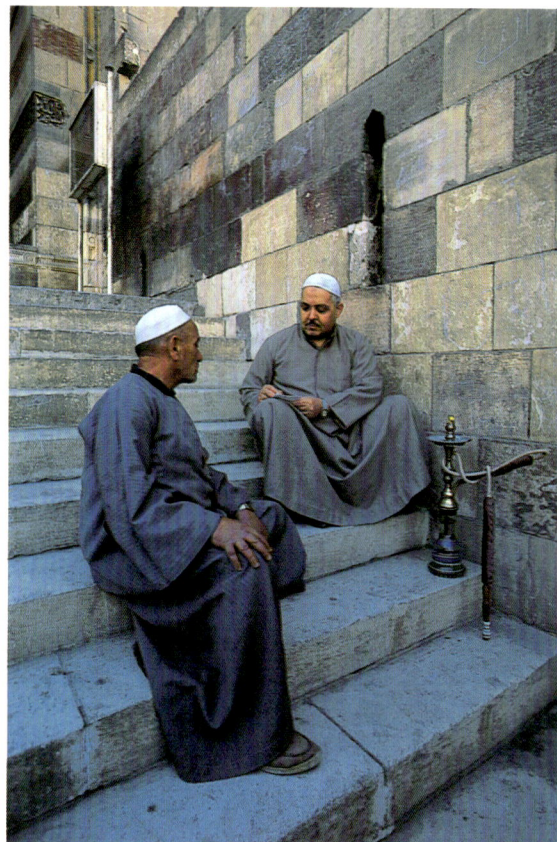

From David Roberts's journal:

4th January - Having heard from my servant of my indisposition, Colonel Campbell came to see me, and I spent a very pleasant hour with him. Later I wrote a long letter to my friend Hay, and spent the rest of the time profitably, retouching the drawings I had done in the past few days.

The Letter Writer, Cairo.

THE SILK VENDORS' BAZAAR
AND THE RELIGIOUS COMPLEX
OF SULTAN AL-GHURI

Plate 94   *6th January 1839*

On the 6th of January, Roberts, now entirely recovered, finally went out dressed "Turkish-style," ready to visit the interior of as many mosques as possible. Escorted by two armed guards, he went (among other places) to al-Azhar Mosque, the most important architectural relic to survive in Cairo from the Fatimid period. Built in 972 by Vizier Jawhar al-Siqilli and once used, at least in part, as a theological college, it was rebuilt in an even more impressive form after the earthquake of 1303. During Ottoman rule, when the Mamluk madrasas had fallen into decline, al-Azhar became the center of Islamic teaching in Egypt, and it is still the most famous religious university in the Arab world. Although its name means "The Splendid," Roberts felt that it was in an appallingly dilapidated condition, and did not even draw it. He received a better impression from Saiydna al-Hussein Mosque, rebuilt in 1792 on the site of a much older place of worship; as the head of Mohammed's nephew Hussein, who died in the Battle of Kerbela in 680, is buried there, the sanctuary is still considered one of the most sacred, and is magnificently decorated during Ramadan, the month of fasting. The same day he also entered the funerary mosque of Sultan Qaytbay, dating from 1474, where he was shown an exquisitely illuminated copy of the Koran. During his visit to the bazaar quarter, Roberts was particularly struck by a section of the street between two sacred buildings over which wooden boards had been erected to offer shade to the silk merchants, and decided to return there.

Apart from that makeshift roof, this part of the city has remained almost unchanged. The madrasa and the mausoleum built circa 1504 by Sultan al-Ghuri still stand opposite one another on al-Muizz Street.

Both buildings have a trefoil stalactite work portal in the façade, and alternate rows of white, red and black stone. Numerous shops and kiosks still do a roaring trade along the street, and the rent they pay to occupy public property is used for the maintenance of the complex.

From David Roberts's journal:

6th January - It makes my hair stand on end to think what terrifying punishment would have been inflicted on me for my involuntary crime if it had become known that the sacred drapery had been contaminated by the touch of an infidel, a Christian dog, and I had been caught.

THE INTERIOR OF THE MOSQUE OF SULTAN AL-GHURI

Plate 95

6th January 1839

Roberts was able to enter and draw the interior of the madrasa-mosque of Sultan al-Ghuri, richly decorated with colored marble. This lithograph is of particular interest because it shows the appearance of a mosque built on the qa'a plan, the same one used by Sultan Hassan to build his masterpiece. Very briefly, an atrium with some degree of decoration leads to an unroofed square courtyard, which may have a fountain for ritual ablutions in the middle; four prayer rooms (iwans) with vaulted or coffered ceilings surround this courtyard. The main iwan, in the end wall of which is the mihrab or prayer niche, is larger than the other three. This cross-shaped plan is typical of the madrasas-mosques built during the 13th century, in which the rooms used for study and the students' lodgings are usually built around the iwans to form a square. The rooms were lit by countless oil lamps and great bronze chandeliers similar to the one portrayed by Roberts; the few surviving specimens are now mostly housed in the Cairo Museum of Islamic Art. Dressed as a high-ranking army officer, the artist visited the mosque accompanied by two guards, who waited at the door, and one of the pasha's young officials who had been educated in England. This official's quick thinking proved providential when Roberts got into a scrape that could have had very serious results. Entrance to a mosque for a non-Muslim was strictly prohibited and subject to very heavy penalties; Mohammed Ali had granted permission to Roberts provided that he dress and act in such a way that he would not be recognized as a Christian. However, overcome by curiosity, after a while the Scotsman entered a room where a number of people where working on a large silk cloth with magnificent gold embroidery. He knelt down as he had seen other onlookers do, not to kiss the fabric but to examine it more closely. The menacing silence that suddenly fell was enough to make him realize that he had done something terrible; when he looked up, he saw his young escort put a finger to his lips and then draw it across his throat. With a glimmer of good sense he prostrated himself again and began to move backwards, while the official covered his retreat. Once outside the mosque he took to his heels and ran through a couple of districts. Later, he was told that the cloth was the sacred drape woven specially for pilgrims to lay on the tomb of the Prophet at Medina.

THE CITADEL GATE

Plate 96

7th-8th January 1839

On the 7th of January Roberts climbed the heights of Moqattam to see the famous petrified forest. The next day his attention was attracted by the preparations taking place in the square in front of Bab el-Asab, the main entrance to the Citadel. Here, caravans bound for Mecca were being prepared, and crowds of pilgrims were flocking from all over the city and the surrounding area.
One of the camels was to take to Medina the precious cloth that was to be placed on the Prophet's tomb. As far as the eye could see, the windows and even the roofs of the houses were packed with onlookers, mainly women and children, watching the spectacle with great excitement.
Now, the great square Midan Salah el-Din has lost its original function, but has remained one of the nerve centers of the great metropolis. It is overlooked by the Mosque of Pasha Mahmud and the adjacent madrasa, Qani bey Amir Akor, shown in the lithograph on the right-hand side of the Citadel Gate.
Opposite Bab el-Asab stands the great Mosque of Sultan Hassan, with al-Rifai Mosque facing it. Completed in 1912 by order of Princess Khoshiar Hanem, it contains (among others) the tombs of King Farouk, last sovereign of Egypt, and the Shah of Persia Reza Pahlavi.

THE DEPARTURE OF PILGRIMS BOUND FOR MECCA

Plate 97

8th January 1839

*R*oberts also drew the departure of the caravan bound for Medina and Mecca. In the lithograph, the pilgrims are leaving the city in the direction of Suez; the huge bulk of the Citadel is silhouetted in the background. The great fortress, which stands on a rocky eminence on the slopes of Jebel Moqattam, where it overlooks the city, was built in 1176 by Saladin; part of the outer layer of the minor pyramids of Giza may have been used as building material. The building was extended several times over the centuries; inside its mighty enclosure wall Mohammed Ali erected a magnificent residence, now used as a museum. The same sovereign started work on a great mosque in Ottoman style in 1824, which was far from complete when Roberts saw it; in fact, the Alabaster Mosque was only finished by his son Said in 1857. The pasha is said to have built it to redeem his soul, tormented by a horrific crime. Mohammed Ali, who was of Albanian descent but born in Greece, went to Egypt with Turkish troops to liberate the country from the Napoleonic occupation. His boundless ambition led him to proclaim himself pasha in 1805, and in 1811, wishing to get rid of the Mamluks, who constituted an obstacle to his political ambitions, he invited them to the Citadel on a pretext and had them slaughtered.

From David Roberts's journal:

8th January - Today I made some sketches of the departure ceremony of the caravan which will take the sacred cloth to be placed on the Prophet's tomb. This evening I dined with friends in accordance with the local customs, in other words sitting on cushions around a very low table, and using my fingers to pick up meat cut into small pieces.

THE INTERIOR OF THE MOSQUE OF SULTAN AL-MUAYYAD

Plate 98

9th January 1839

The religious complex built by Sultan al-Muayyad behind Bab Zuwailah included a mosque for Friday prayers, a madrasa *and two mausoleums. Roberts visited it on the afternoon of the 9th of January, after spending the morning painting studies in oils of the interior of the funerary mosque of Sultan Qaytbay.*

The interior of the mosque, which was built between 1416 and 1421, is a huge hypostyle room divided into a nave and two aisles, supported by columns with Corinthian capitals of pre-Islamic manufacture, certainly reused. The coffered ceilings made of painted and gilded wood, the windows with their elegant stucco frames, the finely decorated wood and ivory pulpit and the dikka *(the imam's dais), visible in the center of the lithograph, which rested on slender marble columns, make the mosque one of the loveliest in Cairo. It is a sad loss that only part of the complex has survived to the present day; in fact, the present mosque only occupies one of the four original* iwans. *At sunset Roberts hurried home so that he would have plenty of time to tidy up and change into* sufficiently elegant clothes, as he had been invited to the inaugural performance at the city's opera house. The building was "small but tasteful" and he enjoyed the opera, sung in Italian.*

228

Interior of the Mosque of the Metwalys

229

A COFFEEHOUSE

Plate 99

10th January 1839

*D*uring his long
strolls through the city streets,
Roberts was enraptured by the
picturesque scenes of local life.
In one spot old men dozed near a
stall crammed with nameless
goods, a little further on an
interested crowd watched a
juggler's performance, and just
around the corner a shopkeeper
was fighting a losing battle,
sweeping into the street the dust
that had just covered the worn
shop floor.
Here and there, from some
mysterious recess, came scents
of spices and grilled meat that
mingled with the aroma issuing
from the countless coffeehouses,
popular meeting places that
were crowded at all hours of the
day with an all-male clientele.
Here, colorfully dressed men
spent their time drawing on a
long chabouk or bubbling
shisha and lazily blowing out
curls of blue smoke, lost in
thought, or idly indulged in
endless discussions around a
cup of coffee prepared Turkish
style and sipped slowly
according to an ancient ritual.
Fascinated and delighted by this
exotic world, Roberts confided
all his impressions to his faithful
sketchpad.

David Roberts, R.A.   Sheghe Lith.

THE TOMBS
OF THE CALIPHS

Plate 100

11th January 1839

*D*uring the
second half of the 13th century,
huge monumental necropolises
were built to the east of the
Fatimid walls; as in the case
of the burial grounds situated
to the west of the Citadel,
they have now been swallowed
up by the continually
expanding metropolis. Here too,
the expanse of bulbous domes
and minarets houses a large
proportion of the poorer
segment of the population,
in strange coexistence between
the living and the dead.
On the 11th of January, Roberts
drew some attractive views of
what are still incorrectly called
the Tombs of the Caliphs; in
fact, the caliphate came to an
end in 1258 with the death of
the last Abbasid sovereign in
Baghdad, while these
mausoleums date from the great
period of the two Mamluk
dynasties. The title of caliph
(which literally means
"successor") was attributed to
the successors of Mohammed,
who acted as his deputies; these
"princes of believers" and
defenders of Islam held
executive and legal power,
governing as absolute rulers.
The sultans, originally less
important than the caliphs,
acquired the role of monarchs
with the advent of the Mamluks.
The lithograph, which is
pervaded by decadent
romanticism yet does not
indulge in pathos, constitutes
an excellent example of the
descriptive skills mastered by
the Scottish artist.

Tombs of the Caliphs, Cairo.

233

THE RUINS OF A MINARET NEAR THE CITADEL

<u>Plate 101</u>

11th January 1839

As he strolled among the Tombs of the Caliphs, Roberts was particularly struck by a ruined minaret standing alone, surrounded by the weather-beaten remains of some other funerary mosques. An atmosphere of melancholy desolation hung over these mute witnesses of past grandeur. Engrossed, Roberts observed the extraordinary variety of forms and decorations surrounding him and the myriad of lines multiplied endlessly, no two of which were alike, in supreme contrast with the severe geometry of the Pyramids, towering on the horizon.

The oldest mosques had no minarets, and the muezzins issued their call to prayer from the rooftops. The first to be built in Cairo was the spiral minaret of the Mosque of Ibn Tulun, designed on the Mesopotamian pattern.

Tall, graceful buildings with a square plan, surmounted by a kiosk with a domed roof, began to appear in the 11th century. Increasingly complex designs developed from these early specimens, and their development passed through various stages, from a square to an octagonal, and later a round shape, and finally multistorey buildings in which the individual elements freely overlapped.

Slender, pencil-shaped minarets, usually with a single balcony, only became fashionable after 1517, following the Turkish conquest. As soon as it was imported into Egypt, Ottoman architecture assimilated some of the local building styles, including the use of two-color-striped masonry called ablaq, which had been imported to Egypt from Andalusia in the 14th century with great success. Whenever it was impossible to obtain different-colored building materials for financial reasons, the ablaq pattern was painted on the plaster.

From David Roberts's journal:

11th January - Today I sketched the Tombs of the Caliphs.
I have received a letter from my dear Christine who tells me that all at home are well, thank God.

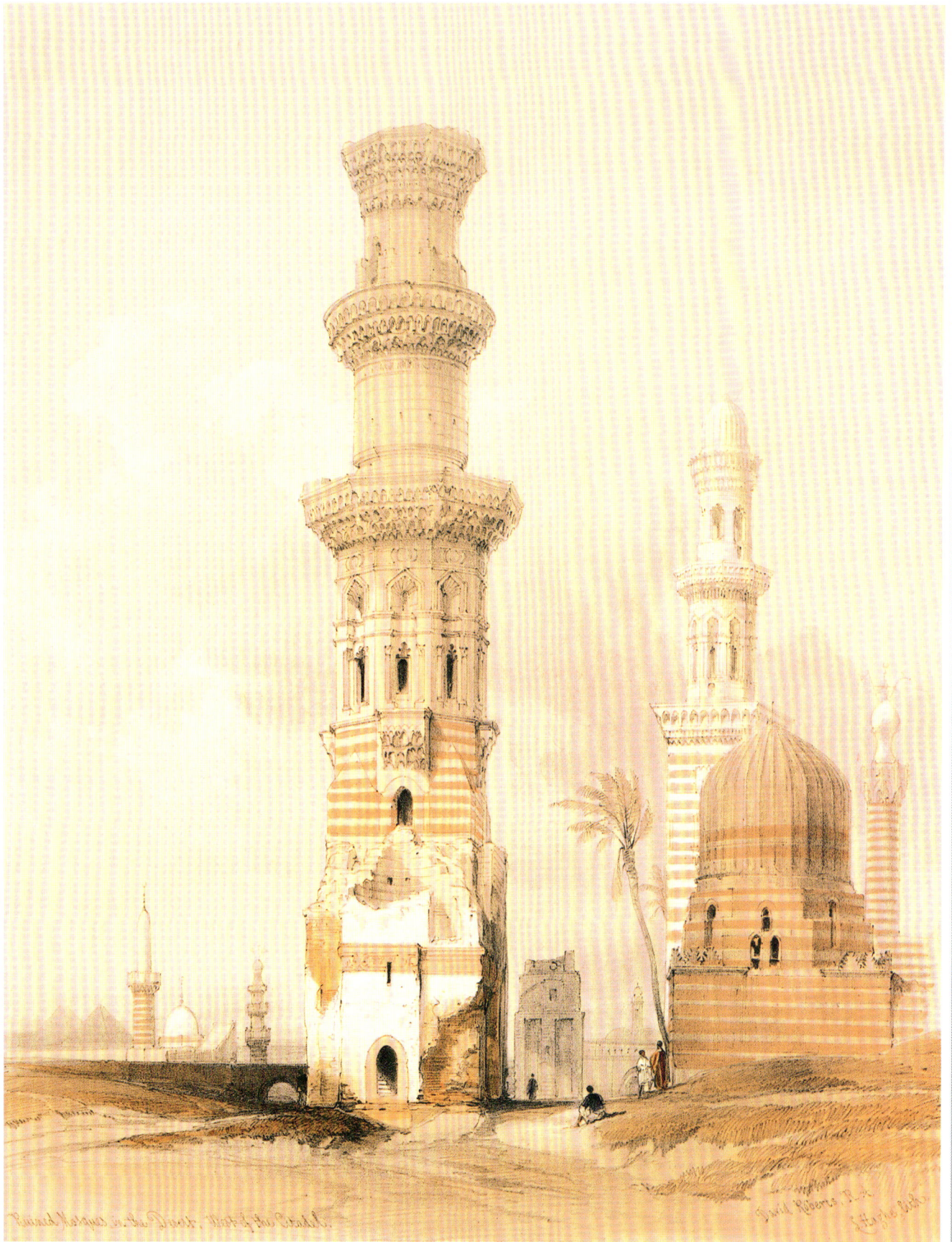

Ruined Mosque in the Desert, West of the Citadel.

David Roberts R.A.

L. Haghe Lith.

THE INTERIOR OF THE MOSQUE OF SULTAN HASSAN

Plate 102

12th January 1839

*A*lthough Sultan Hassan never completed his mosque, the harmony of the building and the elegant understatement of the decorations make it a masterpiece that has no equal in Egypt for grandeur and majesty. The building has an irregular pentagonal plan in which the cross-shaped structure of the madrasa is inserted. Inside is a square central courtyard adorned with the fountain shown here, and the four iwans (prayer rooms) with their high barrel vaults are distributed around this well of light. The play of light and shade, the purity of the lines and the huge volumes are highly conducive to prayer.

On the 12th of January, while Roberts was drawing the inner courtyard of the mosque, a good-looking young man spoke to him, interested in his activity. His name was Hanafee Ismail Effendi and, to the artist's great surprise, not only did he speak excellent English, but he had also been baptized in Glasgow during one of his journeys. Brought up and educated in the European style, he was a member of the pasha's entourage. The two immediately struck up a friendship that was to have important future developments: Ismail accompanied Roberts on his journey to the Holy Land and kept in touch with him by letter for many years afterwards.

THE SLAVE MARKET

Plate 103

13th-14th January 1839

*A*ccompanied by some of his new friends, such as John Pell and Frenchman Linant de Bellefonds whom he had already met several months earlier in Alexandria, Roberts set off into the desert, a few miles from Cairo, at dawn on the 13th of January. Here, the pilgrims bound for Mecca were preparing to strike camp and begin their long journey. There were "roughly 2,000 camels and at least two or three hundred horses." Surrounded by an incredible throng from all the Islamic tribes, among which those from Constantinople were particularly numerous, stood the emir's tent.

Confusion was rife, but the great crowd constituted an impressive sight. Wild-eyed, half-naked dervishes, their skin and even their lips transfixed by skewers and daggers, mingled with the other pilgrims. After the midday prayer a gunshot was fired, and at that signal the seething mass moved eastward amid a cacophony of sounds issuing from instruments of all shapes and sizes, which gave the caravan a joyful appearance quite foreign to what should have been a very solemn moment.

The scene reminded Roberts of the Biblical passage describing the journey of the children of Israel through the desert. Although he had brought his drawing materials with him, there was such chaos that he was unable to get much work done. However, the experience was an unforgettable one, and there was a great deal to talk about on the way back. Roberts spent the next day procuring the materials he needed for his imminent expedition to the Holy Land; he bought water bottles, blankets, some pistols, a saber and various other articles. Although he admired the beauty of Cairo, as he strolled in the maze of the bazaar and the streets of the city center he could not reconcile himself to the appalling poverty he saw all around him and the frequent scenes of tyranny against which his indignant spirit rebelled. He was always horrified by the sight of beggars lying in the middle of the road, young conscripts led to the barracks in chains, and hanged men dangling from a rope in the middle of the main square, exposed to public scorn as a terrible warning of the pasha's justice. What really made his blood boil, though, was the degrading spectacle of the slave market, a barbarous custom that shamed the whole country.

A MOSQUE IN THE SUBURB OF BOULAK

Plate 104

15th January 1839

*A*lthough his knowledge of the Islamic world was rather sketchy, Roberts paid great attention to the superb architecture of the mosques, which greatly appealed to his aesthetic sensibility.

He had already come into contact with Arab art during his journey to Spain years earlier, but the delicate colored masonry, the lightness of the stuccos and the carved stone lacework, and the purity of the lines that appeared before his dazzled gaze every day were absolutely unrivaled.

While he was strolling through the alleys of the port suburb of Boulak, which he visited on the morning of the 15th, this interest continued to predominate, so that in this lithograph the eye is drawn to the sanctuary in the background, right in the focal center of the composition.

Mosques, the most important architectural works in Islamic art, can be divided into three categories: the jami, *the mosque used for community prayers on Fridays; the* masjid, *the place of prayer and meditation, from which the modern word mosque is derived; and the* sawiya, *or commemorative chapel. As there were no major conflicts between the religious, dogmatic and social rules of Islam gradually defined by the four main schools already*

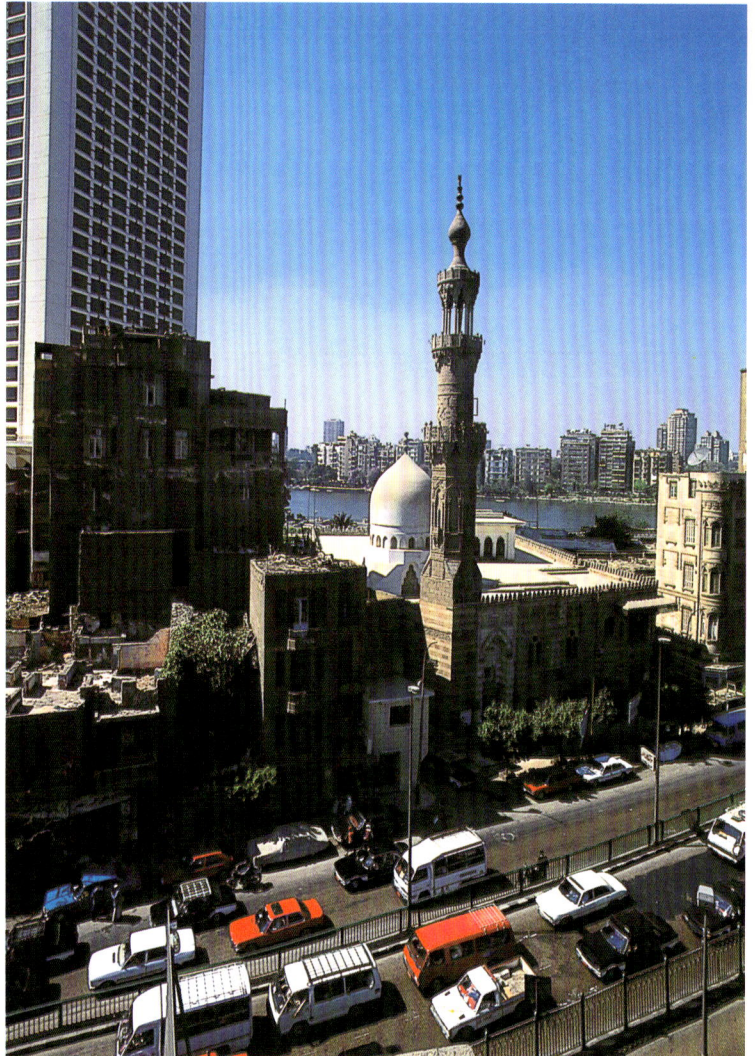

mentioned, it was sometimes possible to hold different rites in the same building.

Another type of building was the khanqa, *a sort of* madrasa-monastery *where those who preferred a mystic and esoteric approach to religious doctrines lived and studied, and where solitude and asceticism played*

fundamental roles.

Mosques, madrasas *and* khanqas *were often associated with the mausoleums of important people to form a single complex.*

From Boulak, Roberts was ferried to the Isle of Rhoda, an oasis of greenery in the middle of the Nile.

David Roberts R.A. Louis Haghe lith.   Boolack, Cairo

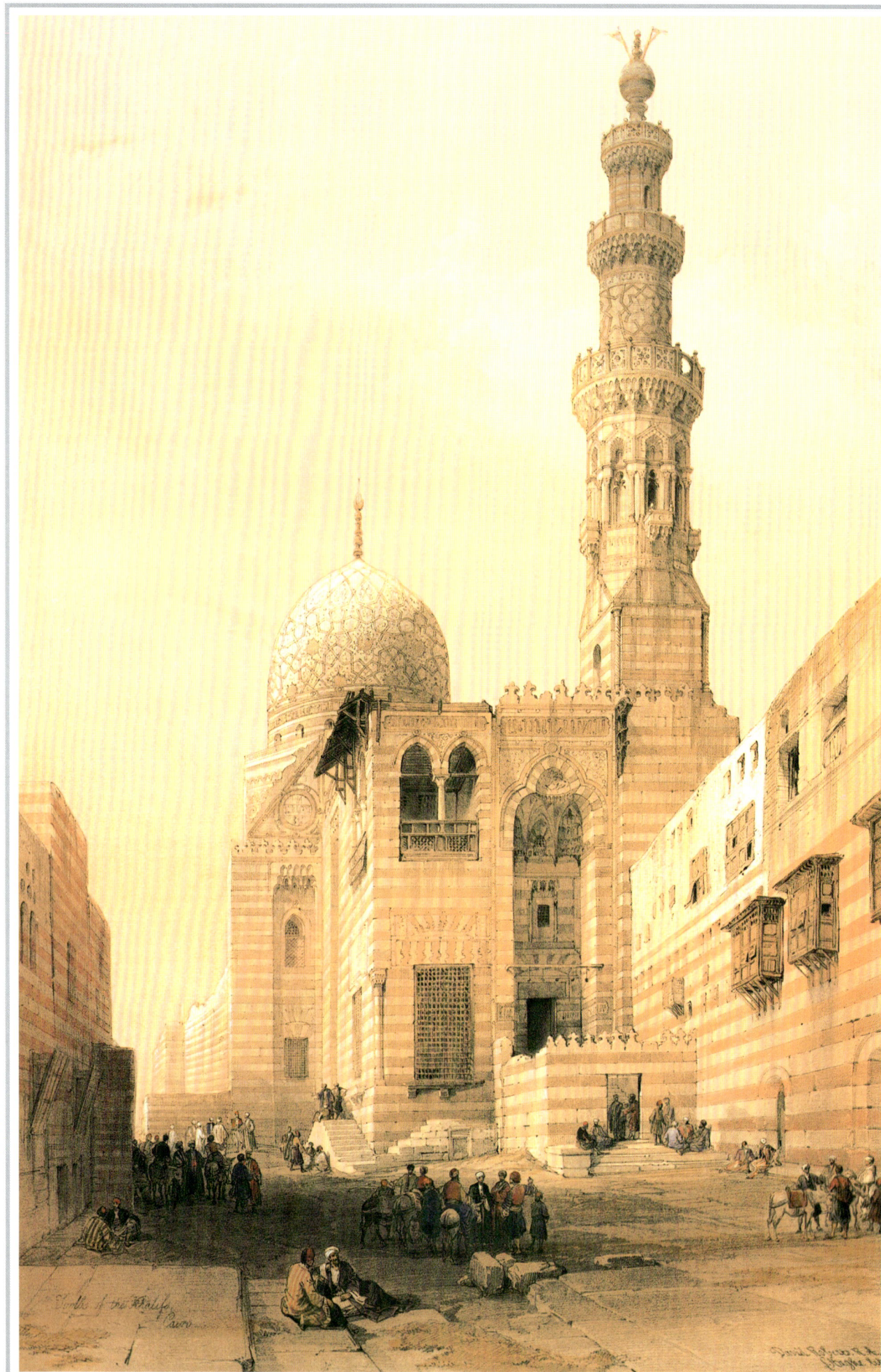

The Mosque of Sultan al-Ashraf Qaytbay

Plate 105

16th January 1839

The surreal atmosphere emanating from the Mamluk necropolises evidently had a special appeal for the Scottish artist, as he returned to draw there on the 16th. One of the most famous of the Tombs of the Caliphs is that of Sultan al-Ashraf Qaytbay, consisting of various structural elements that culminate in the splendid funerary mosque; it was the custom of the sovereigns of that period to build a mosque or a madrasa *next to their mausoleum. The underground funerary chamber in which the body was placed with its head wrapped in a white cloth, facing Mecca, was usually bare of ornament, while the domed room above it abounded in decoration.*

Sultan Qaytbay, whose long reign marked the apogee of the Circassian Mamluk period, built himself a particularly magnificent tomb, featuring an architectural style that paid more attention to detail than to the gigantic structures of the past. The decorative taste of the period also brought a golden age in the carving of marble, which was widely used on façades too.

Built between 1472 and 1474, this monument is considered one of the greatest masterpieces of Mamluk architecture, in view of the sublime balance of its proportions and its wealth of ornament; the fine latticework covering the surface of the dome like lace, and the elegant shape of the 130-foot-tall minaret, are particularly exquisite. In the interior, the prayer room has a splendid mosaic floor made of with multicolored marble pieces. Alongside Sultan Qaytbay's mausoleum is a vestibule in which the tombs of his four wives were placed, bathed in the soft light that enters from the stained-glass windows.

The character of the sultan contrasts strangely with this delicate elegance; ambitious and obstinate, he extorted huge sums of money through crippling taxes to finance an expensive building program in the capital and an interminable battle against the Ottoman Empire, which only concluded with the peace treaty of 1491. Though an aesthete and a lover of the fine arts, he was sadly famous for his sudden, apparently uninstigated fits of terrible violence.

THE KHANQA OF SULTAN FARAJ IBN BARQUQ

Plate 106

16th January 1839

When Roberts visited Cairo, many of the most glorious monuments of the past were in a sad state of neglect, and all memory of many had been lost. The artist also had little if any knowledge of the local language, which made it very difficult for him to obtain information about the magnificent buildings he took as his subjects. This explains the rather vague titles sometimes given to Haghe's lithographs. Although this one is simply described as "One of the Tombs of the Caliphs," it is actually the Khanqa of Sultan Faraj Ibn Barquq, one of the greatest masterpieces of Circassian Mamluk architecture. Although he had already built a mausoleum inside the city walls, Sultan al-Zahir Barquq, founder of the Circassian dynasty, asked on his deathbed to be buried next to the tombs of the Sufis, in the cemetery to the east of the Fatimid city. In order to grant his request, his son al-Nasir Faraj built a great khanqa with two mausoleums, one for his father and the other for himself.

Even though he had been a brave warrior who repulsed the Ottomans and Tamerlane's Mongol hordes, al-Zahir was attracted by the ascetic-mystic practices of the Sufis, which explains his request. Sufism, though originally opposed by the orthodox schools of theology, became popular in the 11th century, and came to exercise considerable political and social influence over Islam, giving rise to the cult of the saints, religious brotherhoods, and Arabic-Persian poetry that speaks of divine love in the guise of amatory and Bacchic verses. The khanqa, built between 1400 and 1411, is a huge structure with a square plan, with two minarets and a dome surmounting each mausoleum. The symmetry of the whole is almost perfect, and quite rare for the architecture of the period. The lithograph shows the north entrance of the building, and the nearby arched gallery supported by columns, called a sabil-kuttab.

The funerary complex was intended to include a camel market and other commercial buildings, which were never completed because of the premature death of al-Nasir, executed by his emirs on the instigation of Sheik al-Mahmudi, the future Sultan al-Muayyad. What might seem a strange mixture of functions was by no means unusual, as cemeteries were not considered to be the sole province of the dead. They even included residential blocks and mansions, where the wealthy resided on the occasion of festivals in honor of the dead and during their regular visits to the tombs of their loved ones.

THE PYRAMIDS OF GIZA SEEN FROM THE NILE

Plate 107

17th January 1839

On the 17th of January, the day he returned to the Pyramids after his first visit on the 3rd of October, Roberts wrote in his journal, "I cannot express my feelings at the sight of these gigantic monuments." His emotional reaction is shared by all those who have ever stood in the shadow of these giants, with their geometrically perfect lines. Since ancient times the great tombs of the pharaohs of the 4th dynasty (2570-2450 BC) have inspired a huge amount of literature, full of hypotheses about their construction, the mysterious significance of their proportions, and the esoteric secret of the orientation on the basis of which they were aligned on the low plateau of the Libyan desert. The travelers of the past began to wonder what their purpose was, while in more recent times, self-styled pioneers of the new and fascinating, though dubious, science of pyramidology have emerged. Now that the burial function of the pyramids has been established, modern archaeologists are not very interested in imaginative speculation, but are endeavoring to discover the engineering techniques that enabled the builders to overcome physical and organizational problems that are difficult to solve even today. Roberts drew this view from the east bank of the Nile, near the landing stage of the Giza ferry. From there, the pyramids appear to be arranged in order of size: from right to left can be seen the pyramid of Cheops, then the pyramid of Chephren (which appears to be the tallest because it is built on a rise in the ground), and finally the pyramid of Mykerinus, followed by the minor pyramid of a queen, the proportions of which were exaggerated by the artist. Until the 19th century, travelers could only reach the area of the Pyramids without too much difficulty when the Nile was low and the surrounding canals empty; it took just over an hour to travel from Cairo to Madiah, cross the river by boat and reach the village of Giza. The journey became much longer and more complicated during the floods, when the area turned into a swamp.

THE PYRAMIDS OF CHEOPS AND CHEPHREN

Plate 108

17th January 1839

Greek historian Herodotus, who visited Egypt in 450 BC, tried to find an answer to the numerous questions posed by the Pyramids and their construction. In his second book, Histories, he tells how the Great Pyramid was built. According to his account, 100,000 men, working in three-month shifts, first built a succession of steps, hauling the stones with the aid of wooden machines, and then covered the structure with well-polished blocks of stone. Cheops is described as a tyrant who imposed on his people "ten years' hardship spent on this mammoth task."

Similar comments were made by another historian, Diodorus Siculus, who lived four centuries later. In fact, neither of the two accounts is true; it has now been established that the workforce, consisting of 50,000 men, was recruited for only three-and-a-half months a year, at the time of the floods, over a period of 22 years. Peasants and young men from all walks of life constituted the backbone of the seasonal army that worked on the building site for the pharaoh, whose divine nature justified the huge size of the tomb and the effort required to build it.

According to current theory, accusations of slavery are unjustified, because the workmen volunteered their labor in return for the deceased's intercession with the sun god Ra. Like the people of medieval Europe who expiated their sins by building great cathedrals, the ancient Egyptians agreed to be divided into squads and supervised by government-employed engineers in order to acquire merit with the gods.

The techniques used to build these extraordinary monuments are not yet known - perhaps overlapping ramps, raised as the work progressed - but the statistics are astonishing. The pyramid of Cheops occupies a larger volume than any other building erected in ancient times (over 3,000,000 cubic feet), and its original height of 485 feet was unequaled until the construction of the bell towers of the Gothic cathedral in Cologne, four thousand years later.

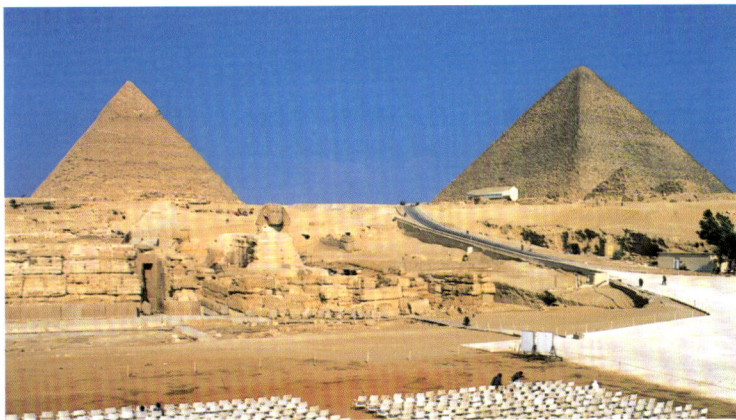

The Sphinx

Plate 109

17th January 1839

The Sphinx, which is aptly called Abu el-Hol (Father of Terror) in Arabic, stands in the desert sands in front of the east side of the pyramid of Chephren.
The reclining statue is 66 feet tall, and some 188 feet long. The great effigy with the body of a lion was carved from a spur of limestone rock originally used for quarrying, while the paws and tail were made with added blocks.
As shown in the lithograph, for a long time the face was the only part of the statue to emerge from the sand; some 16 feet tall, it still presents traces of color, which were more evident when Roberts saw it than they are now.
At the time of Herodotus, the great monument must actually have been invisible, as the historian makes no mention of it. The colossus had the features of the Pharaoh Chephren, portrayed as the living image of the sun god, guardian of the necropolis of Giza. From the time of the New Kingdom, the Sphinx was identified with the god Harmakhis ("Horus on the horizon") or even, with daring syncretism, with a deity that incorporated the triple form of the sun during its journey through the sky: Khepri at dawn, Ra in the splendor of midday, and Atum at sunset.
The Sphinx has been damaged on various occasions, the last time by musket shots fired by Mamluk soldiers, and has undergone numerous restorations at various periods. The most famous one was ordered by Thutmoses IV, to whom Harmakhis himself appeared in a dream, calling for the statue to be unearthed and restored to its ancient splendor.
A granite stele commemorating the event is still visible between the front paws.

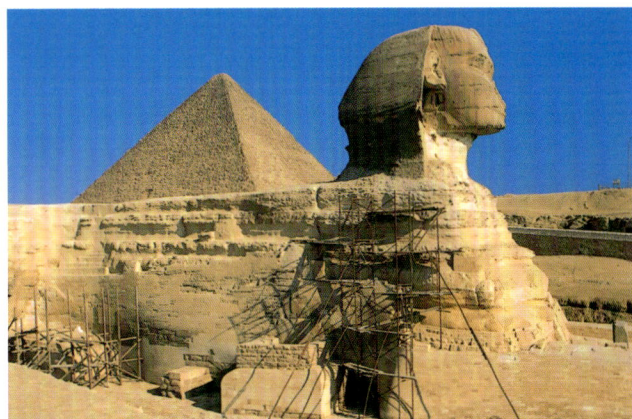

THE SPHINX, SEEN FROM THE FRONT

Plate 110

17th January 1839

Sphinxes *(the Greek name "sphinx" derives from the Egyptian* shesep ankh, *or "living image"), which were very common throughout ancient Egypt, were effigies of the pharaoh or a protecting deity. In archaic times the sovereign had been compared with a lion and portrayed as one, but it was not until the 4th dynasty that sculptors gave the beast a human head, usually adorned by the characteristic royal headgear called the* nemes, *and the* uraeus. *Especially in Thebes, sphinxes sometimes had the head of a ram, an animal sacred to Amun-Ra, or a falcon, the symbol of Horus.*

The most famous of these statues is the great Sphinx of Giza, a monument that has become the emblem of ancient Egyptian civilization. Buried by the sands of the Libyan desert, the colossus was excavated in 1798 by scientists accompanying Napoleon's expedition, and 18 years later, by Italian Giovanni Caviglia, who also found some scattered fragments of the statue, now in the British Museum.

The restoration work that gave the Sphinx its present appearance was performed between 1925 and 1936 by Egyptologists Emile Baraize and Selim Hassan. Note the obviously incorrect date on the picture; the drawing for this lithograph was certainly not made on the 17th of July, 1839, when Roberts was already back in England, but, more accurately, six months earlier.

THE ARRIVAL OF THE SIMÙN IN GIZA

Plate 111

17th January 1839

Roberts very probably made the preparatory drawing for this famous lithograph when he got back home. The composition is a sort of tribute to the mysterious, exotic charm of ancient Egypt in general and the Sphinx in particular, and constitutes one of the few exceptions to the artist's strict rule of portraying a real situation. While the sky is blazing with the last rays of the setting sun, a violent sandstorm is about to overtake the caravan camped at the foot of the Sphinx, whose eternally enigmatic smile seems to express imperturbable indifference to the imminent fury of the wind.

The sky is heavy with sand pushed forward in thicker and thicker waves, and the men are seeking shelter from the fury of the simùn. The moment is fraught with dramatic tension: The enigmatic force emanating from the gigantic face and the mystery of the looming pyramids are actually tangible, yet all is unreal, a magnificent fiction produced by the excited sensibilities of Roberts, who drew on his imagination and fully exploited the poetic license granted to him.

In reality, the Sphinx faces the rising sun, whereas here it faces west and the sun is setting to the south; the pyramid of Mykerinus is too close, and those of the queens are faraway on the horizon, as if separated from their lord and master.

The simùn, a hot, dry wind that rages with indescribable violence for a few minutes, usually blows from the desert in spring, and it is very unlikely that Roberts witnessed a scene like the one portrayed here. Nevertheless, this view is one of the most dramatic in the entire collection, and is certainly among those with the greatest emotional impact.

In January 1850, Roberts gave his friend Charles Dickens a small oil painting of a similar subject. To those who pointed out these anomalies, the great author replied that artists are allowed to take poetic license.

VIEW OF CAIRO
LOOKING WESTWARD

Plate 112

18th January 1839

*R*oberts devoted the whole of the 18th to seeking the best viewpoints from which to draw some general views of the city. Cairo was already a chaotic, complex metropolis in which buildings dating from different periods were jumbled together with no apparent order. The only explanation for such chaos is a history full of radical changes and dramatic events. The first settlement, which the Greeks called Babilonia, stood on the site where the fatal battle between the benevolent god Horus and the treacherous god Seth is supposed to have taken place in ancient times.
The capital of Egypt was then Memphis, and later moved to Thebes. After the conquest of Egypt by Alexander the Great in 332 BC, royal power was transferred to the recently founded Alexandria, which maintained its primacy under Roman rule and during the rapid spread of Christianity.
In 639 Babilonia was conquered by Amr Ibn al-As, the Arab general who introduced Islam into the country; two years later, Caliph Omar Ibn al-Khalab decided to found a new capital, which he called al-Fostat, near the ancient Byzantine fortress. In 750 the Abbasid dynasty deposed the Omayyads and began the construction of the city of al-Askar, a military capital that soon expanded and merged with al-Fostat to form a huge metropolis. One hundred twenty years later, Ahmed Ibn Tulun founded a third fortified capital, which absorbed the previous two cities within a few decades. The true foundation of Cairo, by Fatimid General Gobar al-Sikkili, dates from 969, however; the city then took the name of al-Qahira (The Victorious), and a long period began during which the urban area spread north and east as far as the slopes of Mount Moqattam. The reign of Saladin, which began in 1176, initiated a new era in the history of Cairo; during his rule the city walls were extended and the Citadel was built. The Mamluk era also

256

brought with it a major period of urbanization, which was enthusiastically continued by the Ottoman rulers when Egypt became a province of the Turkish Empire. The development that brought Cairo to its present stage began in 1805, under Pasha Mohammed Ali, after the brief Napoleonic occupation.

From David Roberts's journal:

18th January - Today I received a letter from my dear friend Durrant, from whom I heard that my dear Christine is well.

VIEW OF CAIRO
LOOKING EASTWARD

Plate 113

18th January 1839

*T*he city is portrayed looking east, from the point where the crowded district of el-Saiyda Zeinab now lies; the huge bulk of the Mosque of Sultan Hassan can be seen on the left, the Citadel on the right, and the Citzenib Gate in the foreground. From the surrounding heights, the immense conurbation looked like an ocean of earth-colored houses, permanently veiled by a patina of fine desert sand carried on the wind. The sight was made even more astonishing by the slender silhouettes of hundreds of minarets soaring towards the sky. Roberts was fascinated yet dismayed at the sight of a world so incomparably distant and different from his own.
In Cairo the most extreme contrasts could be seen every day: Coptic Arabs, Bedouins, Turks, Berbers and fellahin formed an indescribable mixture ceaselessly flowing along the streets, while in the silent mosques, white-gowned muezzins leafed through the pages of the Koran. In the meandering streets of the city, relics of a legendary past mingled with everyday poverty, and elegant architecture clashed violently with the barbaric sight of slaves taken to market.

THE FAÇADE OF A HOUSE

Plate 114

19th January 1839

*I*ncreasingly
fascinated by Islamic
architecture, Roberts devoted
a whole day, the 19th, to
studying the typical
construction and decoration
techniques used in Cairo. First
he visited a number of houses,
including an old mansion that
must have been magnificent in
its day, but had been soarly
neglected. He described this
condition as being sadly
common to much of that
unfortunate country, which
had fallen into decay after a long
period of maladministration and
continual wars. After lunch,
he went to the main city square,
where the pasha had opened
several building sites. The stone
blocks and the bowls used to
prepare the mortar were carried
on the shoulders of numerous
young women, supervised by a
guard who meted out rather
generous lashes of his whip with
equanimity. The scene was
accompanied by a continual
buzz of noise, to which only the
superintendents, sitting cross-
legged in front of their
inseparable chabouks, seemed
to be oblivious.
The start of Islamic architecture
in Cairo dates from the 9th
century, with the construction
of the Mosque of Ibn Tulun
and the Nilometer on the Isle of
Rhoda, although they betray an
evident Mesopotamian
influence. Only with the advent
of the Fatimids did an
independent style begin to

develop, with a clear preference
for highly complex decorations
in which arabesques in
geometrical frames and the
entwined star motif
predominate. The influence of
Syrian art was mainly evident
during Ayyubid rule and the
first Mamluk period; among
other things, stucco ornaments,
the use of stained glass,
masonry with bands of
alternating colors, and
stalactite-work pendentives
(which from then on became a
characteristic feature of
Egyptian architecture) were
introduced. The Circassian
Mamluks preferred marble
facing, and took the technique of
building great domes to the
height of perfection. Apart from
a few exceptions, Turkish rule
marked the decline of
monumental building activities
and led to a general regression
in decorative taste.
However, it was European
interference that struck
the final blow at the creativity
of local architecture, which
became very similar to that
of the great western cities.
Most private homes, unlike the
mosques, were sadly demolished
starting in the mid-19th
century to make room for high-
rises; before that, houses rarely
had more than two or three
storeys. Typical features were
the richly decorated entrances
and mashrabiyas, wooden
verandahs jutting out over the
street.

THE SACRED TREE
AT MATARIYAH

Plate 115

20th January 1839

On the 20th, a Sunday, Roberts woke early, and with a hired donkey and a young guide went to Matariyah to see the great sycamore under which the Holy Family is said to have rested during its flight from Herod's soldiers. In fact, what is known as the Tree of Mary was planted in 1672 to replace an older one, already the venue of devout pilgrimages in the Middle Ages. The large village of Matariyah, situated seven and a half miles from Cairo, is still famous today for the chapel dedicated to the Virgin Mary. The sacred tree stands right in front of it, in the middle of a garden with a spring that, according to legend, gushed forth at the command of the baby Jesus. This legend is associated with a far older cult; in nearby Heliopolis, at the time of the great sanctuary of Rameses, there was a sacred tree under which Isis was supposed to have suckled the baby Horus. Roberts carved his name on the bark of the ancient tree and cut off a branch to take as a souvenir to Christine. Although it was a Sunday, Roberts made an exception to the custom of not working (which he did not observe very strictly) and drew the ancient sycamore.

As a rather strong wind had started to blow and the sky was full of storm clouds, he decided to hurry to the obelisk, which stood alone on the plain nearby, the sole surviving relic of the glorious ancient city of Heliopolis.

The Holy Tree, Matareah.

THE OBELISK OF SESOSTRIS I, AT HELIOPOLIS

Plate 116

20th January 1839

*F*rom Matariyah, Roberts went on to Heliopolis, the place where the historian Herodotus was initiated into the mysteries of the Egyptian priesthood. Founded in ancient times with the name of Iunu and soon afterwards becoming the center from which the worship of the god Ra spread, the native city of the sovereigns of the 5th dynasty is often mentioned in the Bible by the name of On. Heliopolis was one of the main cultural and religious cities in the whole of Egypt; there, the falcon-headed sun god, Ra-Harakhti, Atum, and Mnevi, who had the features of a bull, were worshipped with great devotion. A huge temple, which by the time of Rameses had become the second most important after the one in Thebes, was consecrated to this triad. Its priests were famous throughout the ancient world for their wisdom, and legend has it that even Plato went there to learn from them. Nothing remains of the great sanctuary, built by Amenemhat I on the foundations of an older building, apart from one of the two obelisks that his son and successor, Sesostris I, placed in front of the pylon. The monolith, made of red Aswan granite, is 68 feet tall, and bears the same inscription on all four sides, stating that the sovereign built it to celebrate his first Jubilee. As Heliopolis was near Cairo, the ruins were probably used as a source of building materials over the centuries, which would explain the absence of other monumental remains on the site. As the weather was rapidly deteriorating, Roberts hurriedly sketched the obelisk and mounted his donkey again. Shortly afterwards a violent storm broke, and poor Roberts was soaking wet by the time he reached Cairo.

From David Roberts's journal:

20th January - On the way back I was caught in a downpour of exceptional violence, and got so cold that my teeth did not stop chattering for quite a while after I returned home. At the thought of how cold I was, I sincerely feel sorry for all those poor people I have seen clothed only in light cotton garments.

The Nilometer on the Isle of Rhoda

Plate 117

21st-22nd January 1839

*A*lthough he was engrossed in his drawing, Roberts did not neglect the complex organization required for his imminent journey to the Holy Land. A few days earlier he had reached an agreement with the vice-consul, Mr. Walne, for the supply of four camels with which he intended to travel to Syria, and on the morning of the 21st, after packing up the works he had completed so far, he awaited their arrival to conclude the deal. However, the vice-consul brought bad news, all the more shocking because it was totally unexpected; rumor had it that plague had been raging in Jerusalem for three months. A cordon sanitaire had been erected around the city, which meant that if Roberts tried to enter it, he would be placed in quarantine. As he admitted in his journal, "A journey to the Holy Land without seeing Jerusalem would be like visiting England without seeing London." This bad news upset him, but Colonel Campbell suggested that he should make no decision at least until the 24th, when he expected to receive reliable information as to how serious the situation really was. While he waited, Roberts recommenced his explorations, and the next day he returned to the Isle of Rhoda to draw the Nilometer. The adventure proved riskier than expected, as the structure had been converted into a powder magazine, and access was prohibited to all except the guards. Despite the risk of stopping a bullet or having a bad fall, Roberts was determined to complete the task he had set himself. He therefore scaled the outer wall of the structure and from the top hurriedly sketched a study of it, which he completed when he was safe and sound again. Erected circa 715 by the Omayyid Caliphs, who had come from Arabia as conquerors during the 7th century, the Nilometer was similar in concept to those built all over Egypt by the pharaohs, and performed the same task of measuring the level of the river so that the amount of the taxes could be adjusted accordingly. The structure that now survives was built in 861 by Abbasid Caliph al-Mutawakkil. This Nilometer, which is quite sophisticated in design, works on the principle of communicating vessels; the graduated central column is surmounted by a Corinthian capital, and the Kufic inscriptions on the walls are the oldest known in Egypt. The wooden dome was added during a modern restoration.

THE ANCIENT AQUEDUCT ON THE RIGHT BANK OF THE NILE

<u>Plate 118</u>

22nd January 1839

*R*ight opposite the Isle of Rhoda, on the right bank of the Nile, stand the ruins of an ancient aqueduct with the characteristic pointed arches, whose use in the Islamic world preceded Gothic architecture by four centuries; it was 3 miles long, and conveyed water from the Nile to the Citadel. Its route can still be distinguished for a long stretch in the southern districts of the city.

Until the 19th century a canal called the Khalij, which ran alongside the medieval city, conveying water from the Nile to irrigate the fields to the west of Cairo, existed near the massive structure drawn by Roberts, which contained the pumping station of the plant.

The canal, which in 1899 was filled in to become one of the main roads of the metropolis, Sharia Port Said, came into operation when the level of the Nile rose after the summer flood; during the warmest months countless dahabiehs (luxury yachts that once concealed the clandestine vices of the wealthy Cairo bourgeoisie) sailed on the canal. During the rest of the year the entrance to the canal was closed by an earth dike so that its bed could be maintained; the opening day was marked by the most important civil celebration in Cairo, Fath al-Kahlij (the Canal Opening Festival). The pasha himself presided over the ceremony, and the celebrations continued for several days, with music and dancing galore.

The Tombs of the Caliphs and the Mausoleum of Emir Qurqumas

Plate 119

23rd-25th January 1839

While waiting for better news, or at least to dispel the tension created by the consul's visit which was becoming more agonizing with every day that passed, Roberts visited friends and dined "Turkish-style" with them.
In the meantime John Pell tried to persuade Roberts to go with him to Petra, the fabulous Nabataean capital, before continuing to Palestine and Jerusalem. Roberts was very hesitant, however, because he was afraid that this diversion would take too long and would also represent a financial problem for him. In a shrewd move, Pell took the artist to see Linant de Bellefonds, who had painted a series of excellent watercolors of Petra some ten years earlier. Roberts was so struck by them that his resolve wavered considerably.
On the 25th of January Pell and de Bellefonds accompanied

Roberts on yet another excursion to the Tombs of the Caliphs, where the artist sketched what was to be the last of his drawings devoted to the monuments of Cairo. The lithograph portrays a view of the scenic funerary complex built by Emir Qurqumas between 1506 and 1507. The arrangement and appearance of the buildings are very similar to those of the monumental complex erected by Sultan Qaytbay 25 years earlier, and almost seem to be a faithful copy of the same design.
Here again, the minaret stands on the right-hand side of the stalactite-work portal, and the **sabil-kuttab** *is built on the left. The quality of the decorations is far inferior, however, and this is particularly evident in the dome over the mausoleum, the outer surface of which is covered with a simple zigzag pattern on a diamond base instead of delicate lacework.*

From David Roberts's journal:

25th January - After the Tombs of the Caliphs, we visited a convent of Dervishes, and went over to the establishment. The cells, which are numerous, seem so small that I should not think it possible for men to lie in them. A small mosque contains the tomb of the saint, covered with a tattered awning. In the evening I drank tea at Mr. Pell's and made two drawings of Egyptian ladies.

A GROUP OF DANCING GIRLS

Plate 120

26th January-6th February 1839

On the 26th of January no news had yet arrived about the situation in Jerusalem; Roberts was increasingly undecided about what to do, and became more and more restless every day. That evening he was invited to dinner by John Pell, and the evening was enlivened by a generous supply of champagne and a performance by pretty dancing girls wearing revealing dresses. Always susceptible to female charms, Roberts did not hesitate to immortalize the scene, and the fact that this picture concludes our journey to Egypt makes the author seem less austere than Victorian morality and his puritanical daughter might have wished. The days were becoming increasingly tedious, despite the fine weather, when at last the news came, on the morning of the 28th, that the situation in Jerusalem was rapidly improving, and the cordon sanitaire had been lifted. As the financial problems he was worried about had also been solved by a generous loan of forty pounds from the vice-consul in Alexandria, Robert Thornburn, Roberts finally agreed to accompany Pell as far as Petra. John Kinnear, the son of an Edinburgh banker, also joined the expedition; he formed a deep and lasting friendship with the artist, and dedicated to Roberts a slim volume of travel memoirs published in 1840. The route to Syria took in Mount Sinai, Petra and, of course, Jerusalem.

Pell promised to be ready in a week, and Roberts, having made arrangements for his departure with the diligent Ismail, decided to spend the time left checking over his equipment and painting in oils a view of the city that he intended to give to a friend on his return home.

On the 29th of January Colonel Campbell provided him with two letters of introduction to the consuls in Jerusalem and Damascus, and a safe-conduct signed by the pasha. On the 6th of February, when the last preparations had been made and Roberts had said good-bye to his friends, he and his new traveling companions set off for Suez, bound for more adventures. But that, as they say, is another story.

THE HOLY LAND

YESTERDAY AND TODAY

INTRODUCTION

277 In this map, which was also published in the first edition of "The Holy Land," printed by Francis Graham Moon, we can see the route that David Roberts followed. The three colors correspond to the chapters of this volume.

Although versatile and prolific, ranging widely in his choice of subjects, David Roberts nowadays owes much of his fame and popularity to his lithographs of the Middle East. In particular, the fruit of his wanderings in the Holy Land, which during Roberts's lifetime won him great and lasting acclaim, is now considered to be a masterpiece and has survived the test of time and fashion. This volume contains the 123 lithographs realized from the sketches that Roberts executed during his voyage through the Sinai Peninsula to Jerusalem and, finally, to the spectacular city of Baalbec.

The illustrations, large in format, are reproduced from the first edition published in London between 1842 and 1849 by Francis Graham Moon with the original title of "The Holy Land, Syria, Idumea, Egypt, Nubia." The most important new development in this edition of the work is that the lithographs are shown, for the first time, in strict chronological order beginning with Roberts's arrival in Suez on the 10th of February 1839 and running all the way through to his departure from Baalbec, which took place on the 8th of May of the same year. It has thus become necessary to resolve many of the considerable problems in the dating of each and in its precise place in this work. The previous editions have always emphasized the purely visual aspects of the creations of this artist, and have done so to the detriment of an accurate reflection of the historical and geographical details involved, so that the illustrations have been arranged in various ways by various publishers. Roberts himself tended not to pay too much attention to these matters, and it should also be kept in mind that the publication of his works was a process that stretched out over eight years, a length of time that necessarily generated a number of "oversights." Some of the lithographs - which were executed by the Belgian plate maker Louis Haghe, working on the sketches that Roberts made during his travels - bear no dates, while a great many others have inaccurate dates. An example: plate 48 in this edition bears the indication "19th April 1841," in the margin. This is necessarily an erroneous date because by that time Roberts had already been back in London for twenty-one months. In some cases, these inaccuracies can be attributed to the artist's momentary distraction; in other cases, to a careless oversight on the part of Louis Haghe who, it seems logical to guess, must have been tempted in more than one instance to "complete" his plates with chronological notations, thus causing glaring contradictions with the information contained in Roberts's travel journal.

We have split up the route that Roberts took into three separate phases, which are indicated on the map shown here in three different colors that correspond to the three different chapters. It is no accident that each of the chapters opens with one of the original frontispieces from the volumes of the first edition, portraying the most intriguing places that Roberts visited: Petra, Jerusalem, and Baalbec. It is, moreover, not out of line to suggest that for the Scottish artist, the three trips from Suez to Jerusalem - with his exploration of the mythical capital of the Nabateans, his tour of the Holy City and descent to the Jordan River, and, lastly, the trip from Jerusalem to the ancient Heliopolis - constitute three different emotional experiences.

We should, however, point out that the original edition overseen by Roberts began with lithographs of Jerusalem, and that it did not include his travel diary, the well-known journal that proved to be so useful in the work done on this present edition: the journal, in fact, has allowed us to amend gaps in the chronology so that the sequence of pictures presented here is as close as possible to the actual travel experiences that Roberts himself enjoyed. If, therefore, we have not been entirely faithful to the first edition, we believe that we have at least restored to this remarkable artistic enterprise that degree of "legibility" which for many years was entirely lacking. We have also chosen to provide a commentary to each plate with brief historic and geographic notations in order to provide a narrative of the episodes described and shown by Roberts himself. In each case, with a view to philological accuracy, we have chosen to accompany many of the illustrations with major excerpts from Roberts's journal, giving some indication of the Scottish artist's gifts for brevity and description. The reader may notice that those commentaries that emphasize the historical background of the places visited by Roberts tend to emphasize the distant past rather than the recent past and the present.

A bridge spanning the distance between past and present is offered by the splendid photographs that correspond with the lithographs. This unusual mingling of such radically different pictures is particularly informative regarding the inexorable results of the passage of time. These photographs have no commentary: the reader can draw his or her own conclusions, or imagine a modern trip through what is certainly one of the most appealing and perhaps mysterious regions in the world. Before such eloquence, we shall leave the pictures to speak for themselves.

Fabio Bourbon

MAP
to Illustrate
THE ROUTE OF
DAVID ROBERTS, ESQ. R.A.
IN
THE HOLY LAND, PETREA & SYRIA.

NOTE—*The Route is indicated thus* _____

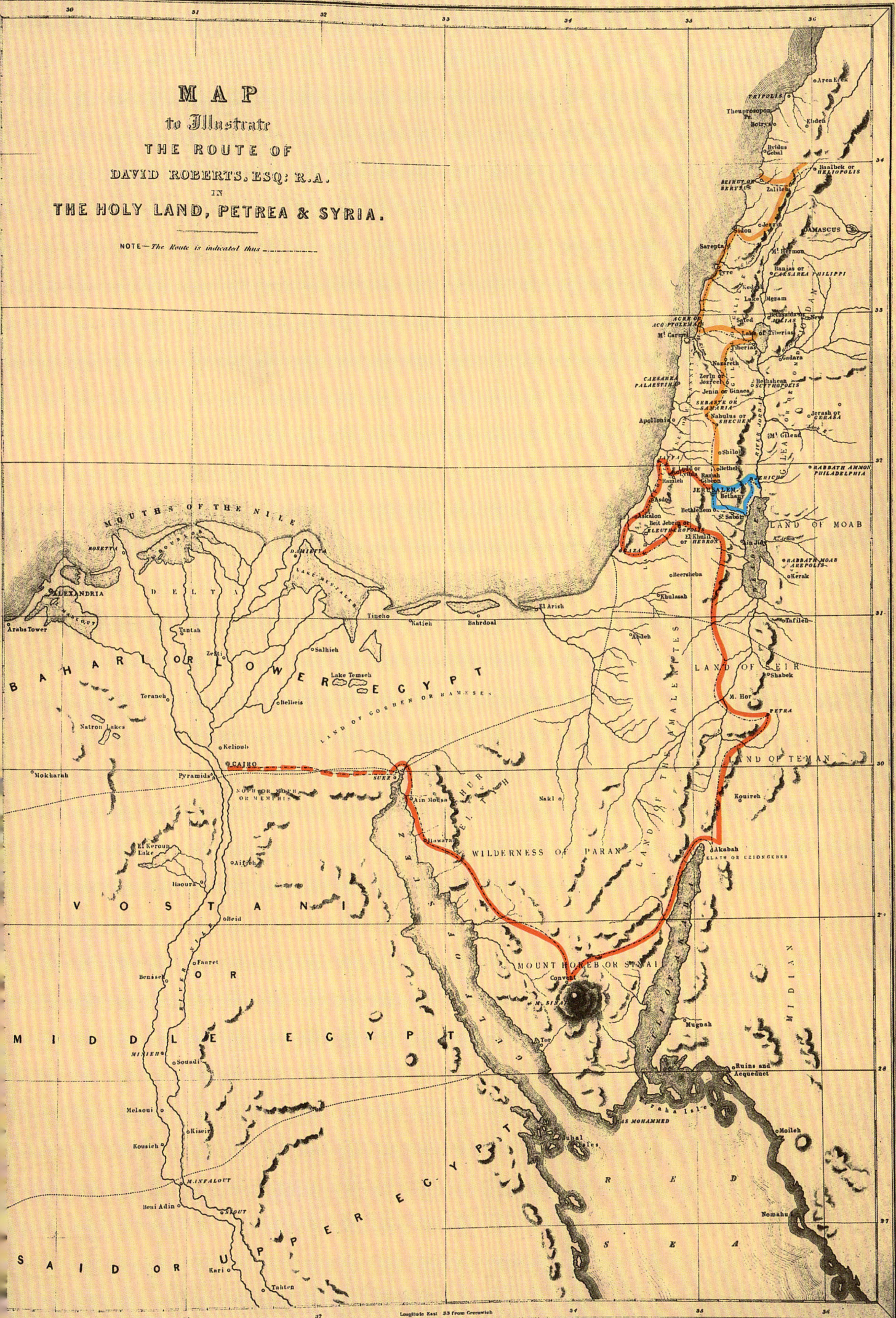

MOUTHS OF THE NILE

BAHARI OR LOWER EGYPT

ROSETTA
DAMIETTA
LAKE MENZALEH
ALEXANDRIA
Arabs Tower
DELTA
Tantah
Salhieh
Zefta
Teraneh
Natron Lakes
Kelioub
Lake Temseh
Tineho
Katieh
Bahrdoal
El Arish
PYRAMIDS
CAIRO
SUEZ
Aim Mousa
Hawara
Nokharah
OLD MEMPHIS OR MEMPHIS
LAND OF GOSHEN OR RAMESES
VOSTANI OR
El Kheroun Lake
Aitfeh
Haoura
Benihassen
Fanret
oBeid
WILDERNESS OF PARAN
Nakl
MIDDLE EGYPT
Minieh
Souadi
MANFALOUT
Melaoui
Kiseir
Kousich
Beni Adin
Siout
SAID OR UPPER EGYPT
Kari
Tahter
MOUNT HOREB OR SINAI
Convent
M. SINAI
Tor
Mugnah
RAS MOHAMMED
Jubel Zeles
Moileh
Nomahu
Ruins and Aequednet
RED SEA

TRIPOLIS
Area Esk
Theuprosopon
Botrys
Eden
Dvidus
Gebal
Baalbek or HELIOPOLIS
BEIRUT OR BERYTUS
Zalileh
Sidon
Jexria
DAMASCUS
Sarepta
Mt Hermon
Tyre
Kedes
Danias or CAESAREA PHILIPPI
Lake Megam
Mcas
Neve
ACRE OR ACO PTOLEMAIS
Safed
Lake of Tiberias
Mt Carmel
Tiberias
Nazareth
Gadara
Zerin or Jezreel
Bethshean SCYTHOPOLIS
CAESAREA PALESTINA
Jenin or Ginaea
SEBASTE OR SAMARIA
Nabulus or SHECHEM
Jerash or GERASA
Apollonia
Shiloh
Mt Gilead
GILEAD
RABBATH AMMON PHILADELPHIA
Lydd or Diaspolis
Bethel
Ramah Gibeon
JERICHO
JERUSALEM
Bethany
Ramleh
Azdod
Bethlehem
St Saba
LAND OF MOAB
Askalon
Beit Jebrin
ELEUTHEROPOLIS
El Khulil or HEBRON
Ain Jidi
Gaza
RABBATH MOAB AREPOLIS
Beersheba
Kerak
Khulasah
Tafileh
Abdeh
LAND OF SEIR
Shabek
LAND OF THE AMALEKITES
M. Hor
PETRA
LAND OF TEMAN
Kouireh
Akabah
ELATH OR EZIONGEBER
MIDIAN

London Published by F. G. Moon, 20 Threadneedle Street
Longitude East 33 from Greenwich

FROM SUEZ TO JERUSALEM

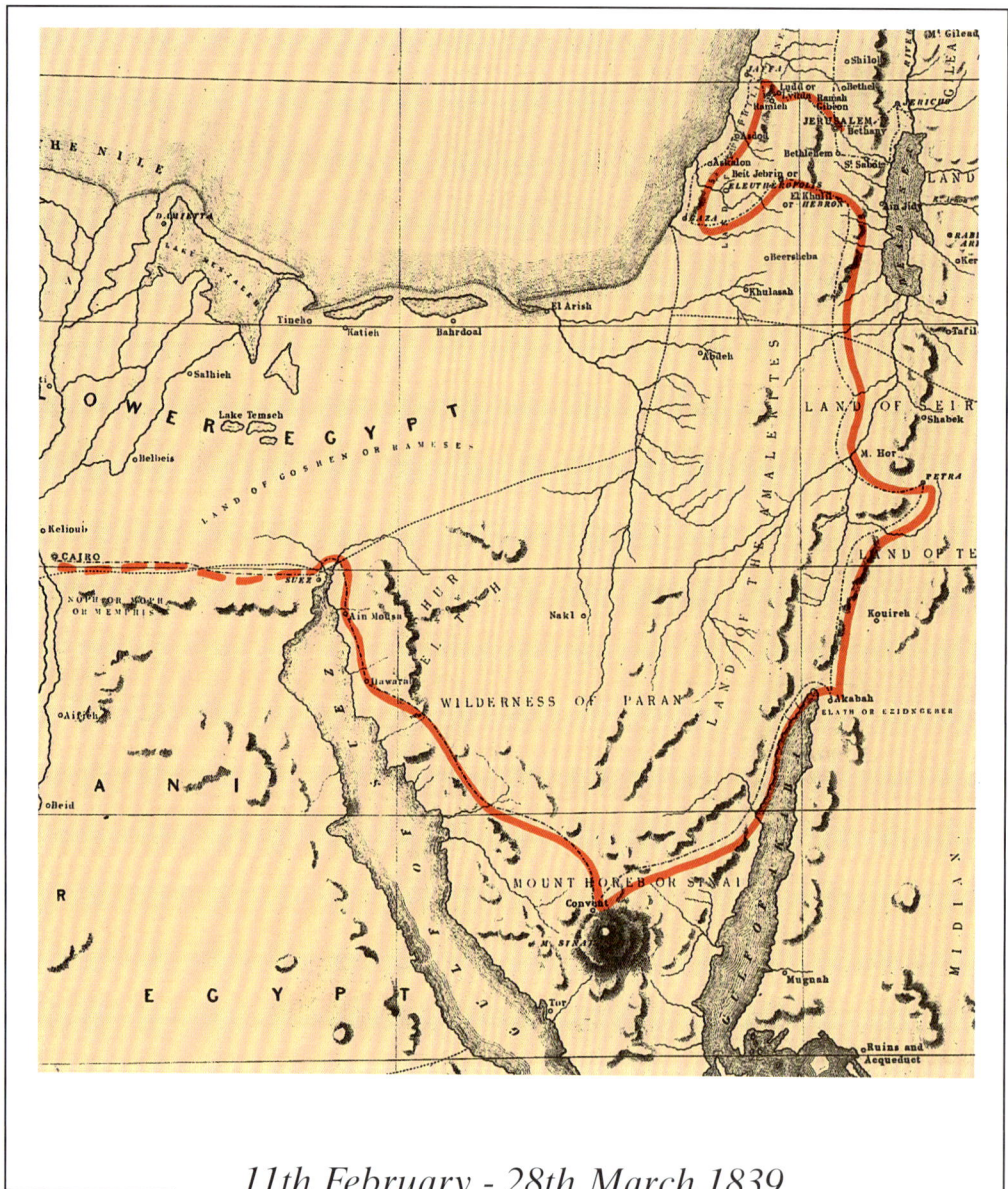

11th February - 28th March 1839

David Roberts. R.A

HOLY LAND.

Syria, Idumea, Arabia, Egypt & Nubia.

FROM DRAWINGS MADE ON THE SPOT BY

David Roberts, R.A.

WITH HISTORICAL DESCRIPTIONS BY

THE REV? GEORGE CROLY, L.L.D.

LITHOGRAPHED BY

LOUIS HAGHE.

VOL. 3.

LONDON, F. G. MOON, 20 THREADNEEDLE STREET,
PUBLISHER IN ORDINARY TO HER MAJESTY.
MDCCCXLIII.

ARRIVING IN SUEZ

Plate 121

10th February 1839

Having left London on the 31st of August 1838, and having touched at ports in France, Italy, Malta, and the Greek islands, David Roberts reached Alexandria on the 24th of September. From here, Roberts set off along the Nile Valley; during that trip he sketched all of the principal monuments of the pharaohs. Returning to Cairo on the 21st of December, during the first days of the year Roberts decided to continue on to Syria, and to visit Jerusalem and the Holy Land. By the 21st of January, he had arranged for a number of camels and the appropriate equipment. On the same day, however, he received word of a serious outbreak of the plague in Judea, and that there was a strict "cordon sanitaire" around Jerusalem. To his great disappointment, Roberts decided to wait out events, and in the meanwhile he continued preparations for this new adventure. A week later, he finally learned that the time seemed ripe. On the 29th of January, he received from Colonel Campbell - the English general consul at Cairo - two letters of presentation to the consuls of Jerusalem and Damascus, and a safe-conduct signed by the pasha in person, so that anywhere he might need it he would immediately be supplied with an armed escort. In the meantime, Roberts had in part modified his plans, agreeing to join forces with two other English travellers, John Pell and John Kinnear. The new plan was to reach Palestine by following the route believed used by Moses, from Suez to Aqaba through the Sinai, and then following the valley of El Ghor all the way to Petra, and thence on to Hebron. The three Europeans decided to wear local garb, so much more practical in the brutal heat of the desert. Roberts, who intended to pay visits to a number of mosques, was also obliged to shorten his thick sideburns. The caravan was formed of twenty-one camels and escorted by nearly the same number of armed Beduins. The baggage included a number of tents, blankets, and weapons, along with adequate quantities of munitions and foodstuffs. The group left Cairo on 7th of February and was within sight of Suez and the Red Sea three days later, after following for a considerable distance a track marked only by the fossilized carcasses of camel after camel. On every hand was a featureless sun-beaten desert without a hint of tree or shrub in any direction. The city of Suez lay along the sea, and walls protected the side that was exposed to the interior.
On the opposite side of the Gulf and in sharp contrast with the motionless surface of the great body of water, stood the mountains of Sinai, reflecting the rays of the setting sun in a red fireball.

SUEZ. Feby 11th 1839

From David Roberts's journal:

7th February - Left Cairo for Mount Sinai, and slept in the desert.
8th and 9th - On our way. Overtaken by a rain storm on the evening of the 9th, and before we could get our tents pitched everything was in a big mess.

SUEZ

Plate 122

10th February 1839

Roberts described Suez as being fairly picturesque, and was particularly impressed by the unusual shape of the boats in the port. The city, which stands on the site of the ancient city of Kolsum, was already fairly important in bygone eras as the way station in passing from the Red Sea to the Mediterranean, but it had declined to little more than a unassuming village when the English, in a joint undertaking with the pasha of Egypt, established regular trade with their colonies in the Far East across this isthmus. Suez thus became the destination of steamers arriving from Bombay and even from China. In a very short time, it had attained great importance, and the construction of the canal only increased the importance of the port city. In reality, the first efforts to drive a canal across the isthmus date from the age of the Pharaohs, and the maritime link was routed through a branch of the Nile all the way to Cairo, and through a manmade canal from Cairo to Suez. The passage was operational under Trajan, as well, and for a brief period during Arab rule. An early plan for a direct canal was developed during the sixteenth century in Venice, which wanted to attract the South and East Asian trade to the Mediterranean, but difficulties of all sorts hindered the project. The project actually got underway only when Napoleon had his engineers begin to make studies and draw up plans.

This preliminary work was rudely interrupted by the thunder of war, and it was not until 1833 that work started again, under the aegis of Mohammed Ali Pasha. Although Mohammed Ali was in favor of the project in principle, he did little more than to equivocate. In November 1846, the "Societé d'Études du Canal du Suez," which worked under the direction of the Italian engineer Luigi Negrelli, proceeded by fits and starts until 1854. Years later, the "Universal Company of the Suez Canal" was set up, with the engineer Ferdinand de Lesseps as the director. Actual digging began in April 1859 and continued for ten years. The canal was finally inaugurated on the 17th of November 1869 in the presence of the empress of France, Eugénie; in celebration of the occasion, of course, Giuseppe Verdi composed "Aida."

Quay at Suez. February 11th 1839.

From David Roberts's journal:

10th Sunday - Suez picturesque. Made a few sketches. Boats curious in form; sea limpid and pure.

David Roberts R.A

ARABS OF THE DESERT

Plate 123

11th -12th February 1839

*R*oberts began his voyage toward the Holy Land on the morning of the 11th of February, after clearing up a troublesome misunderstanding with his Arab companions. The Englishman had in fact discovered that a considerable portion of the grain that had been included in the baggage borne by the camels was not meant, as he had assumed, for their nourishment, but would be given to the tribes they met along the way for planting, because the harvest of the previous year had been extremely scanty. A few hours' ride out of Suez, the caravan was caught by surprise in a sandstorm so brutal that by noon Roberts and his travelling companions were forced to pitch tents and take shelter. In contrast, the following day was beautiful. The track ran along the coast, with an imposing mountain range rearing up in the distance. This was the place where the waters of the Red Sea supposedly opened up to let Moses and the people of Israel through, crashing closed again upon their persecutors. Their trip proceeded without any major surprises, and as the landscape rolled past Roberts was able to observe their surroundings in

perfect calm. Among the Arabs who made up his entourage, the most noteworthy individual was certainly a certain Beshara, a native of the tribe of Beni Sa'id. Beshara was gifted with an agile intelligence, and he accompanied Roberts all the way to Aqaba. His portrait was of particular interest, chiefly because it faithfully reproduces the clothing that the guide wore. Like all desert Arabs, he wore an ample shirt or smock, gathered

at the waist with a leather belt, and a heavy wool mantle over that. His legs were bare, and he wore simple sandals on his feet. His turban denotes an elevated rank, since the more ordinary sort of headgear is made up of a simple strip of rough cloth fastened with a loop of twine or twisted cloth. This simple but eminently functional outfit is completed by the ubiquitous broad-bladed curved knife, and a blunderbuss.

Arabs of the Tribe of the Benisaid, Feb 17th 1839.

The Wells of Moses

Plate 124

On the afternoon of the 12th of February, the caravan reached the so-called Wells of Moses, a group of freshwater springs barely marked by a few scraggly palm trees. Biblical tradition has it that this was where the people of Israel reached the shore after their miraculous passage through the Red Sea.

The pools vary in number from season to season, ranging from a minimum of seven to a maximum of fifteen. The level of the water and its flow also vary greatly. At times, the pools overflow and produce little rivulets, while at other times the water is little more than a dampness in the soil. Though eminently drinkable, the water has a brackish taste that is less than appetizing, and only the blast of desert heat can persuade one readily to drink. Not far from the oasis, a number of fragments and the remains of walls indicate that in antiquity a small village once stood here. Eyun Mousa is the name of the place in Arabic; this is the only source of fresh water for miles around and is also the only place in this section of the Gulf of Suez where any planting is done. That evening Roberts noted in his journal that, although the spectacle of Beduins gathering around the evening fire might be picturesque and romantic, his weariness after travelling twenty miles across the desert by camel prevented him from drawing anything at all.

Wells of Moses. Wilderness of Etsh. February 1st

From David Roberts's journal:

12th - In two hours we reached the Wells of Moses, which are fifteen in number. They are surrounded by a few stunted palm-trees, and the waters are not sweet but bitter...

David Roberts. R.A.

12th February 1839

From David Roberts's journal:

13th - Our route still near the shore of the Red Sea - the desert mountains, though barren, are picturesque in form. 14th - We leave the coast, and enter amid the mountains, of which to-day I made a coloured sketch.

THE APPROACH TO MOUNT SINAI

<u>Plate 125</u>

13th–14th February 1839

The travellers broke camp at sunrise and the caravan set out once again along the track that ran along the coast of the Gulf of Suez amidst a landscape that was totally arid, but which had its own strange allure. The 13th passed without any noteworthy events and by four in the afternoon the tents had been pitched not far from a source of fresh water, Wadi Howara. Again, the next day, nothing occurred to interrupt the tranquil monotony of the voyage:

a cup of coffee upon rising, two hours of travel, and the customary halt to pray in the direction of Mecca, which the Arab entourage never forewent. Lunch meant finishing off the remains of the previous evening's meal and a few gulps of water from the waterskins. With some surprise, Roberts noticed that he ate these frugal meals with an enjoyment he had not experienced since childhood. At sunset, the tents were set up in the oasis of Marah, where the fresh water was as welcome as a benediction amidst the desert blast. Upon the horizon, the travellers could already make out the outlying slopes of Mount Sinai—an improbable and solemn setting, where nature is the only lord, and, at the same time, the only witness, unchanged over the millennia to the passage of time. For time out of mind, despite all of the controversy fueled by historians and archaeologists, the Sinai has been associated with the Exodus, with the wanderings of the House of Israel, and with the Tablets that the Lord handed down to Moses: "And they took their journey from Elim, and all the congregation of the children of Israel came unto the wilderness of Sin, which is between Elim and Sinai, on the fifteenth day of the second month after their departing out of the land of Egypt." (Exodus, 16:1) Nonetheless, the Sinai has been more than simply the setting of biblical stories; it has been the backdrop for one of the most important events in human history—the development of the acceptance of the laws of a single God, although this was a people that grew and learned amidst a polytheistic society.

THE TEMPLE ON GEBEL GARABE

Plate 126

15th–16th February 1839

The 15th of February proved to be one long, grueling march of fifteen hours through the savage desolation of the Sinai. The solitude of the place was such that, although they had been on the move for five days, in all that time Roberts and his fellow travellers had encountered only two wayfarers, both heading for Egypt.

The track led on and on, driving ever deeper into the interior. The following morning before starting up the mountain called Gebel Garabe, the Arab guides sent ahead the camels with the tents, as from that point

twisting upwards to the peak of the rough hill. Here Roberts had the good fortune to stumble upon an ancient Egyptian temple, still exceedingly well preserved. The walls were covered with numerous hieroglyphics, royal cartouches, and symbolic figurations. Amidst the ruins stood about fifteen large stelae, and dozens more lay broken and scattered. These artifacts must have performed a votive function since the entire complex seems to have been a place of pilgrimage and may have been dedicated to Hathor. This supposition would seem to

forward they would only be a burden and no longer a help. For the first stretch, the path followed the bed of a wadi that had recently dried up, the sides of which were softened by a remarkable burst of desert blooms. Then the path led on through rock formations with the most unexpected shapes and curious colors; it then led

be supported by a number of capitals bearing the effigy of the good goddess, mistress of beauty and music. One of them can be seen clearly in the illustration, in the foreground. On the architrave, on the other hand, we can see the winged sun disc, symbol of the god Horus, exceedingly common in Egyptian temples.

Temple on Gebel Garabe, called Sarabit el Khadim. Feb.

From David Roberts's journal:

15th - Made three sketches, and travelled fifteen hours through the wilderness of Sinai, where the Israelites were condemned to wander for forty years...
16th - After much fatiguing climbing, we reached the summit of the mountain; and, to my amazement, instead of a few stones, we found an Egyptian temple in excellent preservation...
I made a sketch of this, and felt very much pleased at our discovery.

THE ENCAMPMENT
AT THE FOOT OF MOUNT SERBAL

Plate 127

17th February 1839

Mount Sinai appeared almost suddenly in all of its majesty on the morning of the 17th of February; the path continued to become steeper and more hazardous. That evening, Roberts and his fellow travellers halted not far from an Arab camp, the first that they had encountered thus far in their journey. All around the camp, sheep and goats grazed unfettered. The new arrivals were greeted in a friendly way by the tribe of Aulad Sa'id, which extended its rule over the surrounding region. The men of the tribe boasted the title of Defenders of the Monastery of St. Catherine, and had done so for centuries. A baby goat was slaughtered in honor of the new guests, and soon the servants of the English artist were intent on roasting the goat over a brightly burning campfire.
The entire camp - in the midst of which the brightly colored tents of the expedition seemed quite garish in comparison with the austere shelters of the Beduins - was steeped in an immense quiet, even during a great variety of activities: a number of women were engaged in milling grain, other women baked bread, and crowds of youngsters were rounding up the livestock to be led to the pens. Overhead, the moon moved slowly across the sky. The tribe of Aulad Sa'id had taken up residence at the foot of Mount Serbal, an imposing massif of red granite, entirely bare of vegetation; many scholars have identified this as the Mountain of the Laws mentioned in the Bible. The fact that this is the first sizable mountain to be seen when arriving from the Gulf of Suez, the isolated location of the mountain, and its distinctly threatening appearance all combine to suggest that this peak, and not Gebel Mousa, may have been the peak upon which Moses received the Tablets of the Ten Commandments from God. The debate is still quite alive, and is probably destined to remain so forever. Nor could it be otherwise.

From David Roberts's journal:

17th - Mount Sinai burst upon our sight in all its splendour; and here we met, for the first time, with an Arab encampment, surrounded by flocks of sheep and goats.

THE ASCENT OF THE LOWER RANGE OF SINAI

Plate 128

18th February 1839

The caravan left the Arab camp around noon, heading for the Convent of St. Catherine; gradually, as the hours passed, the path became increasingly difficult, and the group of travellers were overwhelmed by fatigue. The trail itself, long ago a remarkable piece of engineering, but now damaged extensively by landslides and collapses, wound up steeply along the sheer crumbling walls of a dark and savage gorge. The spectacular view of the mountain peaks shimmering in the last light of sunset, in unsettling contrast with the darkness in which the deep belows lay swathed, indicated that night was falling quickly, and darkness was upon them long before they had sighted the monastery. The track was broken and perilous, and often blocked by rubble that had tumbled from the high surrounding walls. For the group of travellers, dazed by fatigue, picking their way through that succession of rocky detritus was rapidly becoming a hazardous undertaking; finally the walls of the Convent of St. Catherine hove into sight not far away. In a short time, the caravan had succeeded in attracting the attention of the monks, who inquired as to the identity of the English traveller and his entourage.

The monks lit torches to illuminate the path and lowered a stout rope from a cabin that stood at a considerable height There was, in fact, no other way into the monastery, and so the various members of the expedition were hoisted up to the monastery by brute force, and they all had bruises to show for it. After being led through a maze of corridors and passageways, Roberts was welcomed with solemn courtesy by the abbot himself, who honored the customs of hospitality by offering the entire entourage rice soup and dates. A short while later, the artist was fast asleep in a comfortable bed.

From David Roberts's journal:

18th - Supper of rice and dried dates was set before us, and never did a poor pilgrim sleep more soundly than I did under the hospitable roof of the monks of Saint Catherine, Mount Sinai.

THE MONASTERY OF
ST. CATHERINE

Plate 129

19th February 1839

We find the earliest information about the Monastery of St. Catherine in the chronicles of the patriarch of Alexandria, Eutychios, who lived in the ninth century. It is narrated here that Queen Helena, the mother of Emperor Constantine, during her pilgrimage to the holy places described in the Bible, came to the Sinai, and was able to find the exact place where the Burning Bush had appeared to Moses. The queen ordered a small chapel to be built, had it dedicated to the Virgin, and in a short while a monastic community gathered around the chapel.

In the years that followed, the convent increased in wealth, with ever more numerous ecclesiastical donations. As a result, the monastery increasingly fell prey to the incursions of desert pirates. In A.D. 530, Emperor Justinian ordered the construction of a great basilica, which later became the Church of the Transfiguration. In order to protect the monks from further attacks, he ordered that a veritable fortress be built around the complex. Following the Arab conquest of Egypt in A.D. 640, the convent became the last enclave of Christianity in the burgeoning Muslim world, ensured by the safe conduct issued to monks by the Prophet Mohammed himself. The monks still exhibit what they say is a copy of the very document Mohammed drew up. In A.D. 726, the iconoclast Emperor Leo III ordered the destruction of all sacred images, but the convent of St. Catherine, protected by its absolute isolation, was alone in conserving intact the enormous artistic patrimony. The tiny Christian diocese, still today the world's smallest, passed intact through the bloodiest years of the Crusades and over the ensuing centuries remained an oasis of peace and traquillity, periodically receiving the visit of one or another illustrious personality attracted by the allure of biblical places and the holy nature of the Church. Following Napoleon's expedition to Egypt, the Convent of St. Catherine was described widely in Europe, the beginning of a widening fame that has come down to the present day.

From David Roberts's journal:

19th - The convent is a large square enclosure, the walls and flanking towers built of hewn granite. Inside, it looks like a small town, for beside the apartments and store-houses there is a chapel and a mosque...

Convent of St. Catherine with Mount Horeb. Feby 18th 1839.

David Roberts R.A.

THE ASCENT TO THE SUMMIT OF SINAI

Plate 130

From David Roberts's journal:

20th February 1839

20th - To-day we ascended to the summit of Sinai, which took us two hours... The view from the top is the most sublime that can be imagined.

The mountainous massif that occupies the southern area of the Sinai peninsula, generally referred to as Mount Sinai, is in reality made up of four main peaks, all of them standing taller than six thousand five hundred feet above sea level; there are also a number of smaller peaks. It is impossible to establish which of these peaks is the one referred to in the Bible, where God gave the Tablets of the Law to Moses, but tradition tells us that the mountain in question is the Gebel Mousa, the peak that towers above the Convent of St. Catherine. Further obstacles to a straightforward interpretation derive from the fact that, in the Old Testament, Sinai - which is to say, the "mountain of God" - was often referred to as Horeb. Both names - Horeb and Sinai - are cited as the location of the vision of the Burning Bush, the Alliance, and the handing down of the Ten Commandments. This dual set of names has given rise to a set of differing interpretations, the most widely accepted among them being that Horeb was the name for the massif as a whole, and that Sinai was the name for the individual mountain that Moses climbed. Roberts must certainly have been persuaded by the last-mentioned hypothesis, as we can see from the notes that he made at the foot of his drawings. The day after he first reached the Convent of St. Catherine, the

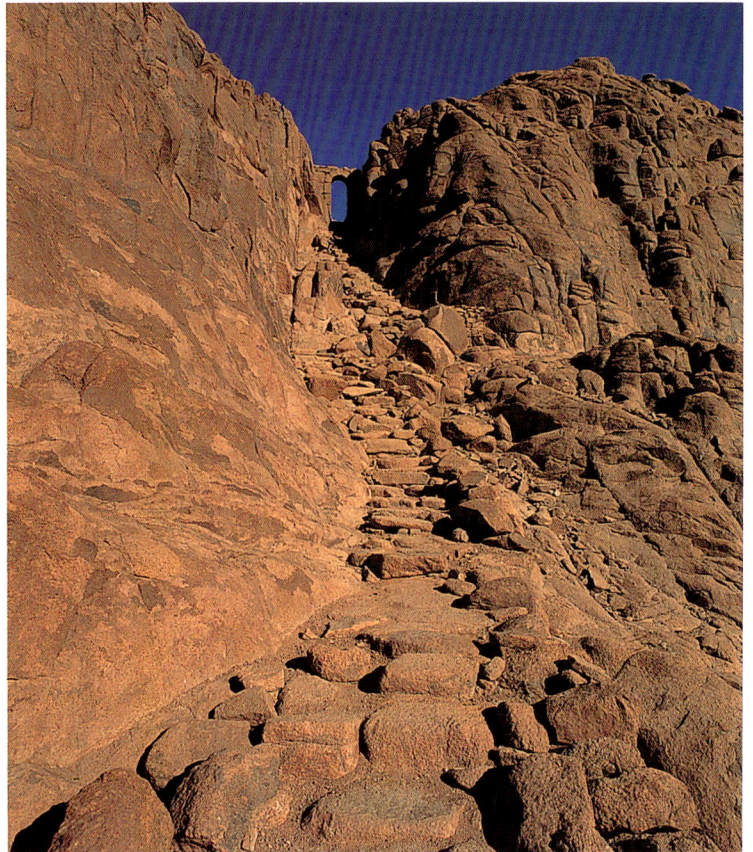

artist decided to climb the mountain that was considered sacred to the three great monotheistic religions of the world. The climb took only a couple of hours. This was no mere outing, and the climb seems all the more daunting to a modern tourist if we consider that the path, which is extremely steep at points and quite precarious, was crumbling and exposed to avalanches in a number of points. The so-called "Stairway of Moses," shown here, covers the most difficult portion of the climb, and consists

of more than three hundred steps carved out of granite. Legend narrates that a single monk did the enormous labor involved, in order to keep a vow he had made. The stairway leads to the "Gate of Confessions," an arch where pilgrims made confession to one of the monks of the convent. Only after absolution could the faithful continue, reaching the "Gate of the Faithful," where they would remove their shoes and, barefoot before God just as Moses had been, finally climb to the summit.

The Chapel of Elijah

Plate 131

20th February 1839

*A*fter passing through the Gate of Confessions, the path rises over a little saddle or basin atop the ridge that separates the valley of St. Catherine from the parallel valley of El Leja. The peak of Gebel Mousa can at last be seen a short distance away, while further off rises the huge bulk of Gebel Katrina. From this point, the view penetrates freely all the way to the monastery below and to the nearby plain of El Rahah, over the expanses of peaks of the Sinai, and across the bone-dry wadis sunken in the bottom of the valleys. In the middle of the hill there grows a solitary cypress tree, not far from a fairly deep well and a boulder covered with inscriptions, the relic of an Islamic pilgrimage. Here, where the last stretch of the trail begins, stands a low construction known as the Chapel of Elijah, built upon the spot where the prophet supposedly sought refuge from the persecution of the Queen Jezebel, the idolatrous wife of Ahab, a follower of the god Ba'al and an enemy to Israel. Inside the small building, an altar marks the entrance to the cavern where Elijah supposedly lived until God appeared before him, comforting him and suggesting that he travel to Syria where he could continue his prophetic mission.

Chapel of Elijah on Mount Horeb. Feby 20th 1839.

THE SUMMIT OF MOUNT SINAI

Plate 132

*T*he summit of
*Gebel Mousa, a massif formed
predominantly of porphyry and
of a distinctly colored red
granite, is some 6,993 feet above
sea level. Here, in the sixth
century A.D., Emperor
Justinian built a small chapel -
destroyed and rebuilt any
number of times - upon the spot
in which Moses supposedly
received the Ten Commandments
from God. In a singular
counterpoint with the Christian
structure, a mosque - similarly
small in size - marks the point
from which, according to the
lore of the Sinai Beduin, the holy
prophet Nabi Saleh was elevated
to Heaven. The mountain is
sacred to Islam because
Mohammed made a halt there
during his night-long journey
from Mecca to Mount Ararat.
As a relic of this remarkable
event, a pawprint of the
Prophet's flying camel, Burack,
is impressed in the living rock.
Roberts, who had heard of this
legend, wished to see the magical
footprint with his own eyes.
He had to agree that the
impression looked exactly like a
camel's pawprint, through some
freak of nature. At the time of
Roberts's visit, both the chapel
and the mosque were in a state
of sad disrepair, but during the
1930s, extensive repair work
was done. Today, most pilgrims
and tourists prefer to spend the
night high on the summit, until
the light of dawn illuminates all
the surrounding peaks and inches
its way out to the Gulf of Aqaba.*

Mahomedan Chapels on the Summit of Sinai   Feb 20th 1839.

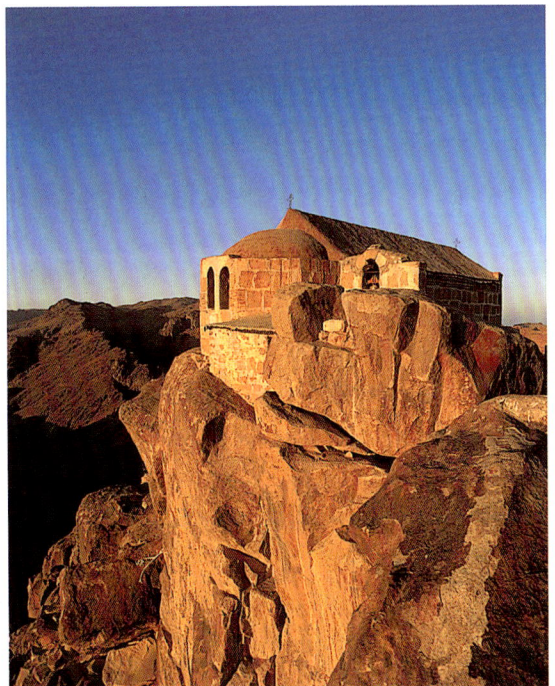

From David Roberts's journal:

20th - Near the top are two small chapels. One covers the cave where Elijah passed the night...
On the summit are other two - one where Moses received the tables of the law, the other belongs to the Mahometans, and under it is pointed out the foot-mark of the camel that carried the prophet...

20th February 1839

The Convent of St Catherine Mount Sinai, looking towards the Ruins of the Encampment. Feby 21st. 1839.

THE MONASTERY OF ST. CATHERINE AND THE PLAIN OF THE ENCAMPMENT

Plate 133

21st February 1839

Downhill from the convent, along the wadi, there spreads a broad plain where biblical tradition holds that the people of Israel set up camp while waiting for Moses to descend from Mount Sinai. The Bible states, as a matter of fact, that "So Moses went down unto the people and spake unto them. And God spake all these words, saying, 'I am the Lord thy God, which have brought thee out of the Land of Egypt, out of the house of bondage. Thou shalt have no others gods before me.'" (Exodus, 19, 25; 20, 1:3.) Although it is extremely difficult to determine whether the story as told in the Bible corresponds to actual history, a series of careful scientific investigations has made it possible to cast new light on the daunting exodus of the Jews in the desert, a forty-year continual search for wells or a luxuriant oasis.

It is impossible to determine how many Jews left Egypt during the reign of Rameses II, but it is certainly unlikely that they were three million as the Bible states in Exodus. It is much more realistic to believe, as most scholars now do, that there were thirty thousand individuals, who in all likelihood did not pass by the base of Gebel Mousa at all, but rather much farther north, where the oases are far more common. In any case, whatever the route that was followed by Moses and his people, these sites have always emanated an attraction that cannot be explained by reason alone. Roberts himself remained greatly impressed by the Sinai, and in particular by the Monastery of St. Catherine, which he sketched from a number of different angles. In this plate, where it is possible to see among other things the two tents used by the expedition, we can clearly see the minaret of the mosque that stands alongside the Church of the Transfiguration. In fact, inside the walls, a small Muslim community coexists in perfect harmony with the Christians—this unusual cohabitation is a result of the fact that the mountain is also greatly venerated in Islam. The need to protect the pilgrims of both religions helped to contribute to the preservation of the convent far more than the document signed by Mohammed, who is also believed to have founded the mosque.

THE WALLS OF THE MONASTERY OF ST. CATHERINE

Plate 134

21st February 1839

Nestled at an altitude over five thousand feet above sea level at the end of a narrow valley, the Monastery of St. Catherine is made even more noteworthy by the setting of spectacular mountains that stand majestically circling it. In this illustration, the complex is portrayed in all the powerful splendor of its fortifications. The appearance of the structure is believed to have changed very little since the Crusades.

The stout enclosing wall made of red-granite blocks girds an area that is roughly rectangular in shape, two hundred seventy-eight feet by two hundred forty feet.

The height of the walls ranges from forty to fifty feet; they attain a width of five and a half feet at the base. Numerous Maltese crosses are cut into the wall along its entire perimeter, with some of them dating from the reign of Justinian.

The eastern corner is protected by the Kleber Tower, while a number of other towers with square or circular plans soften the severity of the construction. Upon the northwest wall, at a height of about thirty feet off the ground, one can still clearly see the jutting cabin depicted by the English artist. Inside the cabin was a winch, which originally allowed visitors to enter the convent, as well as permitted supplies and other materials to be brought in. The original gate, which opened just slightly to the right in the walls, had in fact already been walled up since the Middle Ages so as to leave absolutely no openings in the walls at ground level. Modern-day visitors can enter the monastery through a narrow cranny, cut in the twentieth century and located beneath the trap door of the winch; a number of wells provide the convent's water supply.

The most important of these wells stands just to the right of the entrance on the inside and is known as Bir Mousa, or the Well of Moses. Tradition has it that it was here that Moses met the daughters of Jethro. The eldest among them, Zipporah, eventually became his wife. On the interior, the Monastery of St. Catherine seems almost like a medieval village made up of tiny courtyards, stairways, catwalks, vaulted galleries, and narrow corridors. The constructions are built one jutting up against the other, as if they had sprung up spontaneously with no particular order or intent in a remarkable mixture of varied styles and proportions.

THE CHURCH OF THE TRANSFIGURATION

Plate 135

21st February 1839

The saint to whom this monastery is consecrated was born in Alexandria in A.D. 294 with the name of Dorothea. She was born into a rich and aristocratic family. Extremely learned and well versed in philosophy, she became a Christian and was baptized Catherine. She confounded a great many wise men in a public debate in the presence of Emperor Maximinus Daia. She miraculously escaped death on the wheel, but was then martyred through decaptitation. She was buried in Alexandria, and five full centuries elapsed before a monk of the Sinai had a vision of the body of the saint, transported by angels to the peak of a nearby mountain, where the body remained, sweet-smelling and intact. In time, the monks decided to transport the saint's body to the nearby monastery, which from that moment forward took the name of the saint, as did the mountain, still known as Gebel Katrina. The saint's left hand and her skull, girt by a crown made of gold, studded with precious stones, were sealed up in exquisite silver coffers and placed in a sarcophagus next to the altar of the Church of the Transfiguration. This is one of the most ancient Christian basilicas to survive intact, as it originally appeared. The interior, one hundred thirty-one feet in length, is split up into three naves, punctuated by twelve monolithic granite columns which represent the months of the year. Each column is adorned with a massive carved capital, different from the other eleven, and bears an icon of the saint who is venerated during the corresponding month. The central nave terminates in an apse whose basin is covered with an exquisite mosaic dating from the sixth century, depicting the transfiguration of Christ; each of the side naves terminates in a chapel. Hanging from the eighteenth-century wooden ceiling, decorated with gold stars on a green background, are about fifty lamps made of gold-plated silver. In line with Greek Orthodox tradition, the altar is hidden from the sight of the faithful by the iconostasis, an exquisitely decorated partition. The iconostasis is formed of four wooden panels, with carvings and gold-leaf decoration, with icons of Christ, the Virgin Mary, Saint Catherine, and St. John the Baptist. High above the iconostasis stands an imposing Christ on the Cross. Both this Christ and the rest of the iconostasis were painted by Jeremiah of Crete, during the seventeenth century, and donated to the monastery by the Patriarch of Crete. Roberts was able to sketch the interior of the church through the kind intervention of the abbot; this same abbot, however, was reluctant to allow Roberts to sketch the chapel of the Burning Bush.

Chapel of The Convent of St. Catherine on Mou

Feb 21st 1839

David Roberts R.A.

THE MONKS OF THE MONASTERY OF ST. CATHERINE

Plate 136

21st Febraury 1839

Even now, the Monastery of St. Catherine is under the administration of the Greek-Orthodox Church. Most of the monks that live there are Greek Orthodox, and they practice the cult of St. Basil the Great, the bishop of Caesarea, who lived from A.D. 329 to 379. It is customary for the abbot of the monastery to be chosen by a majority vote, by a council formed of four archimandrites, then to be consecrated by the Patriarch of Jerusalem - one of six ecumenical Greek-Orthodox patriarchs (the other five are the Patriarchs of Rome, Moscow, Istanbul, Alexandria, and Antioch). In this illustration, which shows the courtyard of the monastery, Roberts devotes special attention to the clothing of the monks. The abbot, the archbishop of the Sinai, can be easily picked out from the crowd, as he is wearing a long black mantle, different from that of his brother monks. The garb worn by the entire community, in fact, was cut from a cloth made of camelhair and goathair, very similar to the clothing worn by Beduins; this cloth was made in the monastery. The monks, who never numbered more than twenty, saw to all their needs, and produced all the things that could be needed in that tiny universe. As the need arose, each monk became a carpenter, a woodsman, a tailor, a cobbler, a baker, and a chef. Most monks spent from three to five years at the Convent of St. Catherine, but some of the monks spent their entire lives there. The rules called for them to attend mass twice a day and never to eat meat. Roberts spent a great deal of time talking to the superior, an extremely learned and courteous individual, who had travelled extensively throughout Europe and to England; he had only the most pleasant memories of his travels.

The Rock of Moses

Plate 137

22nd February 1839

On the 22nd of February, Roberts bade farewell to the hospitable monks of the Monastery of St. Catherine, setting off again in the direction of Aqaba, where he expected to arrive within twenty-four hours. That same morning, quite early, the superior had arranged for the caravan to be sent on ahead, along with all the baggage, and by sunset, the English artist - who had stopped along the way to make some sketches - found camp already set up in a wadi to the west of the monastery. After crossing the mountain that separates the valley of St. Catherine from the valley of El-Leja, where the abandoned convent of El-Arbain is located, the artist stumbled upon the Rock of Moses, an enormous boulder that is venerated as the rock mentioned in the Bible, when the people of Israel were left without water, and began to complain. When this happened, Moses supplicated the Lord, who ordered him to take the rod with which he had caused the Red Sea to open, and told him "Behold, I will stand before thee there upon the rock in Horeb; and thou shalt smite the rock, and there shall come water out of it, that the people may drink." (Exodus, 17:6). Roberts believed that the boulder must have tumbled down from the side of the mountain in the distant past, and noted that on the surface of the rock there were a dozen or so fairly regular channels. Careful observation led him to decide that this was not the work of human beings. Rather, he felt, when the boulder had been part of some cavity or cavern deep in the mountain, worn away by streams of water. More likely, however, the unusual shape of the Rock of Moses was the result of the continuous action of desert winds, which blow constantly here.

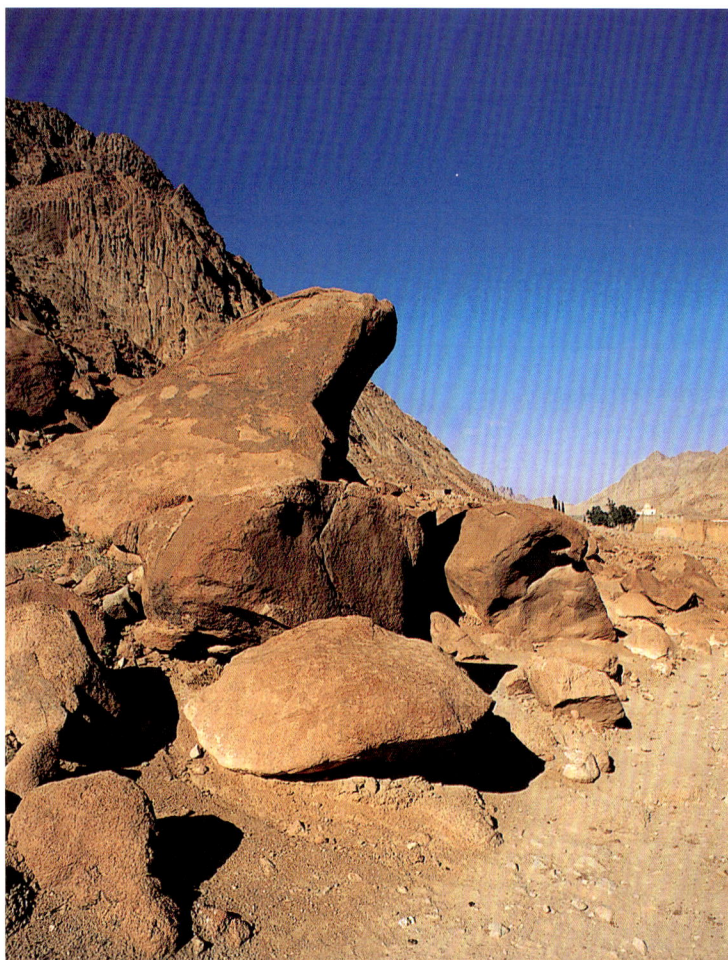

From David Roberts's journal:

22nd - Made a drawing of the Rock of Moses, said to be that from which the water gushed forth to the thirsty multitude. Took leave of our friends the monks of St. Catherine's, of whose kindness it is impossible to speak too highly...

Mount Haib, Feb 22 1839.   David Roberts, R.A.

THE ISLE OF GRAIA, GULF OF AQABA

Plate 138

23rd -27th February 1839

Isle of Graia, Gulf of Akabah — Arabia Petraea

With a lively eye for details, Roberts mentioned in his journal that the 23rd of February began with a hike of a couple of hours' duration, followed by a halt to eat something: bread baked by the monks of St. Catherine, cold meat, butter from Cairo, dates, olives, and water diluted with a bit of brandy to soften its bitter taste. After smoking a pipeful of the finest Turkish tobacco, the caravan proceeded on its way through the hills of the Sinai; they pitched their tents at five in the afternoon, in the middle of a broad valley. The idea of reaching Aqaba quickly had evidently become impracticable, given the conditions of the track, and Roberts prepared himself cheerfully to continue riding for stretches of ten hours over the following days.

On the 24th of February, a Sunday, the expedition finally left the Sinai massif behind; now the landscape was reduced to a succession of low sandy hills dotted with bushes of wild thyme, with a fragrance that filled the heated air. In the afternoon, the track finally began to descend along a ravine that was savage and gloomy in appearance, and when they reached the end of it, suddenly, there were the coast and the crystal-clear waters of the Gulf of Aqaba. The following day, the scirocco wind that had sprung up in the south in the earliest hours of the morning had soon stiffened into a raging sandstorm, in the end forcing Roberts and his fellow travellers to pitch their tents in a sheltered bay. The heat was distinctly oppressive, and toward evening, the thermometer continued to hover at about 85 degrees F. The weather improved during the night, and by daylight the expedition was able to travel on with no further hindrance. On the evening of the 26th of February, finally, they made camp just before the Island of Graia, close to Aqaba. On the island, which was little more than a large rock, it was possible to make out the remains of a fortress or a city that - it was said - had flourished long before the Crusades. In effect, it is thought that the Citadel of Graia once formed part of the fortifications of nearby Eilat. Both Eilat and its neighbor, Aqaba, take their origins from Ezyon Geber, the Biblical port that was built by Solomon on the shores of the Red Sea. Occupied by Nabateans, Romans, Byzantines, and Arabs, it was finally destroyed by a Crusader army around 1116, during the siege of Eilat.

THE FORTRESS
OF AQABA

Plate 139

The drinking water that the caravan had carried with it had long since run out when the caravan finally came to the walls of the fortress of Aqaba, at midday on the 27th of February. The garrison welcomed the unannounced visitors with great courtesy and offered them beds and blankets in the barracks room.

The English artist nonetheless preferred to pitch his tent outdoors and sleep there. After washing up and changing his clothing, he paid his respects to the local governor, an extremely genial and kind individual who offered the visiting foreigner some excellent coffee and tobacco.

After enquiring as to Roberts's route and destinations, he immediately ordered that a messenger be sent to the chief of the Alloueens. He said that without the authorization of the chief, the expedition absolutely could not proceed in the direction of Petra. The fortress, a massive structure with a square plan and a tower at each of the four corners, had been built around the middle of the sixteenth century by the Egyptian sultan el Ghoury, and served to protect pilgrims heading for Mecca, or returning from there to Egypt and to Syria. The strategic importance of the fort consisted largely of its proximity to a number of freshwater wells, the only ones for a great distance around, which represented a

fundamental and vital supply resource for the caravans. Although Roberts was unsuccessful in his efforts to find remains or inscriptions that dated back previous to the foundation of the fortress, he felt reasonably sure that this was the site of the ancient Aelana, the city of the Edomites, conquered by David. Near Aelana, Solomon founded Ezion

Geber, which became one of the most important mercantile and commercial centers in the ancient world. While waiting for the chief of the Alloueens to reach Aqaba to begin negotiations, Roberts spent a couple of days bumming around the area and resting up for the tiring march to Petra.

From David Roberts's journal:

27th - We hurried on to the fortress of Akabah, where we arrived about 12 noon, our camels and Arab attendants apparently making a great impression on the inmates of the pigmy fortress... March 2nd - This morning the sheikh of the Alloueens arrived, when a grand palaver took place. After much beating about the bush, we came to terms, and he guaranteed our safe passage to Hebron, by the way of Wady Mousa or Petra, staying at the latter place as long as we chose...

27th February–1st March 1839

THE APPROACH TO PETRA

Plate 140

2nd-5th March 1839

The lively discussion between Roberts and the sheik of the tribe of the Alloueens, who had reached Aqaba during the morning of the 2nd of March, lasted for quite a while and ended on the following terms: If forty-five hundred piasters - equivalent to about forty-five pounds sterling at the exchange of the time - were paid, the caravan would be allowed to continue toward Hebron, crossing Wadi Mousa, and stopping at Petra for the amount of time Roberts would need to sketch the main monuments there. After striking this bargain, Roberts invited the sheik and the governor of Aqaba to dine in his tent, along with their lieutenants. Later Roberts bade farewell to the men of the tribe of Beni Sa'id who had accompanied him to that point, and began to prepare for his departure the next day. The new caravan, consisting of twenty-three beasts of burden, set off at dawn, and soon left behind the Gulf of Aqaba, striking out along what had once been the bed of the Jordan River thousands of years before. The plain was enveloped in a dense, suffocating fog, which made the desert that much more grim. The travellers moved along in silence until it was time to pitch tents; that same night the pale light of the full moon and the mysterious appearance of the mountains all around them cast Roberts into a strange state of mind, filling him with a yearning homesickness. The sheik's camp appeared on the horizon during the afternoon of the following day, and a few hours later the caravan was received with great joy. As a mark of hospitality to the three Westerners, a suckling goat was served, and they gladly accepted this kindness. After a peaceful night, the expedition set off once again at the first light of dawn, drawing closer to the outlying slopes of Mount Hor. At three in the afternoon, they set up camp beneath an ancient watchtower, set to guard the valley of El Ghor, one of the routes giving access to the city of Petra. The building, two stories high and absolutely free of adornment, stood in a remarkable location, at the peak of a rocky ridge jutting out over the level of the wadi. The tower must have once formed part of a series of watchposts or even a complex signalling system set up to guard the city. It should be noted that the date set on the plate, just as is the case elsewhere in the work of Roberts, is strangely inaccurate, and does not agree with what Roberts noted in his journal.

ch to PETRA – An Ancient Watchtower Commanding the Valley of El Ghor   Feby. 5th 1839

From David Roberts's journal:

4th - About 4 o'clock we arrived at the tents of the sheikh, where we were received with great kindness, and kissed on each cheek by every Arab present...
5th - Started early, as usual. About 12 o'clock we struck into a chain of mountains on our right, forming part of the range of Mount Hor. At 3 o'clock we pitched our tents at the entrance to Wady Mousa...

MOUNT HOR

Plate 141

5th March 1839

Made impatient by emotion, Roberts wished at all costs to climb to the peak of the hill that dominated the campground in order to take a first look at the mythical city of Petra, but his hopes were soon dashed by a further series of hills - completely unlooked for - which stood in the sight of the spot. The landscape, in any case, was spectacular, and the English artist felt wholly repaid for the effort involved in reaching the top of the hill. Beneath his feet were the ravines of El Ghor and Wadi Arabah, the rocks of Mt. Seir glittered in the splendid sunset, and in the distance, directly before him, towered the majestic bulk of Mt. Hor, at the foot of which the people of Israel pitched their tents after the flight from Egypt. It was here that the destiny of Aaron was fulfilled, when the Lord ordered Moses to lead him to the summit of the mountain. "And Moses stripped Aaron of his garments and put them upon Elea'zar his son; and Aaron died there on the top of the mount: and Moses and Elea'zar came down from the mount. And when all the congregation saw that Aaron was dead, they mourned for Aaron thirty days, even all the house of Israel" (Book of Numbers, 20, 28-29).

Gebil Hor March 5th 1839

R.A

THE ENTRANCE TO PETRA

Plate 142

From David Roberts's journal:

6th - Petra. To-day we encamped in the centre of the remains of this extraordinary city, which is situated in the midst of mountains, surrounded by the desert, but abounding in every vegetable production...

6th March 1839

*A*t dawn on 6th of March, after the sheik tried in vain to persuade Roberts to leave his camels and baggage behind him in the camp and to continue on foot, the caravan set off once again and began to climb a steep trail that led along the edge of a precipice, amidst patches of oleander and laurel. After climbing a particularly difficult ridge, and as they were about to descend into the valley of Petra, Roberts and his Alloueen guides were stopped by a group of Arabs belonging to the tribe of Wadi Mousa, who commanded the city in the rock and all the surrounding region. Following a violent quarrel, their sheik informed the foreigners that there were ancient feuds between the two tribes and that the Alloueens had no right to enter Petra, nor to bring foreigners with them to Petra. Negotiations continued for a long time in extremely tense language, and in the end Roberts agreed to pay a tribute of three hundred piasters in exchange for permission to camp for five days in Petra without being disturbed. The time agreed upon was sufficient for the needs of the artist, but Roberts was forced to work during the entire time of his stay there. After passing by the barrier of the armed men, the caravan was able to descend to the floor of the valley, where they pitched their tents and watered their camels and then led them to pasture.

The place where Petra stands is shaped like an amphitheater closed in by sheer cliffs, measuring roughly two-thirds of a mile from east to west and a third of a mile from north to south. The bed of a stream runs through the place and, with its tributaries, marks a low ridge upon which the proper city once stood. The cliffs that surround it, and which in certain points stand over nine hundred eighty feet tall, were used as a medium in which to cut both tombs and habitations. Atop the surrounding peaks were located a number of places of worship and small forts that surveyed the roads leading into the town. The cavea of the theater, which can be seen in the foreground in the illustration, could hold as many as three thousand spectators and was entirely cut out of the side of the mountain.

CONFERENCE OF ARABS AT PETRA

Plate 143

6th March 1839

As soon as camp had been set up amidst the ruins of Petra, Roberts had an opportunity to witness an odd dispute amongst the very same Beduins who just a few hours before had so rudely blocked his way. One of the Arabs had been accused of stealing an ass, and in order to settle the matter, three sheiks of the tribe were asked to deliver their opinions. One of these sheiks, an elderly man held in great estimation by all, had the parties to the dispute sit upon the ground, arrayed in a circle, and began the council by reciting in the most solemn imaginable manner a part of the introductory chapter of the Koran, and a number of phrases that seemed to the ears of Roberts to be enunciations of fundamental laws. During the whole time he was speaking, the old man brandished a sword in his right hand, and the others listened carefully, occasionally nodding in silence. When the first sheik had set forth his view of things, he passed the sword to the next, who spoke in turn; this ceremony continued until all those who were present had spoken. During all this, no one had at any time dared to interrupt the speaker who had, as it were, the floor.

Once a decision had been handed down, the Arabs disappeared silently amongst the rocks. Although his curiosity was greatly aroused, Roberts was unable to find out what the verdict of that odd court had been, nor what the penalty inflicted might have been.

PETRA

Plate 144

Located in southern Transjordan, Petra is mentioned several times in the Bible by the name of Sela, while the Arabs refer to it as Wadi Mousa, i.e. the Valley of Moses. Although the earliest habitations in the area date from the Iron Age, the city became important when the Nabateans occupied the region, during the period of Persian rule. Setting up their stronghold high atop one of the rocky spurs in the area, the Nabateans managed to hold out against the attempt by Antigonus I of Syria, in 312 B.C., to take the place by storm. Petra developed as a rock city at the intersection of three mountain gorges. Later it became a center offering haven and defense for the local nomadic populations.

The decision by the Nabateans to choose Petra as their capital was therefore based on considerations of security. Hidden as it was in the mountains, with a very few, easily guarded points of access, Petra constituted a secure safeguard for the wealth that the Nabateans had accumulated with their caravan trade. The ease of communications with the Red Sea made it possible for the Nabateans to trade extensively with Arabia and with Mesopotamia, while the track through the Negev Desert to Gaza gave them access to the Mediterranean and to Syria.

The continuing development of major trade routes and the growing prosperity of the Nabateans themselves led to the growth of Petra, and to its eventual Hellenization. In particular, during the first century A.D., the Nabatean kings embellished the town with splendid monuments, most of which were carved into the living rock. Roman occupation and the creation of the Arabian province slowed the development of Petra, but failed to halt it entirely.

In the third century A.D., however, with the transfer of the Nabatean capital to Bosra, and the growth of new caravan centers, such as Gerasa and Palmyra, in particular, the importance of Petra declined greatly, even though Emperor Hadrian bestowed upon the town the honor of the title of "metropolis."

For a number of centuries, the rock-cut city continued to be a major power, the see of a bishop, and, following the reorganization of the empire at the order of Diocletian, the capital of the province of Palaestina Taertia. After the Arab conquest, however, Petra declined greatly, though it was fortified and inhabited by the Crusaders. Following the thirteenth century, it was abandoned, and all knowledge of Petra was lost until the beginning of the nineteenth century.

EL KHASNÈ

Plate 145

6th March 1839

Just as soon as camp had been been made, Roberts decided to go and see the Khasnè, certainly the best-known monument in Petra, as well as one of the wonders of the ancient world. In order to better understand the profound impact that the sudden appearance of this superb creation of human genius has upon the visitor, it should be noted that Petra is located in an extremely secure location, since the only easy access to the place is set to the east, and consists of a narrow stream bed enclosed by two cliff walls that are separated from each other in certain points by no more than twelve feet. This passage, now known as the Sik, is about two and a half miles in length. In ancient times, the water that once ran in the stream was channeled through a gallery carved into the rock some two hundred thirty feet in length, and its waters were partly conveyed in the city aqueduct. At a number of different points, caravansaries and spaces were set aside for the encampment of arriving caravans. About halfway up, at a point where the Sik suddenly changes direction, carved into the cliff, one can see the Khasnè, a funerary temple that has no rival on earth. The contrast between the delicate pink facade of the building and the shadowy Sik is quite impressive. The symmetry of the facade is absolute, the proportions are exquisitely tasteful, and the degree of conservation is practically perfect. Roberts tended to believe that the Khasnè had been a mausoleum rather than a sanctuary, and yet, in connection with the age-old question of just what had been the real purpose of the similar structures lined up along the main valley, he expressed the opinion that they had been neither tombs nor temples, but built simply to titillate the refined esthetic tastes of the Nabateans, endowing the city with an openness of perspective that its remarkable natural location would otherwise have denied it. Excavations and careful studies have instead allowed us to determine that the rock-cut structures were put to a great number of uses and that a number of them were simply houses, often made of a large room with columns and niches on the sides and a raised triclinium in the center. A number of these residences are decorated with painted frescoes depicting grape vines and floral motifs

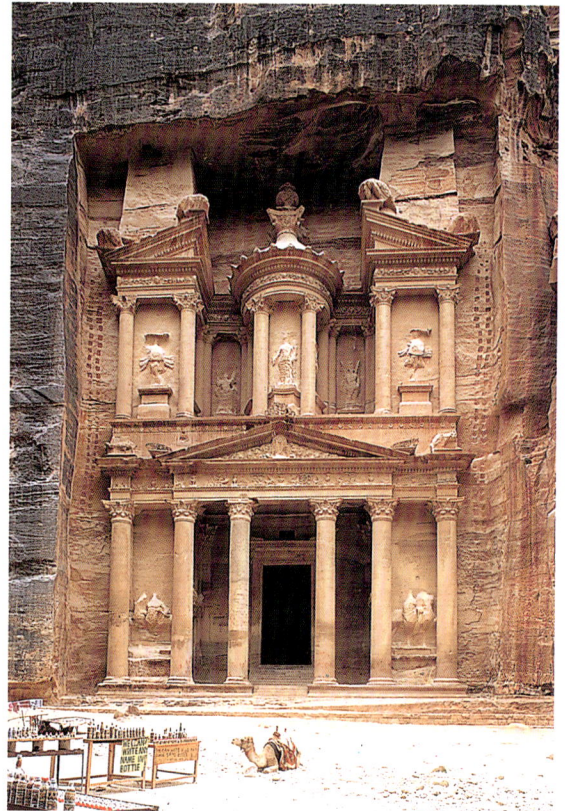

From David Roberts's journal:

6th - Our first stroll was to the Khasnè, and I cannot say whether I was most surprised at the building or its extraordinary position. It stands, as it were, in an immense niche in the rocks, and the fine colour of the stone, and perfect preservation of the minute details, give it the appearance of having been recently finished...

VIEW OF EL KHASNÈ, OR THE TREASURY

Plate 146

7th March 1839

*L*he facade of the Khasnè, one hundred thirty-one feet high and eighty-two feet long, is divided into two stories, the lower story consisting of a portico with pediment, with six Corinthian columns, over forty feet tall each. Between the two outer pairs of columns are two colossal equestrian groups executed in high relief. The design of the frieze consists of a series of pairs of gryphons facing each other, while the pediment, at the center of which stood an eagle with outspread wings, was completed by a scroll decoration. At the corners of the architrave, two lions served as acroteria.

The second story, of an airy elegance, is split into three pavilions. The central pavilion was a round tholos, practically a small-scale temple, with a conical roof surmounted by an urn. It is worth noting that this detail gave the building its name: In Arabic, El Khasnè means "treasury."

The Beduins believed that great wealth was concealed inside the urn and they regularly fired their rifles at it in order to shatter it, believing that a shower of riches would ensue. The tholos is flanked by two semi-pediments, each supported by four corner columns. In the niches stood reliefs representing female figures and four giant eagles served as acroteria. The interior of the building consists of a vestibule some forty-six feet wide and nineteen feet deep, and a stairway with eight steps leads to a central chamber. The chamber is a large cube, thirty-nine feet to a side, with three smaller rooms on each side. Two other smaller rooms lead off from the vestibule. It is this arrangement of interior rooms and the absence of any altar whatsoever, as well as the location of the building in the narrow gorge - which would certainly have hindered its functions as a temple - that leads us to suppose that the Khasnè was actually a monumental tomb, rather than a temple as had long been believed.

Louis Haghe Lith.   Temple called El Khasné Petra March 7th 1839

PETRA March 7th 1859.

THE EXCAVATED MANSIONS

Plate 147

7th March 1839

It was said that the Nabateans were the descendents of Nabath, the firstborn son of Ishmael. They did speak an Aramaic dialect, known as Mendaic, belonging to the northern branch of the Semitic languages. Originally, nomads from the Arabian peninsula, the Nabateans settled down and quickly organized themselves into a powerful centralized monarchy, and in a brief time prospered greatly.

The greatest point of expansion of the Nabatean kingdom came during Hellenic and Roman times, when the city of Petra flourished in a particularly spectacular manner.

The splendid capital of the Nabateans was, even in antiquity, the object of great amazement and surprise because of its unusual and spectacular appearance. What is now the bed of the Wadi Mousa was then the main street of the town, beginning near a pool for the bath, alongside a nymphaeum; further on stood three marketplaces arranged on terraces one atop the other with shops arranged along the sides, a great Corinthian temple, baths, the Roman arch, and a several-storied gymnasium.

The rock cliff across from the theater contains a great many rock structures, all built with remarkable craftsmanship. The structure shown in the illustration is certainly one of the most interesting of them, both in terms of high quality of the workmanship and because of the setback of the facade with respect to the natural profile of the mountain face. There was certainly an unusual technical solution in the use of a double order of vaulted galleries to support the broad terrace between the two lateral colonnades cut into the living rock. The conscious attempt to attain a spectacular effect is hard to miss, and the result is made even more impressive by the warm tones of the stone.

From David Roberts's journal:

7th - I am more and more astonished and bewildered with this wonderful city, which must be five or six miles each way in extent; and every ravine has been inhabited, even to the tops of the mountains. The valley has been filled with temples, public buildings, triumphal arches, and bridges, all of which have been laid prostrate, with the exception of one arch, and one temple, and of this temple the portico has fallen. The style of the architecture varies from all I have ever seen and in many of its parts is a curious combination of the Egyptian with the Roman and Greek orders. The stream still flows through it as heretofore; the shrubs and wild-flowers flourish luxuriantly; every crevice of the rock is filled with them, and the air is perfumed with the most delicious fragrance.

EL DEIR

Plate 148

8th March 1839

On the morning of the 8th of March, Roberts started down a long ravine, accompanied by a small platoon of armed men. He was following an extremely rough trail, which soon turned into a steep stairway nearly a mile in length. After climbing nearly a thousand feet, the little group finally reached the astonishing rock-cut monument known as El Deir, which means the Monastery, one of the buildings in the ancient Nabatean capital that is less frequently visited, although it is certainly the most imposing. Cut entirely from living rock, the facade of the temple is one hundred and sixty feet in width and one hundred and twenty-eight feet in height; the decoration is very similar to that of the Khasnè, if only more elaborate. The lower floor is punctuated by eight columns that frame two arched niches, and a portal with a pediment in the center. Through the entrance, a double flight of steps leads to a square chamber. At the center of this chamber, the altar once stood, and is now almost entirely destroyed. Roberts observed a roughly painted cross upon the altar, a clear indicator that the pagan sanctuary had been used as a Christian church for a certain period. On the upper story, the facade, which is purely decorative in function, presents a central tholos, and the pediment, and two pillars at the corners, while a handsome Doric frieze crosses the entire facade. Facing this remarkable building, in a commanding position high on a natural base, stand the ruins of a second temple, preceded by a colonnade of which only the plinths survive. Roberts was intrigued by the incredible view that one enjoys from that rock balcony, projecting out over the valley of El Ghor. Indeed, Roberts became quite discouraged, and felt that he was not adequate to the challenge of depicting such marvelous creations.

8th - To-day we wound our way up a steep ravine, a broken staircase extending about a mile. We reached a bulding, rarely visited, called Deir, or Convent, which is hewn out of the face of the rock...
The view here is magnificent, embracing the valley of El Ghor, Mount Hor (the tomb of Aaron crowning the summit), and the whole defile, leading through rocks which make you giddy to look over; while the ancient city, in all its extent, is seen stretching along the valley...

THE EASTERNMOST POINT
IN THE VALLEY

Plate 149

8th March 1839

The first rock-cut monuments of Petra presented a smooth, extremely simple facade, surmounted by one or two rows of step pinnacles, at the base of which a door opened, at times framed by half-columns (this type of architecture can be seen in Plate 24). This sort of sepulchre, the oldest instances of which can be dated back to the end of the second century B.C., constituted a typically Nabatean adaptation of models that had become common in nearby Syria. During the two following centuries, more complex types of facades were developed. At the origin of this new development lay the adoption upon a broad scale of Hellenistic architectural motifs, such as the frieze, the architrave, and the pilaster strip. In the meanwhile, a special type of capital had been developed, which was known as the Nabatean capital, and an increasingly widespread use of structural elements with a purely ornamental purpose had spread. The extremely provincial nature of local art, which had developed in an area on the far boundaries of the civilized world, in open desert, nonetheless justified the persistence of local features in decoration that could be said to be completely obsolete, such as rosettes and animals used in a heraldic manner. In the second half of the first century A.D. a new type of facade finally made its appearance, enjoying its greatest degree of development in the following decades.

A noteworthy enrichment of an architecturally oriented range of figurative elements corresponded to an effort to develop the theatrically spectacular, which is so typical of Roman influence.

The cliff facades attained a colossal scale, with stacked orders of columns that served to emulate elevations of temples and theatrical "scenae."

During this period of great architectural production, the two tombs shown here in the illustration by Roberts were built, and still stand at the easternmost extremity of the valley: the so-called Tomb of the Palace, with four entrances with alternating arches and pediments and four orders of small columns and pillars on the upper order, is one; the other is the adjacent Corinthian Tomb, not unlike the Khasnè, but with a smaller, intermediate story between the pediment and the tholos.

THE RUINS OF A TRIUMPHAL ARCH

Plate 150

8th March 1839

Not far from the gymnasium, before which stood a great temple, the road passed under a triumphal arch characterized by three openings of considerable size. Although the structure had long since been reduced to a heap of rubble, the function it clearly served and the surviving bits of architecture that could still be deciphered indicated that this was a work dating back to Roman times. Numerous fragments of sculpture scattered all about showed that the arch had possessed a rather exuberant ornamentation. Amidst the ruins, among other things, there was a winged figure of remarkable workmanship that may well have had a place in the pediment. All through the area of what was once Petra, in fact, the presence of a great many decorative elements, which clearly reflected a Greco-Roman influence, leads us to think that after the Roman conquest of Petra in A.D. 106, master craftsmen who had come from the West were active in Petra. Nonetheless, the local style had characteristics of its own so distinct and recognizable that a clear identity arose without getting confused with the foreign styles. This illustration is dated the 8th of March, the third day of Roberts's stay in the Nabatean capital. That afternoon, while Roberts was away exploring and the servants were busy preparing dinner, a man succeeded in slipping into the camp and stealing a metal soup tureen, probably believing it to be silver. After vanishing among the rocks, the thief suddenly appeared atop a nearby peak and, brandishing his booty over his head, began to boast shamelessly of his prowess, and to promise new feats of thievery. The local tribes had a villainous reputation and their raids could easily end in tragedy for the unfortunate victims.

PETRA, LOOKING SOUTH

Plate 151

9th March 1839

The ruins of Petra were discovered by the Swiss Orientalist and traveller Johann Ludwig Burckhardt in 1812, and they certainly constitute one of the most singular and enchanting monumental complexes of the ancient world. There are two sets of reasons: first, the exceptional quality of the architectural creations themselves; and second, the odd and perhaps unique location of the city, clamped between volcanic hills, set deep in narrow gorges, enhanced by the remarkable color of the rock from which the buildings have been carved. This illustration clearly emphasizes the way in which the most significant surviving ruins line the main valley, perched on terraces at various levels; originally the terraces were linked one to the other by networks of stairways that must surely have been spectacular to see. As mentioned earlier, the stream bed must have been covered with a paved road, and the ruins that can be seen along each of the two banks indicate that this decuman of sorts was lined with a number of remarkable public buildings. On the northern side of the stream bed, in fact, the ruins of a very large temple can be observed, while on the opposite side, it is still possible to distinguish the outline of a monumental portico: not far off, where the main stream bed joins a creek of more modest dimensions, stand the remains of a broad terrace. At one side of this structure stood a small structure with a circular plan. Roberts was the first Westerner to receive official permission to camp at Petra, where he studied the monuments in some depth. He was also the first Westerner to bring back a thorough going graphic documentation of the place, while the first systematic archeological campaign was not carried out until much later, in the years from 1929 to 1935.

THE RAVINE, LEADING TO PETRA

Plate 152

9th March 1839

On the 9th of March, Roberts visited the main entry route to Petra, known as the Sik, a spectacular gorge about a mile in length, which runs right up to the temple of El Khasnè. Obscure, unsettling, and intriguing, the canyon is extremely narrow, perennially immersed in shadows, and clamped between cliff walls that rise from three hundred to six hundred feet high. At certain points the cliff walls almost seem to touch, blocking out any sky whatsoever. The rock appears to be shaped by the erosive action of the wind and by the erosion of a small stream, a stream that swells enormously, however, during the summer thunderstorms.

This unimpressive stream that now gurgles along in the open air, giving life to a tenacious vegetation, was once channeled along in an underground passage that was uncovered centuries ago. The illustration shows an arch that once spanned the bottom of the canyon, connecting the two walls and reaching upwards to a considerable height; the lower section of the arch structure was cut out of the living rock and was decorated with two very deep niches, presumably meant to hold the simulacra of the patron deities of Petra. Although Roberts was unable to ascertain the original function of the striking piece of architecture, a number of fragments of a portal discovered on the canyon floor inspired the idea that this might have been a piece of defensive fortifications. Though Petra had long been uninhabited, Arab traders still made frequent use of the ancient track; in fact, while the artist sat sketching out this view, a caravan originating from Gaza went by on its way to Maan, along the Damascus road. The caravan was made up of about forty camels.

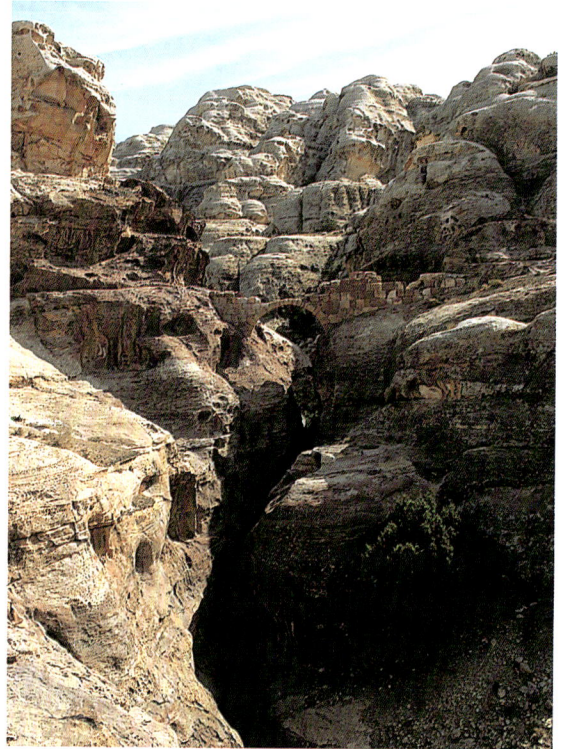

From David Roberts's journal:

9th - Explored the grand entrance to Petra, which may be about a mile in length, winding between the high rocks by which the Valley is enclosed, in many parts overhanging so as almost to meet each other... This was the grand entrance into Petra, and is still used by the Arabs.

THE ACROPOLIS
AND THE KUSR FARON

Plate 153

9th March 1839

*I*mmediately following the great theater, the gorge known as the Sik opens out into a broad and brightly illuminated valley, once packed with homes and temples, many of which have been unfortunately lost due to the violent flooding of the stream. During the time of Petra's greatest glory, the population must have ranged from thirty to forty thousand, most of whom were merchants and traders. At the center of the valley stands the hill now called El Habis, the site of the ancient Acropolis. From the slopes of this hill ran a wall that served to protect all of the main public buildings. The huge blocks of stone, which can be seen in the drawing, formed part of the triumphal arch; nearby a paved plaza once stood, though only a few scanty traces remain of it. At the extremity of the plaza closest to the Citadel stood an impressive building called Kusr Faron, which means the Castle of the Pharaoh. Although the complex stands for the most part in ruins, and we are uncertain as to its true function, its importance is noteworthy because we can draw some understanding from its overall appearance as to just what the appearance of the elevations of the buildings of ancient Petra must have been. Because the entire region is often subject to earthquakes, only the structures cut deep into the rock faces have remained much as they originally appeared, while virtually all of the other buildings have been destroyed. The facade of Kusr Faron presented a portico with four columns and with a single entrance leading to a fairly spacious hall within.

From this area, by climbing three stairways, one could enter as many different smaller rooms. The fact that the central hall should possess a sort of naos or "sancta sanctorum" surrounded by columns, leads us to believe that the so-called Castle of the Pharaoh was in fact a sanctuary. The facade, which measures about one hundred and five feet across, was also decorated with an elegant Doric frieze.

THE SEPULCHRAL MONUMENTS

Plate 154

9th March 1839

The rocky cliffs that surround the city served as raw material for the construction of both residences and tombs. And, as tombs go, the most remarkable and interesting monumental structures were carved out of solid rock along the great flank of the mountain, Gebel el Kubtha, to the west of the city proper. The earliest rock-cut tombs at Petra, dating from the third century B.C., or earlier, usually feature tall rectangular facades lined with lined battlements, clear indicators of Egyptian or Assyrian influence. Belonging to the Hellenistic and Roman era, on the other hand, a time that was so much wealthier in the creation of remarkable architecture, are the facades that we could almost describe as baroque - they rise several stories, they are distinguished by the free-form alternation of triangular and curvilinear pediments, and diverse architectural orders. These astounding elevations, minutely chiseled into the limestone, show a clear kinship with the fantastic architecture featured in the painting of the second Pompeian style. Just like in those celebrated frescoes, here the manner in which the upper story is conceived reveals an intention of endowing them with a certain added perspective with respect to the ground floor, by means of a meticulous interplay of slight optical corrections. On the interiors the tombs typically possess a number of rooms cut out of the rock: the typical plan is made up of a vestibule that gives access to the funerary chambers, smaller in size. In a number of cases, as Roberts himself noted, previously existing rock-cut habitations were converted into tombs. In the illustration on the left we can see a number of the most remarkable rock-cut tombs in the area. These are enormous monolithic cubes, which emerge from the slope of the mountain's face, as a result of a truly monumental effort in excavation. The tomb in the foreground caught the artist's attention because the plinths of the columns, the capitals, the architrave, and the cornices must all have been carved out of a particularly valuable material, either marble or bronze, and then set in the living rock. The material had long ago been torn away by some tomb robber, and by the time Roberts arrived, nothing was left but the notches which had held the ornamental finish. The rock-cut tomb in the background, still in an excellent state of preservation, is surmounted by four graceful pyramids, the only ones of their sort ever found at Petra. Roberts visited the necropolis on the 9th of March; the following day, the weather turned ugly and a steady rain fell. Nonetheless, the Englishman ventured forth to continue his exploration of the valley and its astounding ruins.

From David Roberts's journal:

9th - The necropolis lies between the main entrance and the meadows; some of the tombs hewn out of the rock, though mutilated, are still magnificent. Several have porticoes and colonnades, and the columns of one I observed were Doric of the purest kind. They seem now to be used as pens for cattle.

THE TOMB OF AARON, SUMMIT OF MOUNT HOR

Plate 155

11th March 1839

On the morning of the 11th of March, the fifth day that Roberts spent at Petra, the camp was suddenly awakened by the shrill yells of desert bandits, who fled with their booty, a pair of pistols and a bag of cartridges. Considering what had happened, Roberts came to the suspicion that the attack had been arranged in advance with the local guides, who in fact seemed quite anxious to turn back at this point. At eight in the morning, the camels were saddled and, shortly thereafter, the caravan was climbing the mountains in a southeasterly direction. The sides of the mountains were dug out and the architectural forms quite resembled those that they had seen in the city. Not far from the peak stood a number of monuments whose significance was far from simple to interpret. At least, keeping Mount Hor on the right, the travellers began to climb back down toward the main valley, along a very steep track cut into the living rock like a rough stairway. Roberts deeply regretted being unable to climb to the Tomb of Aaron, but his shoes at this point were truly too worn for the task. It is therefore rather strange that this plate, dated precisely 11th March 1839, should depict the peak of Mount Hor and the sepulchre of the older brother of Moses, as written in the margin. In reality, the illustration shows the hill that stands at the foot of the mountain, clearly visible in the background. On the peak, in effect, it is possible to distinguish a square and regular shape that may well be all that survived of the structure.

According to the Bible, Aaron, during the passage through the desert, was unable to resist the demands of the people of Israel, and he had the golden calf set up and worshipped; for this reason, God did not allow him to enter the Promised Land and he died on Mount Hor, at the age of 123. His tomb, restored first by the Crusaders and later by the Muslims, is the destination of both Christian and Muslim pilgrims.

David Roberts R.A.

Tomb of AARON, Summit of Mount Hor, March 9th 1839.

Louis Haghe, Lith.

12th - This morning we left at half-past 6, and proceeded towards Hebron. During the day we came upon an Arab encampment, with large flocks of sheep and goats. We bought a goat for about 35...

13th - Started this morning at 7. Our course still lay through the Wady El Ghor, or Wady Araba...

Mount Seir   Wady el Ghor. March 4th. 1839.

The encampement in Wadi Arabah

Plate 156

12th-13th March 1839

*A*lthough they had already left the remarkable cliff city behind them several hours before, Roberts noted that for many miles around the slopes of the hills showed signs of terracing, the unmistakable indicators of a bygone era in which the entire region had been assiduously cultivated.

The night went by without any event, and they struck their tents at dawn; proceeding in the direction of Hebron along the Wadi El Ghor - also known as Wadi Arabah - Roberts and his fellow travellers encountered an Arab camp, around which grazed numerous flocks of sheep and herds of goats. The Beduin proved quite friendly, and many of the women gathered around the strangers to have a closer look at them. By common accord it was decided to spend the night there, and the tents were pitched in an area where there was abundant pasturage for the camels. The landscape, which consisted of limestone and jagged cliffs, seemed to be permeated with an air of melancholy; it all appeared grandiose in its savage desolation. On the following day, the 13th of March, Roberts and his entourage rose early and continued for a great many hours along the bed of the wadi, until they reached a well, surrounded by stands of reeds; the water, however, was stagnant and the camels refused to drink.

The travellers passed on. Towards midday, the caravan began to enter the hills to the left of the wadi, and they were soon able to slake their thirst with cool rainwater that had filled a small pool hidden amongst the rocks.

David Roberts R.A.

351

THE RUINS OF SEMUA

Plate 157

14th - 15th - 16th March 1839

On the 14th of March, after breakfasting at the foot of the mountains that separate Wadi El Ghor from Judea, David Roberts and his travelling companions began the climb upward, which soon proved to be extremely tiring and steep, to the point that the trail at certain points became little more than a sort of stairway carved roughly into the living rock. At the top they found a number of ruins that Roberts was unable to identify as either Roman or Saracen. Once they had moved through milk from the tribesmen, and after so many days of quenching his thirst with brackish water, he found the milk absolutely delightful.

Not far off, they saw the ruins of a tower or a fortress built on the brink of a deep gorge.

The buildings seem to have been crushed by an earthquake; Roberts was unable to learn the age or the origin of the construction. The entire region bracketed by Wadi Mousa and Hebron must once have been densely populated, but when Roberts was there, the

the pass, they finally began their descent into a valley of pleasant appearance, luxuriant and spangled with wildflowers. The trail began to climb upward once again to the top of a hill. From there, they descended again to another valley not unlike the first, where a number of camels were grazing, the property of an Arab tribe. Roberts purchased some fresh countryside and the villages appeared to be in a state of extreme neglect or, in many cases, to have been entirely abandoned. The village of Semua, as well, which was described in the Bible as a prosperous town, was now nothing more than a village of sheepherders. Roberts reached the place on the 16th of March, just before sighting Hebron.

Much of the population had left a few days earlier, taking their flocks with them, in search of new pastures but also - and chiefly - to flee conscription into the Egyptian army. In this illustration, Semua appears atop the hill, overshadowed by the massive ruins of a tower which may well have been part of fortifications dating back to Roman times.

From David Roberts's journal:

14th - After breakfasting at the foot of the mountains which separate Wady El Ghor from Judea, we commenced the ascent, which is very steep, the roadway being partly hewn in steps out of the rock... Overhanging a deep ravine, through which flows a stream, are the ruins of an ancient tower or fort, that seems to have been thrown down by an earthquake...

HEBRON

Plate 158

16th -17th -18th March 1839

Located in the heart of Judea, amidst a hilly landscape, Hebron is probably one of the oldest cities in the world, the site of ancient strife and impassioned devotion. Within the massive city walls built by King Herod, in fact, stands a church - later transformed into a mosque - which was built around 1195 atop the Cave of Makhpelah, where it is believed that Abraham, Isaac, Jacob, and their wives Sarah, Rebeccah, and Leah are buried. Hebrew tradition considers the tombs of the Patriarchs to be the legal foundation for the claim of the Jewish people to this territory. According to the Bible, this city was founded seven years before Tanis, that is, in the eighteenth century B.C., and it was near this city that the Biblical oak grove of Mamre stood, where Abraham lived.

The city was sacked by Joshua, and was the home of David - who was proclaimed King of Israel here - and the center of the revolt of Absalom. Rehoboam fortified the city, but it was destroyed by the Romans during the great revolt. Even after its destruction, however, the Jews never entirely abandoned it. The Crusaders, who called Hebron "Presidium Sancti Abrahe," designated the town an episcopal see in 1168; just twenty-one years later, however, the city fell back into the hands of the Muslims. The period of Mameluke rule constituted for the Jews a period of respite from persecution. Local lore has it that the prosperous business of manufacturing glass, in which Hebron still excels, was introduced by Venetian Jews, immediately following the Crusades.

David Roberts reached Hebron on the 16th of March 1839; he describes it as a city washed by sunlight, so peaceful and pleasant as to remind him of his native England. In particular, Roberts was impressed by the healthy appearance of the children, so different from the Egyptian children of the same age. The group of travellers received the hospitality of the only Christian family in the place, and set off again on the 18th, heading for Gaza. Having learned that an outbreak of the plague yet again prevented him from entering Jerusalem, the English artist decided very cheerfully to head for the coast and wait to see what would happen next.

From David Roberts's journal:

16th - Approaching Hebron, the hills are covered with vines and olive-trees. On turning round the side of a hill, Hebron first bursts upon you...
17th - To-day I made two coloured sketches of the town, but could not get admission to the mosque containing the tombs of Abraham, Isaac, and Jacob...

Ksar Jibam. March 7th 1899.

BETH GEBRIN

Plate 159

19th March 1839

Roberts spent the night of the 18th of March in a small village called Terkumich, and by dawn of the next day he was back in the saddle. At a distance of about sixteen miles from Hebron, in the middle of a prosperous, well-tilled countryside, the small group of travellers stumbled upon the ruins of a Crusaders' castle and a number of ruins from Byzantine and Roman times, the lingering relics of the splendor of ancient Eleutheropolis. First known as Betogabra and later as Beit Gibrin - meaning the "abode of Gabriel - in A.D. 200, the city was raised to the Roman rank of municipium with the name of Eleutheropolis and was endowed with extensive lands. In the fourth century it was mentioned as a major episcopal see and as the capital of the province of southern Palestine. Around A.D. 315, the bishop Epiphanius was born there; he went on to become a prolific ecclesiastical author and to compile compendia of Christian doctrine. In A.D. 796, the region was caught up in a bloody civil war, and the city was razed to the ground. Three centuries later, the Crusaders built a fortress there to fend off attacks from the Saracens in the nearby Askelona. Later the place lost its strategic value and underwent a further and inexorable decline. In modern times, not far from what is now Beth Gebrin, extensive remains of monuments and a number of excellent mosaic floors from Byzantine times were found, perhaps the finest ever unearthed in Palestine. Roberts noted that he had admired a number of handsome Roman columns and the colossal foundations of a fortified complex, as well as a few splendid olive trees that looked to be quite old, and which were growing near the modest Arab village. The travellers set off again and toward sundown set up their tents in a place called Burier. That day, Roberts and his travelling companions had ridden for ten hours and were just two hours' ride from Gaza. It is worth noting here too that the date that appears in the margin of the illustration is certainly apocryphal.

From David Roberts's journal:

19th - Left at daybreak,passing through a richly cultivated country. About sixteen miles from Hebron are the remainsof a castle, and Roman ruins, consisting of a number of marble columns. There is a village, which takes its name from the Roman ruins and is called Bed El Gebrin, the hous of Gabriel...

GAZA

Plate 160

20th March 1839

The last stretch of road before Gaza wound through a region of luxuriant forests, broken here and there by fields of wheat and prosperous olive groves. Roberts considered the city to have an excellent location, spreading across a hilltop some two miles from the sea. A procession of sand dunes separated the city from the sea. Sadly, the city's ancient grandeur had been long ago broken into mere memories, and although it might seem quite imposing from a distance, the inhabitants appeared poverty-stricken. The city itself possessed no buildings worthy of any note. A great many of the houses and mosques, in fact, seem to have been built with fragments of far older structures, and indeed many shards of marble could be seen in the masonry. One miserable hut in particular captured Roberts's attention, since the roof was supported by splendid Roman capitals, piled one upon the other. Despite its humble appearance, the city did indeed boast a glorious past, made up of memorable events and an enviable wealth. It had been the capital of the nation of the Philistines and leading trading center, as well as the site of the legendary feats of Samson. Gaza was sacked by Ezekiah, and thereafter occupied repeatedly by Egyptians, Assyrians, Chaldeans, and Persians. Conquered in 332 B.C. by Alexander the Great and later by Ptolomey I, it was favored by the Romans, under whose rule it prospered as a trading center. Occupied by Crusaders in 1100, it saw them alternately victorious and beaten. In 1516 the Turks routed the Mamelukes there, and in 1799 the city was taken by Napoleon. When Roberts visited Gaza, it had a population of about fifteen thousand - five hundred of these being Christians. Today that population has tripled.

The city's destiny continues to be linked to its strategic location, and to a controversial and troubled history.

The troops which are clearly seen in this illustration were made up of two regiments of Egyptian Light Dragoons and Lancers, equipped and armed European-style, marching from Gaza to Sidon.

From David Roberts's journal:

20th - The approach to Gaza is through extensive forests. The city stands on a height two miles from the sea, from which it is sheltered by hills of sand. Its ancient grandeur is entirely gone; the inhabitants are wretchedly poor, and there are not even the ruins of any building of importance standing...

ASKELON

Plate 161

21st - 22nd - 23rd March 1839

The 21st of March and the following two days passed slowly, as the travellers waited for fresh camels in order to continue their voyage. After the long wait and despite the lengthy negotiations, Roberts was able to procure only five of the nine animals that he had requested. In any case, the Englishman was on his way again on the 23rd of March, dressed like a Turk once again. In the late afternoon, the group stopped in a small village called Burbah, not far from the place where the splendid Askelon had prospered in the distant past; this was the site of the love between Samson and Delilah. Once a capital of the Philistines, according to Greek mythology this town was founded by Ascalon, the son of Hymen, during the conquest of Syria. We have some documentation from Egyptian records that tell of Ascalon's rebellion against the rule of the pharaohs. The town is also mentioned in the Bible, and seems to have been noted more for the renowned products of its soil, than for the political events that occurred here.

The products mentioned are wine and scallion, a type of onion that takes its name from this town. The town came under Hebrew rule after the death of Joshua, and when the empire of Alexander the Great collapsed, it became part of the Kingdom of Egypt, then part of Syria, at which time it became the center of the cult of Astarte. An episcopal see during the early Christian era, it was still a flourishing town under Arab domination. During the Crusades, this was the site of bloody battles. It was destroyed by Saladin and rebuilt by Richard the Lion-Hearted; shortly thereafter it was abandoned once and for all. It is now a major center of archeological research, and finds have been made here concerning the ancient civilizations that succeeded one another until the arrival of the Romans. Roberts notes that he found the city in a state of very grave neglect. The city walls were in ruins, the port facilities had virtually disappeared, and the entire zone inspired one with a great sense of desolation.

The only noteworthy features were the remains of a Corinthian temple, with columns still in place, and a large marble statue of a woman. Not far off stood an ancient Christian church that showed numerous elements of Greek Orthodox influence, including capitals adorned with a cross crowned with laurel.

From David Robert's journal:

21st, 22nd, 23rd, and 24th - The port has been swept away, and the city is quite deserted. Ibrahim Pasha has caused a considerable portion to be excavated for stones to build a modern city...

ASHDOD

Plate 162

24th March 1839

*A*shdod is today one of the most important commercial ports in Israel; it is located about twenty-five miles north of Askelon, not very far from Jaffa. David Roberts reached the place on the 24th of March, and at a first glance, it all appeared quite miserable, despite its excellent location in the midst of an exceedingly fertile countryside. The fact that the town lay along the major coast road seemed to Roberts to suggest a brighter future for the city which, in ancient times, had been one of the five leading cities of the civilization of the Philistines.

It was at Ashdod that the Ark of the Covenant was brought as booty of war after the defeat of the Jews; there the Ark was placed in the temple of Dagon, a pagan divinity in the form of a triton. The power of the Lord, however, was made manifest in a number of different episodes: first, the priests of the temple found the statue of the idol prostrate before the Ark. Then a terrible disease swept through the entire population. The Ark was then taken to the village of Gath, and then to the village of Ekron, but the pestilence continued to follow it. It was thus decided to give the Ark back to the Jews, and it was taken to Jerusalem by David as the supreme religious symbol of his reign.

Jaffa, seen from the north

Plate 163

25th March 1839

Breaking camp at the first light of dawn, Roberts and his fellow travellers first passed through a prosperous little town known as Ibrech, and quite soon thereafter from atop a hill that dominated the coastline, found themselves glimpsing the outskirts of Jaffa which was surrounded by orange groves. Roberts noted that the city, long ago known as Joppa, enjoyed a magnificent location. Southward, the eye could roam freely over the rich plains that extended toward Gaza, while northward the horizon was enclosed by the noble silhouette of Mount Carmel. To the east stretched the hills of Judea, toward Jerusalem, while to the west extended the endless waves of the Mediterranean. In the face of such natural magnificence, however, the narrow alleys of the city itself were a great disappointment. Disease and pestilence had devastated the population and a mere five thousand souls huddled in those white hovels amidst dust and poverty. Only from the outside did the city preserve its proud appearance, the heritage of a truly glorious past. According to Semitic legend, Jaffa was in fact founded by Japheth, the son of Noah. According to Greek mythology, the town was built by a daughter of Aeolus. It is also said that here Noah built his ark; that here Andromeda was left to the mercy of the sea monster; and that here Perseus washed the wounds he received in his battle with the Centaurs.

This was certainly the Joppa of the Philistines, burned by Judas Maccabee in the second century B.C., and later destroyed by Vespasian. The Arabs took the city in A.D. 637, but it was conquered twice by the Crusaders, until finally being expunged by the sultan Baibars and largely destroyed in 1267. The name of the city returned to the spotlight of history five centuries later in 1799 when it was occupied by Napoleon. At the time of Roberts's voyage, Jaffa had just fallen seven years earlier to Ibrahim, the son of Mohammed Ali, the pasha of Egypt. Today it forms part of the urban agglomeration of Tel Aviv and is a lively commercial center known throughout the world for its export of fruit and agricultural delicacies.

The individuals in the foreground of this illustration are Polish Jews returning from their pilgrimage to Jerusalem, waiting to take passage back to Europe.

From David Roberts's journal:

25th - Leaving our encampment by daybreak, we passed a beautiful little town called Ibrech, and arrived at Jaffa, which is surrounded by orange groves, and stands on a hill sloping to the sea.

From David Roberts's journal:

26th - I examined the town carefully, but found very few antiquities.

JAFFA, SEEN FROM THE SOUTH

Plate 164

26th March 1839

On the morning of the 26th, Kinnear bade Roberts farewell and set off for Beirut. Later that day, the English artist had an invitation to a reception at the consul's residence, where he was treated with great courtesy. The two chatted amiably and smoked a few pipes together. That same day, Roberts had wandered extensively through the town, without, however, finding any particular ancient monuments. In any case, Jaffa appeared to be a majestic and even spectacular city, set atop a sheer promontory that jutted out over the sea. This view from the north shows clearly how, due to the extreme steepness of the rough terrain, it was possible to see the entire town at a glance; many of the constructions, some of which were quite large, had foundations that covered several different stories, in a form of terracing, and long stretches of the streets were actually stairways. These features all gave the town a certain charming allure. All it lacked was trees or greenery of any sort, common though those may be in other major cities of the Middle East.

RAMLA, ANCIENT ARIMATHEA

Plate 165

Roberts left Jaffa at ten in the morning on the 27th of March. He was accompanied by his friend John Pell, his guide Ishmael, and three servants.

The group of travellers had eight horses which bore tents and the remaining baggage. The road ran through the gardens and orchards that surround the city, and then crossed the plain of Sharon, well cultivated in the midst of that pleasant countryside, all a-flower and studded with small villages and palm groves. Roberts considered this to be some of the finest countryside he had ever seen. Around three o'clock in the afternoon, the travellers entered the town of Ramla, where they were welcomed joyfully by the Father Superior of the Latin convent. Later the same day the Father Superior accompanied him in a tour of the most ancient monuments in the village. What most caught the English artist's attention was the Great Mosque, which was said to be originally the church of the Knights of the Hospital of St. John of Jerusalem. Nonetheless, the structure clearly showed a strong Saracen influence, while the subterranean sections clearly included structures from the Roman era. Ramla, which remains a town with a predominantly Muslim culture, was founded by the Arabs around A.D. 716. During the Crusades it was often the site of battles, and it was occupied alternately by Christians and Egyptians. Richard the Lion-Hearted made his headquarters here. In 1276 it was

incorporated once and for all
into the Kingdom of Egypt.
It enjoyed a period of great
prosperity under Turkish rule,
and seemed immune to the
general decline that laid low
the other towns of the region,
because of its excellent location
on the great caravan route
between Damascus and Egypt.
In Ramla, which in Arabic
means "sand," a great many
immigrants of Balkan descent

now live; there is also a sizable
Arab community. Of particular
interest are the White Mosque,
the so-called Tower of the Forty,
and the Great Mosque
mentioned above, which was
built on the ruins of a
Crusaders' cathedral, as well
as an interesting complex of
underground cisterns dating
back to the ninth century.

27th -28th March 1839

From David Roberts's journal:

*27th - Left Jaffa at 9 A.M. for
Jerusalem... Our way lay through the
gardens which surround Jaffa, and
across the plain of Sharon, through a
richly-cultivated country. The ground
is carpeted with flowers - the plain
is studded with small villages and
groups of palm-trees, and, independent
of its interesting associations, the
country is the loveliest I ever beheld.
The mountains of Judea bound the
view, and beyond is the Holy City.
About 3 we arrived at Rameh, and
were kindly received at the Latin
Convent by the superior...*

369

Lod, ancient Lydda

Plate 166

28th March 1839

Roberts spent the evening of the 27th of March at Ramla in the company of the monks of the convent, who had shown themselves in the meanwhile to be extremely jovial hosts. The following day the Englishman had a chance to visit the nearby town of Lod briefly. It had once been known by the name Lydda, and was supposedly the birthplace of St. George. In antiquity, it had been a busy local capital, the center of a complex network of roads, and a commercial center of considerable importance, mentioned in the documents of the Pharaohs as early as 1500 B.C. Later, it was united politically with Samaria, and later still with Judea, when it took part in the revolt against the Romans. The town was destroyed by Vespasian and by Hadrian, but it was rebuilt, and was dubbed Diospolis - or the "City of God" - by Septimius Severus. Lod became one of the earliest Christian communities, was an episcopal see under Constantine, but it declined as Ramla prospered. Conquered by the Crusaders, who built a church in Frankish Romanesque style there and dedicated it to Saint George - the ruins of that church greatly impressed David Roberts - the city was destroyed by Saladin and bebuilt by Richard the Lion-Hearted. Sacked by the Mongols in 1271, it declined in importance until the modern day. Israel's national poet, Abraham Shlonski, has described it as the "city of Books, an oasis of peace and of watchtowers." After crossing the last hills of Judea, Roberts finally came within sight of the Holy City and spent the night camped just a short distance from the walls. In his journal, the English artist noted that the surrounding area was immersed in an absolute silence, broken only by the occasional howling of a distant dog and by the scream of a solitary owl, perched on the battlements. Here, too, the date that appears in the margin of the illustration should probably be moved up by a day or two.

Christian Church of St George at Lud

370

da. March 29th 1839

JERUSALEM AND THE PILGRIMAGE TO THE JORDAN RIVER

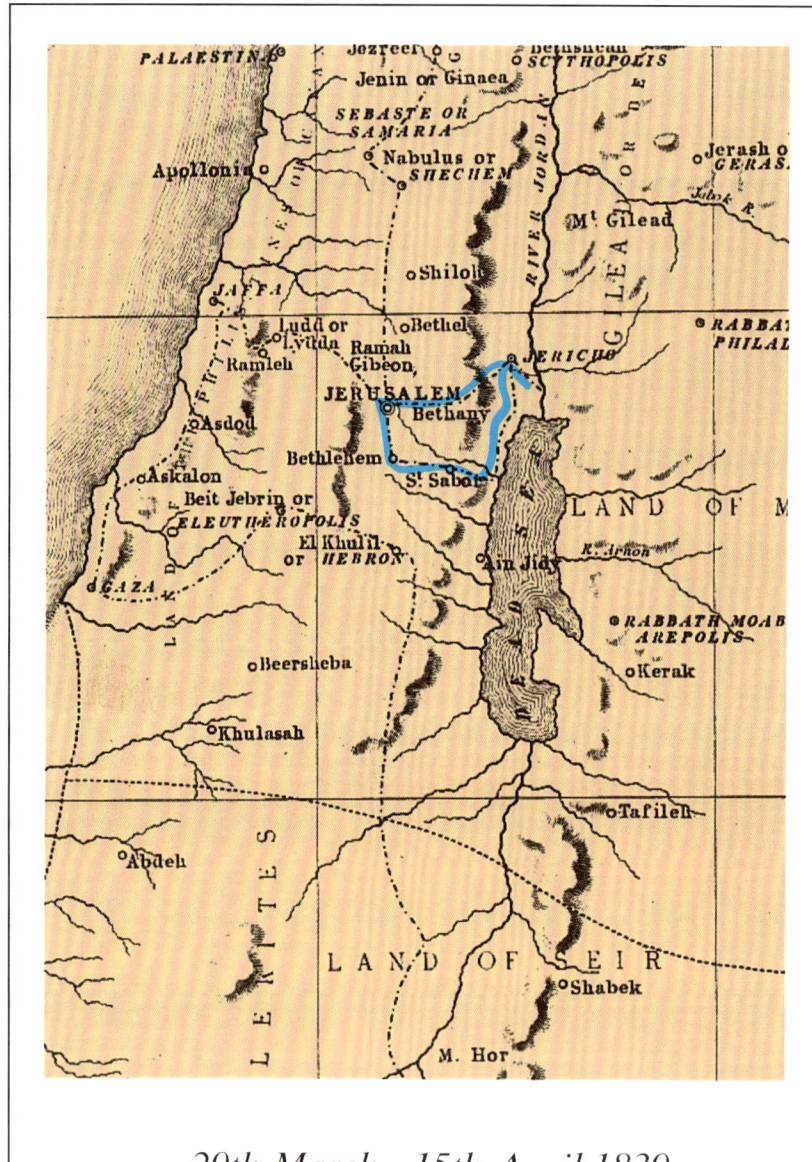

29th March - 15th April 1839

David Roberts. R.A

The

HOLY LAND

Syria, Idumea, Arabia, Egypt & Nubia.

FROM DRAWINGS MADE ON THE SPOT BY

David Roberts, R.A.

WITH HISTORICAL DESCRIPTIONS BY

THE REVD GEORGE CROLY, L.L.D.

LITHOGRAPHED BY

LOUIS HAGHE.

VOL I.

LONDON, F. G. MOON, 20 THREADNEEDLE STREET,
PUBLISHER IN ORDINARY TO HER MAJESTY.
MDCCCXLII.

THE CITADEL OF JERUSALEM

Plate 167

29th March 1839

On the morning of the 29th of March, a Good Friday, the quarantine was finally lifted, and at long last Roberts was able to enter the city of Jerusalem; as he walked into the city, he saw the entire population thronging out of the city gates in a state of joyful celebration. Groups of soldiers marched to and fro, preceded by the pounding of the bass drum and by the brilliant colors of their military banners, followed by crowds of gleeful men, women, and children. Crowds of pilgrims pressed in from all sides, descending upon

of travellers made their way around the walls of Jerusalem, moving from the Damascus Gate toward Mount Zion. In all likelihood, this plate, which depicts the Citadel of Jerusalem, is based on the observations that Roberts made during that first excursion. The imposing fortified complex lies to the right of the Jaffa Gate, which is girt by a deep moat. On this site, around 24 B.C., Herod built three towers to protect his palace; these towers survived the destruction of Jerusalem ordered by Titus, and were subsequently turned into

Jerusalem for the Easter festivities; indeed, the British artist and his entourage had a difficult time finding accommodations. It was their extreme good luck to meet with Elias, the head of a large Christian family, who had received them in Hebron. Elias arranged for them to stay as the guests of his brother-in-law, an Orthodox Greek. In the course of the morning, the little group

barracks for the Twelfth Legion. During the Byzantine Era, this Citadel had fallen into such a state of disrepair that local anchorites had taken it over as a place of refuge and meditation. Rebuilt by the Crusaders, who garrisoned the place, the Citadel was destroyed once more at the hands of the Mamelukes in 1239 and lay in shattered ruins until 1335, a century later when the Turks rebuilt the fortress and

built atop the keep - still the most ancient part of the structure - one of their distinctive little minarets, now known as the Tower of David. Currently, the Citadel contains the Museum of the History of Jerusalem, which documents the many stages of the city's history; sound and light shows are held here during the evenings, providing an impressive spectacle.

Citadel of Jerusalem without the walls

From David Roberts's journal:

29th, Good Friday - "It is better to be born lucky than rich" is an old proverb, and it applies to me. This morning the quarantine has been removed... I made the circuit of the city walls, proceeding northward by the gate of Damascus and the Valley of Jehoshaphat to the hill of Sion,

where the tomb of David is placed... After settling ourselves in our quarters we visited several interesting places, among others the Mosque of Omar, built near the pool of Bethesda, and the Holy Sepulchre, which is approached through a series of narrow streets, the last of which opens into a court...

THE ENTRANCE TO THE CITADEL OF JERUSALEM

Plate 168

29th March 1839

Citadel of Jerusalem April 1914

The walls of Jerusalem, with the Citadel on their western side, boast an extremely complex history, the faithful mirror of the military fortunes of the city over the course of the centuries. The circuit of walls as they stand today, extending over a circumference of roughly two and a half miles, is certainly much smaller than the walls that must have girded the city of Zion prior to the second destruction of the temple at the orders of Emperor Titus. Even Aelia Capitolina, which Emperor Hadrian had rebuilt on the ruins of the Jewish city, occupied a smaller area. Presumably, the walls built by Hadrian served their function until the time of the Crusades, although the city by that time had expanded far beyond that perimeter.

The structure of the walls must have presented some quite evident signs of wear and damage; in fact, in 1178 they underwent extensive repair. Nine years later, Saladin nonetheless managed to overcome the resistance of the city's defenders and took Jerusalem. Victorious though the new conqueror may have been, he still feared the desire for revenge from Richard the Lion-Hearted. Saladin worked tirelessly to ensure that the walls should be reinforced and, where necessary, rebuilt from the foundations up. Six months of hard work, with Saladin himself lending a hand, made Jerusalem an impregnable fortress. By a fluke of destiny, in 1219, the Sultan of Damascus, Melek, fearing that the city might fall into the hands of the Christians and become a dangerous enclave in his realm, ordered that the entire ring of walls be destroyed, with the sole exceptions of the Citadel and the Noble Enclosure. In 1229, without an arrow fired or a sword drawn, a treaty was drawn handing over Jerusalem to the Holy Roman Emperor Frederick II of Swabia. It stipulated that the walls of the city could not be rebuilt. Ten years later, however, the new rulers of Jerusalem felt threatened and reinforced the walls with the help of Pisan master builders. The new walls and turrets could do little to staunch the might of the emir Kerek, who pierced Jerusalem's defenses, massacred all the Latins, and dismantled the entire complex of fortifications. In 1243, a new treaty handed over the city to the Christians, who immediately set out to reinforce the walls. The next year, the Crusaders lost the Holy City for once and all, trounced by an Islamic military coalition. It was not until 1542 that the ring of walls was newly rebuilt, and this time, the walls survived. It is no accident, however, that the structures that now stand possess a number of heterogeneous and alien features, in some cases dating back from Roman times, and in other cases, from the reign of Solomon.

THE GOLDEN GATE

<u>Plate 169</u>

29th March 1839

he eastern walls of the city, at the foot of which lies a Muslim cemetery, are broken by the elegant forepart of the Golden Gate, which Roberts was able to admire during his walk around the walls. The fortification stands several yards higher than the surrounding countryside, and was rebuilt during the Byzantine era on the ruins of a Roman tower from the reign of Hadrian. The lower section of the walls and the vaults of the two twin arches seem to belong to the original structure, which has been renovated and modified extensively over the centuries. The Crusaders expanded and embellished them during their rule over Jerusalem, and the sultan Suleiman the Magnificent had them restored in the sixteenth century, when he incorporated them into the circuit of walls that even today surrounds the Old City.

The Golden Gate, also known as the Gate of Mercy, had been walled up as early as the conquest by the Crusaders, but it was opened once a year, during Palm Sunday, since tradition held that Jesus passed through here during his entrance into the Temple. Nonetheless, it was definitively sealed in 1530 by the Muslims, who even kept a squadron of guards here in the fear of the prophecy that the new king of Jerusalem and of the entire world would enter the city through that very gate.

Even now, many believe that the Golden Gate will miraculously be reopened only when the Messiah enters for the second time the city of David.

Mosquee of Omar Shewing the site of the temple

THE MOSQUE OF OMAR

Plate 170

29th March 1839

*A*fter settling into his new accommodations, Roberts elaborated on his first and cursory tour of the city, going to see the most interesting sights. Among these sights was the celebrated Mosque of Omar, which, perched atop Mount Moriah, dominates the skyline of Jerusalem. Here, on the flat space known as the Noble Enclosure, stood the Second Temple, which Titus destroyed. Following the Arab conquest, Caliph Omar built a small wooden mosque here as a mark of devotion. Jerusalem is sacred to the Muslims because of the magical Night Journey that the Prophet Mohammed supposedly made to the city from Mecca. After reaching the Temple Mount, the Prophet Mohammed went to the sacred rock upon which, according to the Bible, Abraham was about to sacrifice his son, Isaac, when the Angel stayed his hand. On the same night, God transported

Mohammed back to Mecca - this story establishes the Prophet's descent from Abraham. Rebuilt around A.D. 699 by Caliph Abd al-Melik, the Mosque of Omar, also known as the Dome of the Rock, is one of the sacred places of Islam. The splendid gilt dome covers the rock of Abraham, and there a footprint carved into the rock marks the spot from which Mohammed departed for heaven. A masterpiece of Arabic art, the Mosque of Omar glitters with gold and ceramics. Panels of multicolored majolica and strips bearing inscriptions from the Koran adorn the upper portion of the building, while the lower part of the building, octagonal in shape, is covered with marble panels with delicate pastel shades. The pilgrims in the foreground of the illustration are shown on the terrace that stands before the church of St. Anne; at the bottom of the gorge behind them is the Pool of Bethesda.

THE CHURCH OF THE HOLY SEPULCHRE

Plate 171

29th March 1839

As soon as Roberts reached Jerusalem, he received a warm welcome from the governor of the city, Achmet Aga, whose residence was said to be located on the exact spot where the palace of Herod had once stood. This was the beginning, moreover, of the Via Dolorosa, which wends its tortuous way to the Holy Sepulchre. The route is punctuated by a number of "stations," which supposedly correspond to the various episodes recounted in the Gospels in reference to Jesus's painful climb to Calvary and His subsequent Crucifixion. While the entire Via Dolorosa was of considerable interest, as it wound through the narrow streets of the most ancient part of the city, Roberts was keenly aware that the expectations of the faithful might be disappointed at the nearly shabby and certainly unimpressive appearance of the Holy Sepulchre itself. The area that stood before the monument, in fact, was crowded with miserable and tumbledown shacks; at the time of Roberts's visit, the square was used as a sort of bazaar, where a busy trade thrived in sacred images and relics. The English artist noted in his travel journal that with the possible exception of the facade, the exterior of the Holy Sepulchre possessed absolutely no noteworthy features, and appeared nothing more than a jumbled clutter of mismatched elements.

This appearance was without a

Church of The Holy Sepulchre Jerusalem.

doubt in part the product of the necessity of crowding together under one roof all of the fundamental passages of the Passion of Christ. Despite its lack of architectural unity, the Holy Sepulchre remains one of the fundamental sacred monuments in Jerusalem and of all Christendom, for centuries a lightning rod for the faith and emotions of pilgrims who, although of many different confessions, gathered here to pray side by side. The church was founded in A.D. 326; tradition has it that Queen Helena, the mother of Constantine, was for founding the church. She is said to have believed that the church marked the exact site of Golgotha. The original structure of the church, however, was destroyed in A.D. 614, and the current appearance of the Holy Sepulchre dates largely from the Crusades, although major renovation was carried out by the Greek Orthodox monks following the fire of 1808. Inside the Holy Sepulcher, a rotunda stands above the tomb of Christ and, not far away, a chapel has been built on what is believed to be the exact point where the Virgin Mary discovered that her son had been resurrected.

Stone of Unction,
Holy Sepulchre.

THE STONE OF UNCTION

<u>Plate 172</u>

30th March 1839

Most of the sites sacred to Christianity are "jointly held" by a number of religions. There was a time when this co-existence was far from brotherly, and at times ferocious disputes ensued concerning the varied array of rights and jurisdictions. Nowadays, however, it seems that an increasingly ecumenical spirit is spreading. Quite heterogeneous in architectural terms, the Church of the Holy Sepulchre is now under the direct administration of Franciscan monks, with the assistance of Greek Orthodox monks, as well as Copts, and Armenians. Each of the Christian communities runs its own chapels and altars, celebrating their rituals according to different, rigidly planned-out schedules; moreover, each confession oversees the work of restoration of its own sector. In Jerusalem, the religions seem in any case to be complementary one to another, rather than being antagonists in a welter of liturgies and liturgical garb unequalled anywhere else on earth. This predisposition to tolerance, so fundamental to the peaceful coexistence of different ethnic groups, was fostered as far back as during the Ottoman rule. Adherents to moderate policies in the field of religion, and particularly sensitive to the economic benefits to be derived from the regular flow of Christian pilgrims, the Turks never hindered religious functions or restricted access to the Holy Sepulchre. Because of this cannily tolerant behavior, Roberts was able to tour the church quite freely. Inside the church, he depicted with an acutely observant eye the professions of faith being made upon the Stone of Unction. Tradition has it that this unadorned slab of white marble serves to protect the underlying slab of pink limestone, upon which the body of Christ, after the Deposition from the Cross, was sprinkled with myrrh and aloe by Joseph of Arimathea and Nicodemus, and that as it lay upon the slab of pink limestone, the Virgin Mary wept over it before the burial. Even today, the Stone of Unction is lighted by numerous oil lamps and adorned by silver candelabra, smaller nowadays than those that were portrayed by the English artist - back then the candelabra stood about six and a half feet tall. The lamps that can be seen in the plate were gifts from Greek Orthodox, Latin, and Armenian convents, whose monks back then took turns in overseeing the running of the church.

Roberts's journal informs us that on the Saturday in question, the 30th of March, the governor of Jerusalem had invited Roberts to make use of the upper floors in his residence in order to sketch some views of the city.

THE ENTRANCE OF THE TOMBS OF THE KINGS

Plate 173

31st March 1839

On Palm Sunday, after witnessing the procession to the Holy Sepulchre led by the Greek Orthodox archbishop, Roberts visited the Valley of Jehosaphat for the first time. Here, not far from the Damascus Gate, stands the so-called Tombs of the Kings. The actual burial chamber, carved into the limestone wall of the hill, and quite similar to the rock-cut structures of Petra, appears as a deep niche cut in the form of a portal, about twenty-six feet in width.

On either side, two pillars must once have stood, while the same number of columns - which served to support the massive architrave - have evidently been destroyed or lost.

The architrave is decorated with an elegant fascia of floral motifs, now badly damaged; above this strip is a decoration made of metopes and triglyphs and a high cornice. The entire decorative complex clearly reflects the influence of Imperial Roman style.

The space that is marked off by the portal leads to a deep antechamber carved out of the living rock; behind it there are three large burial chambers and two smaller ones.

Here Roberts was able to admire the fragmentary remains of a number of marble sarcophagi, whose excellent reliefs seemed to him to be the only surviving documentation of ancient Hebrew art.

Although the burial chamber was long believed to be the final resting place of a number of kings of Israel, it is far more likely that this is the tomb of Helena Adiabene, a queen of Mesopotamia who converted to Judaism.

From David Roberts's journal:

March 31st, Palm Sunday - To-day splendid processions, in which the Greek Christians took precedence; and led by their bishops, they walked three times round the Sepulchre, bearing branches of palm in commemoration of Christ's entry into Jerusalem. The bishops, ascending the steps to the altar, blessed the multitude. A plenteous supply of holy water was distributed and flowers were strewn on the steps leading to the Sepulchre. Other Christian sects followed, all animated by sincere veneration. Visited the tombs of the three kings of Judea...

JERUSALEM, SEEN FROM THE ROAD TO BETHANY

Plate 174

*T*he governor of Jerusalem, above and beyond his kind welcome to David Roberts and companions, told the artist that within a few days he would personally be escorting a caravan of Christian pilgrims to the banks of the Jordan, and he invited Roberts to come along. The governor offered to give Roberts mounts and a few armed guards, against all events. The trip was to take no more than a week, and in the meanwhile, they could visit the shores of the Dead Sea, Jericho, Bethlehem, and the famous cliff convent of St. Saba.

Roberts happily accepted the invitation and began to prepare for the departure. The caravan set out on the first of April in the early morning hours; after crossing the Valley of Jehosaphat and climbing the slopes of the Mount of Olives, they were soon in sight of the village of Bethany, which is just less than two miles from Jerusalem. Although the illustration is clearly dated the 5th April 1839, it should be placed in the earliest part of the trip. The journal tells us in fact that on the 5th of April David Roberts was already in Bethlehem.

Here, too, we should presume that the plate was not dated by the author and that it was erroneously dated by Louis Haghe or by one of his colleagues just before going to press. At the center of this view, drawn from high atop the Mount of Olives, it is possible to recognize the Mosque of Omar, while to the left is the Mosque of El Aksa.

The depression which begins at the foot of the hill, crossed by the small stream of the Kidron, is the Valley of Jehosaphat, in which it is possible to make out the white tip of the tomb of Absalom.

Jerusalem. April 5th 1839.

From David Roberts's journal:

April 1st - Having got horses, left for Jericho, taking with me my portmanteau, tent, and servant. Crossing the Valley of Jehoshaphat, and ascending the Mount of Olives, we passed close to Bethany, the principal object in which is a building like a sheikh's tomb, called the House of Lazarus...

1st April 1839

BETHANY

Plate 175

1st April 1839

Bethany is mentioned in the Gospel as the home of Lazarus and of his two sisters, Mary and Martha. It was in this small village at the gates of Jerusalem that Jesus supposedly performed the miracle of resurrection. It is to this remarkable event that Bethany owes its fame and also its modern name, El Azarieh, which is Arabic for "Lazarus." Despite the sacred nature of the place, Bethany looked to David Roberts like a rundown conglomeration of miserable huts, many of which were built with material taken from ancient ruins. No more than a few dozen families lived in the town. Then as now, popular lore indicates with great certainty the houses in which Mary, Martha, and Simon the Leper once lived, and of course, the tomb of Lazarus.

The sepulchre in question, which can be easily recognized in the illustration by Roberts, is the small square building topped by a dome to the left of the town itself; in reality it is a deep niche carved into the limestone and can be reached along a steep stairway.

The site was already a place of worship in early Christian times, and the earliest documented mention of it dates from A.D. 333. Seventy years later, St. Jerome describes it as being covered by a church, and in subsequent centuries, a number of monasteries and other sacred buildings were constructed there.

David Roberts R.A. Bethany april 1839.

THE DESCENT UPON THE VALLEY OF THE JORDAN

Plate 176

1st April 1839

From Bethany onward, the road that drops away toward Jericho wends its way through a highly unusual landscape, where neither houses nor plowed fields interrupt the monotonous succession of hills, each as bare and brightly colored as the last and the next, a surreal procession of sun-bleached peaks, among which the track curved and wound as if in a labyrinth, in the bed of arid valleys that seem never to have known the gurgle of water or the presence of any living creatures. An absolute silence, broken only by the stirring of the wind and the rattle of pebbles tumbling down the steep slopes of the hills - this silence weighed down upon the pilgrims, amplifying the terrors of the voyage.

Indeed, this territory was sadly famous for the raids of desert brigands, and the last mountain pass was particularly feared. This illustration shows that last pass, and the spectacular panorama that greeted the travellers after they had made their way through it.

The Jordan Valley, the silvery line of which is barely visible, lay spread out under the fading light of sunset. The glittering surface of the Dead Sea shone on the right, while the brightly colored tents of the pilgrims could be seen in the distance. In the presence of such spectacular beauty, Roberts observed that the scene was more suited to the pen of a poet than to the pencil of an artist. Although the great depression of the Dead Sea is one of the most arid places on the planet, it should be noted that around the southern course of the Jordan River and in the area surrounding Jericho, the presence of numerous springs makes the land remarkably fertile; the English artist, in fact, observed this in his journal.

From David Roberts's journal:

April 1st - Proceeding along the road, which has been all pavemented by the Romans, we first beheld the Dead Sea. Along the whole line, Arab horsemen and Bedouins were stationed. Groups of pilgrims were moving on to the Jordan. On our left is a brawling stream, at the bottom of a deep ravine, the sides of which are perforated with caves, the former abodes of anchorites. Farther on is a pool and stream, said to be that sweetened by Elisha. Jericho lies at the base of the hills...

THE ENCAMPMENT OF PILGRIMS

Plate 177

1st April 1839

*I*n the Gospel according to St. Mark, it is written: "And it came to pass in those days, that Jesus came from Nazareth of Galilee, and was baptized of John in Jordan." It is therefore not hard to understand why over the centuries multitudes of the faithful have ventured to undertake the difficult and perilous journey to bathe and purify themselves, during the Easter time, in the waters of the river, not far from Jericho. And so it happened that in April of 1839 David Roberts was able to produce another one of his early "scoops"; during this period, the entire territory was plagued by the raids of robber brigands, and the caravans of pilgrims usually travelled with the escort of a considerable troop of armed guards, provided by the governor of Jerusalem. This strange mixture of the power of faith and the necessity of weapons can be found even now at Allenby Bridge, just a few miles from the site of the Baptism of Christ, a sensitive crossroads of many different cultures and faiths. Roberts, who until then had travelled with the protection of armed men put at his disposal by Achmet Aga, was finally greeted by Achmet Aga himself, while still in the vicinity of Jericho. Later, the artist noted in his notebook that he had been received, with exquisite courtesy, in the tent of the high official, who had offered him sherbets and coffee. Towards evening, the two men rode together to the banks of the Jordan, where preparations were already under way for the following day. The scene that Roberts portrayed here was remarkably lively. The camp is dominated by the tent of the governor; all around the tent, numerous groups of pilgrims are busily engaged in various activities. A number of horsemen ride their horses at a gallop, while other men from the escort chat idly. In the background is the motionless surface of the Dead Sea.

Banks of the Jordan. April 2nd 1839.

THE IMMERSION
IN THE JORDAN RIVER

Plate 178

2nd April 1839

On the morning of the 2nd of April, the pilgrims set out once again. Later, a cannon shot indicated that the governor too had set off. The caravan stretched out of sight, and the silence of the desert was barely disturbed by the shuffling tramp of all those feet. Nonetheless, as soon as the banks of the Jordan appeared in the near distance, the crowd set off at a mad dash, while women launched shrill shrieks of joy, not unlike those that Roberts had already noted in Egypt. At this point the governor's men arranged a number of carpets and comfortable chairs upon a promontory that overlooked the waters. Achmet Aga took a seat there, and his soldiers began patrolling.

Under the rather curious eyes of David Roberts, women and men began to strip and, in a remarkable display of a total lack of inhibition, they ventured out into the rapid current of the Jordan that runs at that point between sheer cliffs sunk deep below the plain of Jericho. Many of the faithful were entirely naked, while others wore light garments that they would later take home with them, religiously preserving them for the day of their own funerals. Unfortunately, a young Greek was drowned in the treacherous waters of the river and a number of other imprudent pilgrims ran the same risk, as they had ventured out too far into the current. The entire ceremony lasted only a couple of hours until the pilgrims lined up on the route home with the governor bringing up the rear of the procession.

In this illustration, Achmet Aga and his men can be clearly distinguished in the foreground.

From David Roberts's journal:

April 2nd - I was very much struck with the breadth of the plain of Jericho, and the narrow space in which the deep and rapid stream is cooped up between the steep banks. The scene in the river was most exciting. Young and old, male and female, were in the stream in one promiscuous mass...

THE ENCAMPMENT NEAR JERICHO

Plate 179

Situated to the north of the Dead Sea, the city of Jericho boasts an extremely ancient history. According to the Bible, Joshua conquered the city, apparently around the thirteenth century B.C. During Roman times, it was endowed with sumptuous palaces built by Herod the Great, and it later became an episcopal see during the Christian era. After the Crusades, a slow but ineluctable decline began, which David Roberts clearly witnessed during his brief visit. The town appeared to him to be little more than a heap of ruins, a few miserable huts surrounded by small pens for the domestic animals, dominated by the remains of a Saracen tower, somewhat loftily described as the Castle. The few inhabitants farmed a remarkably fertile land, rich in palm trees and vineyards, although the air was heavy and overheated, almost seeming to crush the horizon under a mantle of silence. Roberts had passed through here upon his way to the River Jordan, and he passed through here again at dawn on the 3rd of April, while on his way to the Monastery of St. Saba. This illustration shows an encampment of Beduins, who spent the night not far from the tower of Jericho. Under the silvery rays of a full moon, the surface of the Dead Sea appears smooth, luminous, and unshadowed. Swimming in the pale light of the moon, the desolation of the surrounding desert touches the realm of pure poetry, while the deep and brackish Dead Sea sheds any sense of its harsh three-dimensional reality, until it mutates into an imaginary landscape. This illustration by Roberts contrasts sharply with the image of modern-day Jericho, a luxuriant oasis of bougainvilleas and orange groves. Recent digs have transformed this into one of the most interesting archeological attractions in the region.

THE WILDERNESS
SURROUNDING ST. SABA

Plate 180

3rd April 1839

After taking his leave of Achmet Aga, who had provided him the evening before with guides who knew the area well, Roberts left the plain of Jericho in the early hours of the 3rd of April. At first the road ran along the foot of the highlands, and the group of horsemen rode along with the waters of the Dead Sea on their left. Three hours later, Roberts and his companions made a stop near a spring of drinkable water. A little further along, the coast turned into a scarp and the group of travellers was forced to climb along a very steep trail, which became quite dangerous in certain stretches, winding as it did along the sheer drop into the depression.

This enormous effort was repaid by the remarkable view that they had from the top of the mountain: the surface of the Dead Sea, smooth as enamel, glittered like a mirror, and reflected the surrounding hills. In that motionless and evocative silence, no one in the little group said a word.

They descended along the Fire Valley. Wadi el Naar, in the local tongue, was equally arduous and full of strange allure. Once they had passed the stream of the Kidron, which here runs between equally sheer banks, the group proceeded for a distance along a rough and uneven ground, largely made up of reddish limestone, where an unusually luxuriant vegetation grew. At some distance, they finally glimpsed the towers of the Monastery of St. Saba, a remarkable complex of buildings perched on the walls of the remarkable canyon of the Kidron.

Roberts was so impressed by the spectacle that he wrote in his journal that he could not imagine a more romantic setting.

THE DEAD SEA FROM THE HIGHLAND OF EIN GEDI

Plate 181

4th April 1839

This view of the Dead Sea, dated 4th April 1839, was sketched from high atop Ein Gedi, not far from the monastery of St. Saba, which appears here in all its astounding drama and impressiveness, perched high atop the cliff carved out by the Kidron. The Dead Sea, some fifty miles in length and eleven miles in width at its widest, lies in the deepest tectonic ditch carved out of the earth's surface, at about one thousand two hundred and ninety-six feet below sea level. This surrealistic body of water is surrounded by an extremely arid landscape on both sides, and only in the northern extremity, near the mouth of the Jordan, does the humidity permit some scattered vegetation to survive. Never brushed by the humid breezes that make the area to the west of Jerusalem so fertile, ten times saltier than any other sea on earth, and so dense that it is impossible to dive into its waters, the Dead Sea has no outlet and has no life forms. Amidst such arid desolation - which struck Roberts however as being rich in mystery and majesty - the occasional oasis appears as an improbable mirage, the guardian of a life that is here negated by the hostility of the land and the pitiless glare of the sun. With its freshwater springs and its luxuriant greenery, Ein Gedi attracted the English artist with all the power of an unexpected miracle.

The Dead Sea
looking towards Moab
April 4th 1839

THE CONVENT OF ST. SABA

Plate 182

4th April 1839

Built against the stark rock walls of the gorge dug out by the Kidron River as it flows toward the Dead Sea, the Monastery of St. Saba is a place set aside for isolation and prayer amidst the silent desolation of the desert, a few miles southeast of Jerusalem. Founded in A.D. 492, but destroyed by the Arabs during the seventh century, the Monastery was quickly rebuilt in a radical new version; John of Damascus was ordained a priest here, and he wrote his fundamental theological treatises here. The architectural complex, whose most noteworthy features are the cupolas, painted bright blue, and the enormous enclosure wall, is clearly a piece of defensive construction; the walls are very thick and are well arrayed, the windows are little more than loopholes, and the entrances are narrow and low, and are girded with stout portals. Inside, the relics of St. Saba are preserved; they were brought here from Venice in 1965, after being held there for more than seven centuries. As it was when David Roberts toured it, the Monastery is now run by Greek Orthodox monks, who forbid women from entering there. In Roberts's journal, his first view of and approach to this remarkable monument is described in terms of hushed wonder: aside from the inevitable considerations on the remarkable architecture of the place, the English artist notes that he was pleasantly surprised at the cordial hospitality of the monks and at the astonishing comforts the Monastery yielded. Walls and floors were covered with thick carpets, the air was cool and healthful, and the local wine - made from grapes perhaps harvested from terraces dug into the rocky wall - was pleasing to the palate.

From David Roberts's journal:

April 3rd - The convent consists of a cluster of buildings on the face of the rock, and contains many chapels. The brotherhood is of the Greek persuasion, and numbers about thirty-five monks, who dress the same as those of Mount Sinai.
4th and 5th - On looking from the heights above down on the convent, one could scarcely believe that it could possess so many comforts and conveniences within its walls...

THE CHAPEL OF THE CONVENT OF ST. SABA

<u>Plate 183</u>

5th April 1839

The day after his arrival at St. Saba, David Roberts asked for and received permission to sketch the chapel of the Monastery of St. Saba. With great courtesy, the monks even allowed the artist to complete his work after the religious services had begun. The setting, quite ancient, was heavily decorated in adherence to the ornate style found in so many Greek Orthodox churches. One of the frescoes, which depicts Judgment Day, was the object of particular devotion, while figures of saints adorned virtually the entire surface of the pillars. Just prior to David Roberts's visit, the Russian government, which was particularly sensitive to the welfare of Orthodox churches throughout the Middle East, had sent a huge number of very fine icons to St. Saba, and had also paid for the restoration of the entire building and its adjacent structures. Around noon on the 5th of April, the travellers bid the monks farewell, having left an offering for other, penniless travellers who might happen that way. They then set off for Bethlehem, which they reached after a three-hour ride.

Chapel of the Convent of St Saba.
April 5th 1839.

BETHLEHEM

Plate 184

Bethlehem lies about five miles from Jerusalem, amidst countryside that yields such rich harvests that the area's original name was "Ephrata," or "fertile." Despite the historical prestige of the village, mentioned in ancient Hebrew history as the native home of the family of David, who was probably born there, it boasts no monuments or urban grandeur. Most texts describe the town as small and unassuming.

Modesty and poverty fit well, after all, with the character of the Savior; evangelistic tradition, in fact, has it that Bethlehem was the birthplace of Jesus Christ, who was born in a cave there, according to St. Jerome. It quickly became one of the holy places of Christianity, and the destination of endless pilgrimages. As so often happens in the Holy Land, where history and religion overlap in a setting found nowhere else on earth, Bethlehem is not sacred only to Christians: the Jewish religion also holds the village sacred to the memory of Rachel, wife of the Patriarch Jacob, and archetype of the suffering of all Jewish mothers. Her tomb, just outside of the village, is the object of great veneration because it is considered a symbol of the redemption of Israel. David Roberts arrived in

Bethlehem in the afternoon of the 5th of April. Scrupulous as ever, he writes in his journal that he encountered a great many flocks of sheep during his trip to St. Saba, and that the immediate outskirts of the village seemed quite fertile, with fields of wheat broken here and there by olive groves or fig trees.

5th April 1839

April 5th - The Church of the Nativity crowns the height on which the town is situated, and around it are the Latin, Greek, and Armenian convents. The Church of the Nativity is in form similar to the Basilica at Rome, with a double row of Corinthian columns supporting a wall, above which rises a timber roof. The wall is covered with scriptural subjects, most elaborately executed in mosaic, but much mutilated...

THE CHURCH OF NATIVITY

Plate 185

6th April 1839

From the hills surrounding the city, David Roberts observed that the landscape of Bethlehem is dominated by the hill upon which stands the Church of the Nativity, which is probably one of the oldest churches on earth. It was built at the orders of St. Helena, the mother of the Emperor Constantine, around A.D. 330. The church was restored and partly renovated as early as the sixth century at the orders of Justinian who, it was said, reduced the height of the doors in order to prevent the sacrilegious from entering the church on horseback. In 1479, lastly, the beams of the ceiling were replaced, thanks to the generosity of all the leading Kingdoms of Christendom. The building presents the architectural characteristics of the Roman basilica, and is reminiscent of the church of Saint Paul in Rome; the interior, which is divided into five naves by Corinthian columns and pilasters made of yellow marble, appears sumptuously ornate. Over long centuries of pilgrimage, in fact, the faithful of all the denominations of Christianity have left their mark, in a blaze of votive lamps and icons distinctive to each confession. In this connection, Roberts noted in his journal that the interior of this church is strictly divided into different areas of jurisdiction: while the choir is occupied by the so-called Greek Orthodox Church, the arms of the transept - beneath which lies the Shrine of the Nativity - are instead occupied by the Latin Chapel and the Armenian Chapel. The beginning of the dispute among the three different Christian churches over who rightly possessed the sanctuary dates back to the sixteenth century, but even today the church is surrounded by the convents of the three religious communities, which take turns in officiating at the ecclesiastical rites and ceremonies.

THE SHRINE OF THE NATIVITY

Plate 186

6th April 1839

The Shrine of the Nativity, where Greek Orthodox monks now officiate, is a small and cramped space, its walls partially sheathed in marble yet quite stark when compared with the opulence usually found in Greek Orthodox churches.
In a small apse, the altar of the Nativity of Christ, is adorned with fifteen silver lamps - symbolizing the various denominations of Christianity - and with a silver star, marking the point where Jesus is though to have been born. Upon the star, which represents the comet sighted by the Magi, a Latin inscription explains simply: "Hic De Virgine Maria Jesus Christus Natus Est." Along the sides of the grotto, one after the other, are two small altars: one is the altar of the Manger, in which the Infant Jesus was laid for a crib, the other is the altar of the Magi, who came here to adore the Christ Child.
Tradition has it that the original Manger, brought to Rome at the orders of Pope Sixtus V, is now found in a side chapel of Santa Maria Maggiore. David Roberts writes that, just as he was drawing the interior of the Shrine, a man arrived from Jerusalem carrying the sacred flame; immediately all of the Greek Orthodox faithful clustered around the herald in order to light their lamps at the flame of divine origins.
Roberts's drawing emphasizes the many oil lamps, left as gifts by Christian pilgrims, which then softened the setting with their gentle light, as they do today.

Shrine of the Nativity
Bethlehem. April 6th 1839

JERUSALEM, FROM THE MOUNT OF OLIVES

Plate 187

7th-8th April 1839

On the way back from Bethlehem, on the 7th of April, Roberts wrote that he rode on horseback as far as the so-called Pools of Solomon, which supplied drinking water for the residents of Jerusalem, and which he believed to have been constructed by the Saracens. The following morning, John Pell left the group of travellers and started back to Cairo, and shortly afterwards Roberts returned to Jerusalem. Although the artist writes in his diary that he wandered through the Valley of Jehosaphat and that he had explored the rock-cut tombs that are found here, and which can be seen in the following illustrations - this plate is also dated 8th April. It is therefore quite likely that the drawing - a view of Jerusalem from the top of the Mount of Olives in which it is possible to descry quite clearly the Tomb of Absalom - was executed the morning Roberts returned to the city. The Biblical David came to this long-venerated site to seek refuge, after surviving the revolt instigated by Absalom. At the foot of the Mount is the Garden of Gethsemane, where Jesus was betrayed. In the cemeteries that extend along the slopes of the Mount, thousands of Jews and pilgrims are buried because it is here, according to the Prophets, that the dead will be resurrected. The view created by Roberts shows the eastern quarter of Jerusalem; at the very center lies the Noble Enclosure, where a mosque was built to protect the Rock, from which Mohammed ascended to heaven.

THE TOMB, OF ZECHARIAH

Plate 188

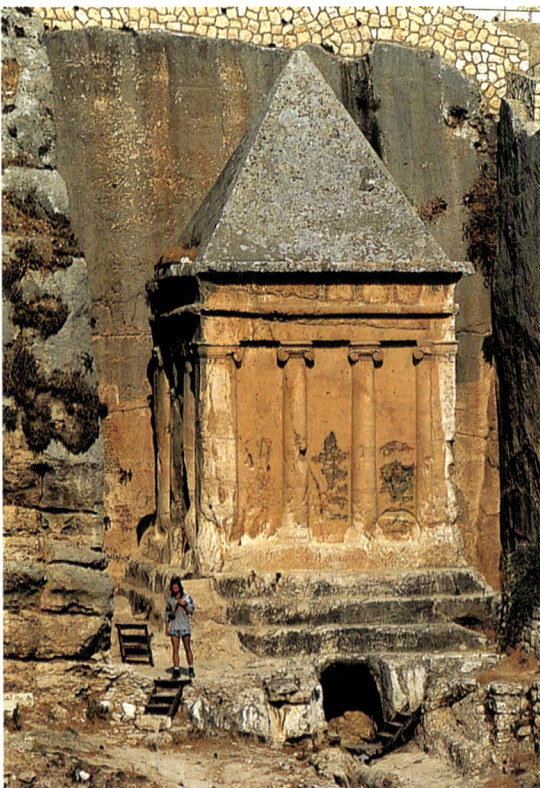

The Valley of Qidron , which winds between the Temple Mount and the Mount of Olives, and which is also known as the Valley of Jehosaphat, features numerous remains of ancient settlements. The upper portion of the valley, with its harsh slopes dotted here and there by small patches of vegetation, was used as a burial ground even in ancient times. Four monumental tombs still stand in good condition. Two of these tombs - that of Jehosaphat and that of St. James - are made of architectural carved into the rocky cliff wall; behind them are the crypts proper. The of Absalom and of Zechariah,

on the other hand, are authentic monumental structures, carved in a single block from the side of the mountain. Despite their clearly Biblical names, these two surprising funerary structures date from Hellenistic times, and once formed part of a vast necropolis in which wealthy and well-to-do citizens from the court of Herod were buried. The correct attribution of the tomb of Zechariah is difficult to

be ascertained, as it is not known whether the Zechariah in question was the prophet - who is said to be buried elsewhere - or Zechariah, the father of John the Baptist. The monument is formed of a cube, some twenty feet to a face, and entirely detached from the slope of the hill.

The faces of the cube are punctuated by half-columns with Ionic capitals and corner pillars. The cornice above, which presents elegant motifs of acanthus leaves, terminates in a jutting molding. Atop the molding is an obtuse pyramid just about ten feet in height. The tomb - which rises on a base made up of three tall stairs, beneath which is the entrance to the burial chamber - was partly buried until the beginning of this century. Roberts, in fact, depicted it as a striking form emerging from the sand. It is interesting to observe that popular tradition holds that not far from the Tombs of the Prophets is the place where the souls will be weighed on Judgment Day, in preparation for the Resurrection of the Flesh.

8th April 1839

THE TOMB OF ST. JAMES

Plate 189

A few yards to the left of the Tomb of Zechariah, and carved out of the same rocky cliff, we find the so-called Tomb of St. James. An inscription identifies this as the burial place of a family of priests in the second century B.C.; nonetheless, tradition holds this to be the place where St. James took refuge and was later buried. Here again, the attribution is complex and obscure, since it is equally common opinion that this tomb was used by this Apostle as a hermitage during the period between Christ's Crucifixion and His Resurrection. Later, St. James supposedly travelled to the Iberian peninsula, where he evangelized extensively, before returning to Jerusalem. Back in Jerusalem, St. James suffered cruel persecution at the hands of Herod Agrippa I, who had him put to death; the saint's body was then supposedly transported to Santiago de Compostela, on the northern coast of Spain, where it was paid enormous honors, and St. James eventually became the patron saint of all Spain. The tomb carved out of the rock wall in the Valley of Jehosaphat is a portico tomb; the architrave is supported by two columns without fluting, with Doric capitals; the facade stands about fifteen feet above ground level, and the tomb runs almost fifty feet into the cliff.

8th April 1839

Tomb of St. James, Valley of Jehoshaphat

THE PILLAR OF ABSALOM

Plate 190

Most of the tombs that dot the slopes of the Valley of Jehosaphat are of fairly recent date, but the surprising time-eroded monument that is commonly known as the "Tiara of the Pharaoh," because of the conical shape of its covering, is presumed to date from the period of the Second Temple, and would therefore be two thousand years old.

The magnificent tomb, which is also partially carved out of living rock, is believed to be that of Absalom, the rebellious son of David; according to the Holy Scriptures, since Absalom had no sons to whom he could leave his name and his memory, he had a monument built not far from Jerusalem, and upon it inscribed his name for posterity. Historical tradition, nonetheless, tells us that Absalom, defeated in battle by his father, fled to the forest of Ephrahim, in the Jordan Valley; there he was caught by the victors, slain, and buried in a simple ditch. As so often happens, here too it is difficult to distinguish fact from legend. In any case, the Tomb of Absalom - its lower section extremely reminiscent of the Tomb of Zechariah - remains a magnificent example of Hellenistic architecture. It appears as a cube roughly twenty feet on each face, entirely detached from the sloping limestone ridge of the hill. The faces of the cube are punctuated by half-columns with Ionic capitals and composite corner pillars.

oms Pillar.
Valley of Jehoshaphat

The architrave, with carved
Doric triglyphs and metopes,
supports a parallelipiped
element, upon which a low
cylinder stands, terminating in
a crown with relief decorations;
all of this is completed by an
odd bell-shaped roof, tall and
tapering. The interior of the
construction consists of a small
burial chamber. David Roberts,
who spent the entire afternoon
of the 8th of April visiting the
Valley of Jehosaphat, was struck
by the remarkable similarities
between these cliff tombs and
the architecture of Petra - in
particular, the habit of merging
half-columns and corner
pilasters seemed identical to him.

8th April 1839

THE FOUNTAIN OF SILOAM

Plate 191

8th April 1839

Around the year 1000 B.C., King David conquered Jerusalem and made it his capital; later David's son Solomon built his temple on the hill overlooking the Valley of the Kidron. This choice of location - which so greatly influenced the later development of the city's layout, and which has recently been documented by archeological finds on the slopes to the south of the Mosque of El Aksa - was probably determined by the presence of a spring, back then the only source of fresh water in the entire region.

The Gihon Fountain, also known as the Siloam Fountain, tumbles forth from a deep cleft in the rock in the higher section of the Valley of Jehosaphat. Today one can still reach the spring only by descending a steep stairway carved into the living rock. The spring lies outside the walls and this was the reason why the Jebusites dug an underground tunnel to conduct the fresh water into the city to the Siloam Pool. It was through this narrow passage that the Jews, led by the young David, made their way into Jerusalem, taking the defenders by surprise. The waters of the Siloam Fountain were used as a votive offering by the priests of the temple during the Feast of the Tabernacles. David Roberts toured the entire Valley of Jehosaphat on the afternoon of the 8th of April; while there he carefully sketched the rock-cut tombs of the valley. Although this plate and the two subsequent plates are not dated, it is fair to suppose that they were all completed on that same day, considering the proximity of the three sites and the burial ground.

Fountain of Siloam. Valley of Jehoshaphat.

THE POOL OF SILOAM

Plate 192

S ince the spring of Siloam bubbled forth at the back of a cave in the Valley of Jehosaphat, outside the city walls and therefore eminently vulnerable to attack, the inhabitants of Jerusalem were afraid of remaining cut off from

water during a siege. Three centuries after the reign of David, when the threat of an attack by the Assyrians began to loom large, King Hezekiah gave the order to dig a new tunnel, in order to channel the spring waters into the city, to what has since come to be called the Pool of Siloam. The spring was thus connected to the new reservoir by a channel some one thousand seven hundred and fifty feet in length. The stream crossed the hill of Ophel and gushed forth in the Tyropoeon Valley. An inscription commemorated the completion of the colossal undertaking, which took place in 701 B.C. When the plaque with the inscription was uncovered in 1880, under Ottoman rule, it was transported to Istanbul, where it is still part of the collection of the Museum of Ancient Orient. The English archeologist Charles Warren, in order to study this remarkable piece of hydraulic engineering, made his

way along the entire length of the tunnel on his hands and knees, jotting down a plan of its course as he went. The fruit of his daring labors is displayed in the Archeological Museum of Jerusalem. The Pool of Siloam appears today as a basin of crystal-clear water, located at the mouth of the tunnel, at the end of a trench bounded by stone walls, which can be reached by a stairway.

A popular legend has it that the Virgin Mary came to wash the clothes of the Infant Jesus in this very fountain, and that the Savior used the same water years later in order to restore the sight of a blind man.

8 April 1839

THE FOUNTAIN OF JOB

Plate 193

8th April 1839

The so-called Fountain of Job is, in reality, an ancient well located just below the point in which the Valley of Jehosaphat joins the valley of Hinnom. It is mentioned in the Book of Joshua and in the Book of Kings, clear signs of an extremely venerable age. Curiously, however, there is no mention of it in any documents dating from the Crusaders' occupation of Jerusalem. One can deduce that the well had long ago fallen into disuse, and that it was restored to operation only following the Arab reconquest. This hypothesis would seem to be supported by the vaguely orientalizing appearance of the structures, as they appear in the drawing and in the description by Roberts. The well, which was roughly one hundred and twenty-five feet in depth, appeared as a large, square basin, fairly irregular, made of massive blocks of stone; one of the sides was occupied by a low building, probably a reservoir, while a taller structure joined it at its corner. Atop this taller structure was a small cupola, and it opened out onto the surface of the water with a spacious acute arch of Islamic style. During the rainy season, the level of the water in the well rose considerably, and the well would even overflow at times. Tradition is divided upon the origin of the name - or even upon the exact name of the fountain. The Christian monks call it the Well of Nehemiah, while the locals called it "Bir Eyub," or the Well of Job. According to the Bible story, this was where the sacred fire of the temple was stored and protected during the Babylonian captivity, until the reconstruction of Jerusalem.

Fountain of Job. Valley of Hinn

VIEW OF JERUSALEM, LOOKING WESTWARD

Plate 194

9th April 1839

In the panorama of the eastern quarter of the city, we can clearly see the precinct, supported by massive walls, where the mosques of Omar and Al Aksa stand. In this handsome view, it is possible to see how other Islamic constructions of different eras are located around the Dome of the Rock. Among them are the Dome of the Chain, a miniature copy of the Mosque of Omar; Sabeel Qait Bey, a small octagonal structure dating back to the fifteenth century; and the Kadi Burhan el-Din, an elegant outdoor pulpit, for use in the summer. The Mosque of El Aksa, to the left in the illustration, dates from the time of Caliph Walid I, who ordered it built between A.D. 709 and 715, upon the ruins of a Byzantine basilica known as the Church of Purification. It was then destroyed entirely by an earthquake and rebuilt in 1034 in the form that it still largely presents today. Sixty-five years later, during the reign of the Crusaders, it was transformed into a church of the Templar Knights, who called it "Templum Salomonis." When Saladin conquered Jerusalem, El Aksa was turned back into a mosque, which it remains to the present day. Its name means literally "The Most Distant One," because, according to Muslim tradition, it marks the furthest point from Mecca that Mohammed reached during his magical Night Journey to Jerusalem. Right at the foot of the Dome of the Rock and of the Mosque of El Aksa stands the imposing Kotel Maaravi, the Wailing Wall, an enormous wall that once formed a support for the foundations of the Temple of Solomon. There is no other place on earth so profoundly venerated by the Jewish people. Ever since the times of Roman occupation, followed by the Diaspora, the children of Israel have come here to pray and to show their grief over the destruction of the House of God. Today, this holy place is an open-air synagogue, and Jewish men must come here with their heads covered.

VIEW OF JERUSALEM, FROM THE SOUTH

Plate 195

9th April 1839

The hill that lies to the east of present-day Jerusalem was inhabited from the third millennium B.C. onward by the Canaanites. As early as the second millennium B.C. we find literary documents that mention the city, which was then called Urusalim. When David, upon the death of Saul, decided to gather the various tribes of the Hebrew people into a single kingdom, he chose Jerusalem as his capital due to its advantageous position, girded it with walls, and had his palace built on Mount Zion, where he also moved the Ark of the Covenant. David's son Solomon subsequently enlarged the city, and built the Temple there; this was razed to the ground in 586 B.C., when Nebuchadnezzar conquered the city and took its inhabitants in captivity to Babylon. Upon the return of the Jews from captivity, Jerusalem was rebuilt and enclosed within new walls, but the city never regained its ancient splendor. Conquered in 331 B.C. by Alexander the Great, it then fell under the rule of the Ptolemies, and then the Seleucids, but the resistance of the Maccabees prevented the complete Hellenization of the city. From 63 B.C., Jerusalem fell under the rule of the Romans, and they placed Herod the Great on the throne: during the reign of this king the Temple was rebuilt, and the Fortress Antonia was constructed.

Later on, because of the rapacious greed of the Roman Procurator Gessius Florus, Jerusalem rebelled; besieged first by Vespasian and later by Titus, the city finally fell in A.D. 70. Titus destroyed the city entirely, burnt the Temple, and drove out the inhabitants. Sixty-four years later Hadrian established a Roman colony there called Ælia Capitolina; it was forbidden to Jews. It was not until Constantine became emperor that the city took back its old name. In A.D. 637, the city surrendered to Arabs led by Caliph Omar, who nonetheless granted freedom of worship to both Christians and Jews. This enlightened approach was curtailed under the rule of the Fatimites and the Seljuk Turks, whose harsh behavior helped to spark the Crusades. In 1099 the Holy City was taken by Godfrey of Bouillon, but the Kingdom of Jerusalem endured for less than a century. In 1187, Saladin beat the Latins at the battle of Hattin. Following the short interval of the rule of Frederick II of Swabia, the city remained in Egyptian hands until 1517, the year in which it was conquered by the Turkish Sultan Selim I. Ottoman rule, which continued right up to the First World War, was briefly broken by the occupation of the city by the Egyptian Pasha Ibrahim, between 1831 and 1840, in the very period when Roberts made his tour of the Holy Land.

THE CHAPEL OF ST. HELENA

Plate 196

10th April 1839

Mount Calvary, the site of the crucifixion of Christ, takes its name from the Latin term "calvaria," which means "skull," as do the Hebrew term "Gulgoleth" and the Aramaic word "Gulgoltha." This place name originated from the odd shape of the land here, as well as from a popular superstition that Adam's skull was buried here. Calvary had long been used for public executions, and in the year A.D. 135, it was leveled at the orders of Emperor Hadrian, who had the capitol of his new colony, Aelia Capitolina, built there. Queen Helena came to Jerusalem in the year A.D. 325 on a pilgrimage, in the company of the bishop of Jerusalem, Macarius, guided by a dream in which she was ordered to have excavations made in that precise spot. The excavations quickly unearthed the Holy Sepulchre of Jesus, and - it was even believed - the remains of the True Cross of Christ and of the two thieves. The following year, Helena's son Constantine began construction of a first basilica with five naves, completed in A.D. 335, for the protection of Golgotha and the Holy Sepulchre. Around the Holy Sepulchre, in particular, he ordered the construction of an enormous rotunda topped by a great cupola and called Anastasis, which means "Resurrection."

The entire building was destroyed by the Persians in 614, and rebuilding began fifteen years later, under Abbot Modestus. The new church was severely damaged in 1009 by the armies of the Caliph el-Hakem, and was restored by the Emperor Constantine IX Monomachus. When the Crusaders conquered Jerusalem in July 1099, the entire building was considered to be unworthy to cover the Holy Sepulchre of Christ. The structure was therefore radically renovated, although the same floor plan and the distinctive rotunda were maintained. The new structure was consecrated in 1149; its appearance remained unvaried until 1808, when a terrible fire - possibly arson - seriously damaged the building. When Roberts visited the monument, the restoration had already been completed by the excessively enterprising Greek Orthodox monks. This illustration depicts the intriguing Chapel of St. Helena, a crypt with three naves, supported by four massive columns; a throne is still to be found here, from which the pious queen is said to have overseen the excavation in search of the True Cross. From this room, a narrow staircase leads to another chamber, in which the slab of marble that covered the True Cross of Christ is still kept.

From David Roberts's journal:

10th - After having made four drawings of the Holy Sepulchre, I waited on the new consul, Mr. Young, who arrived here to-day.

Crypt of the Holy Sepulchre

433

CALVARY

Plate 197

10th April 1839

Unfortunately, the reports of the terrible fire that partially destroyed the Holy Sepulchre in 1808 reached Europe at a time when other disasters occupied the public imagination: Rome and the Papal State had just been occupied by Napoleon's troops, and Spain was invaded shortly thereafter. The following year, Pope Pius VII, who had excommunicated the French Emperor, was arrested and imprisoned at Fontainbleau; the cries for help sent out in the wake of the fire by the various congregations of Jerusalem, therefore, fell upon deaf ears in Europe. The Greek Orthodox monks, who had been vying fiercely with the Latin community for centuries over the rights to the church, took canny advantage of the unlooked-to situation.
The Greeks Orthodox monks easily obtained permission to oversee the reconstruction of the basilica, and thereafter became the true adminstrators of the site. Nonetheless, more than a restoration, this was a veritable work of demolition of everything that could be considered to reek of the Latin world. All of the signs of devotion left by armies of pilgrims over the centuries were thus systematically eradicated, such as the inscriptions and the cross that had been carved around the altars; they were replaced by icons and by other typically Greek Orthodox decorations. Among other things, the beautiful sarcophagi of Godfrey of Bouillon, conqueror of Jerusalem, and of his successors, were all destroyed, as was the beautiful edicule that marked the site of the tomb of Christ. Calvary, as it appears in the illustration by Roberts, was covered by a small and ornately decorated chapel. At the center stood an altar, beneath which was a shaft bordered with gilt silver, where the Cross had been placed. On the sides of the altar, two similar holes indicated the points where the crosses of the two thieves had been raised. Currently, Calvary is formed of two adjacent chapels, one of which is Catholic, and the other Greek Orthodox. In the first chapel, two stations of the Way of the Cross show where Jesus was stripped and where He was crucified; in the second chapel, the Twelfth Station marks the point where the Messiah died on the Cross. Behind the altar, three life-sized icons depict Christ on the Cross, the Virgin Mary, and John the Baptist, while between the two chapels stands the small altar of the Stabat Mater.

THE SHRINE OF THE HOLY SEPULCHRE

Plate 198

10th April 1839

*A*t first sight, the interior of the Church of the Holy Sepulchre is almost intimidating with its arcane atmosphere, fraught with the aroma of incense, veiled in dim light, amidst the constant murmuring of the sacred offices. Nonetheless, once the first impression wears off, the church glitters with an incomparable splendor that no one can easily overlook. The plan of the church is the outcome of a series of the most unforeseeable turns of event in history, far more than the product of the intentions of the architects. The quarrels amongst the various religious orders over possession of the Holy Sepulchre did their fair share to increase the level of architectural chaos. Over the centuries, every corner of the building has taken on a specific and precise meaning, and all of the available space around the main structure has been employed in building small chapels that recall events and individuals who played a role in the Crucifixion and the Resurrection of Jesus. The heart of the basilica is, nonetheless, the marble edicule that stands at the center of the Anastasis, or Rotunda, in which the Sepulchre of Christ is still venerated. The small construction, topped by a strangely shaped cupola, owes its fanciful and over-elaborate style to an unknown Greek Orthodox architect who completed it in 1817.

The interior is split up into two small rooms - the first is the Chapel of the Angel, which contains the stone upon which the angel supposedly stood when announcing the Resurrection of Jesus to the pious women, while the second room is the funerary chamber proper, which is also the last station in the Via Dolorosa. The tomb, dug out of the living rock of Golgotha, was donated by Joseph of Arimathea and Nicodemus so that the body of the Messiah could receive adequate burial. Within this narrow space that cannot hold more than six people, an altar bearing an image of the Virgin indicates the corbel-shaped stone, now covered by a slab of finely polished marble, upon which the body of Jesus was laid. Above the Sepulchre hang forty-three silver lamps; thirteen of them belong to the Latin Christians; thirteen belong to the Greek Orthodox; and thirteen belong to the Armenians. The last four belong to the Coptic minority.

Shrine of the Holy Sepulchre.
April 11th 1839.
David Roberts.

THE KATHOLIKON OF THE HOLY SEPULCHRE

Plate 199

11th April 1839

The central area of the Church of the Holy Sepulchre is formed by the so-called Katholikon, a richly decorated nave, with a rectangular plan and apses, split in two by a tall iconostasis. The iconostasis is a partition or screen upon which icons are placed, separating the sanctuary from the main part of the church; it is a typical feature in Greek Orthodox churches, where the presbytery is always separate, kept out of the sight of the faithful. The iconostasis in question appears as a double row of slender columns. The intercolumnar spaces are blocked by the icons. The nave of the Katholikon is dominated by the "omphalos," a huge cupola from the center of which hangs a majestic lamp. As has been noted elsewhere, following the terrible fire of 1808, the Holy Sepulchre was extensively renovated by the Greek Orthodox monks. With grants from the government of Russia, a country with a special place in its heart for the Eastern Orthodox community in the Holy Land, the Orthodox Greeks became the virtual owners of the church. In this illustration, Roberts is intensely concerned with the exquisite iconostasis and the lavish decorations that encrust the entire interior in a breathtaking, mind-boggling accumulation of wildly different styles. Though the Greek Orthodox forbid any form of sculpture in their churches, what they lack in statues they amply make up for with the profusion of paintings, gilt stuccoes, votive lamps, and fine marble objects. At the center of the nave, below the large lamp, stands a small votive vase with an odd shape, the object of great devotion on the part of all the Christian pilgrims that come here. They believe that the vase in question stands precisely upon the fulcrum, or "belly button," of the world.

The Katholikon as it appears today has varied from the illustration by Roberts; an enormous restoration project has recently restored the church to what is believed to be its original form, dating from the Crusades.

THE POOL OF BETHESDA

Plate 200

12th April 1839

*I*n Latin, the word for pool - "piscina" - was used generically, to describe any basin of water not roofed over, whether that water was used to keep fish or for humans to swim in. In ancient Jerusalem, the great reservoir of fresh water located at the northeast corner of the walls of the temple, not far from the Church of St. Anne, was called "piscina probatica." It must have been a common urge with the earliest Christian monks to give names taken from the Holy Scriptures to just about any important landmark in the City of David; perhaps

while the waterproof lining was made during the Roman period. Nearby, during the Byzantine Era, a large church was built, and later the Crusaders built a chapel there. Unfortunately, all of these subsequent constructions, a veritable microcosm of the complex urban history of Jerusalem, were destroyed over the course of the centuries, and today only a few scattered traces remain. Tradition has it that in the Pool of Bethesda lambs were washed before being sacrificed in the Temple, and the Gospel according to St. John mentions

that urge led them to dub this impressive structure - about three hundred sixty feet in length, some one hundred and thirty feet in width, and about seventy-five feet deep - with the name of Bethesda. The deepest parts of the reservoir date from the era of the Hasmoneans,

that Jesus cured the crippled man here. In the illustration by Roberts, the deep trench appears to be choked with rubble and dirt, and small trees even grew on this pile of detritus. Only a part of the basin contained even a puddle of stagnant water, remaining from the spring rains.

From David Roberts's journal:

April 12th - On my return home after sketching, found that the consul had called for me. To-day I have wandered over the hills, but have not been able to get a good view of the city.

View of Jerusalem, from the North

Plate 201

13th April 1839

During his excursions to the areas surrounding Jerusalem, Roberts had an opportunity to survey the city from a number of different points of view. These views inspired him to draw a number of striking panoramas. This view, in particular, gives us some idea of the exotic allure of the city, which can capture the imagination and spirit of the artist just as well as the ordinary visitor. Rising on the slopes of gentle hills, fragmented geographically and, yet, at the same time, spiritually indivisible, the City of Gold has always been a crossroads between East and West, between worlds and peoples that are radically different one from another. Many consider Jerusalem to be the very center of the Universe. The city has the quality of a timeless symbol. It is a great town of low houses and narrow streets, along which the ancient and the modern live side by side; in much the same way, the most important sacred monuments of the world's three great monotheistic religions are clustered side by side in the limited space available.

The natural backdrop for the very history of modern civilization, Jerusalem boasts a veritable mosaic of cultures. This becomes even clearer when one considers the disconcertingly diverse array of ethnic groups that make up the city's population. Jews, Arabs, Muslims, Christians, and Druses coexist in a delicate state of equilibrium, paradoxically made more stable by their ability to maintain their distinct identities. Perhaps it is in this alchemical equilibrium that we can find the secret of a city that has witnessed bloody internecine battles over millennia, that has been dismembered by political and religious fanatics, but which has always succeeded in reaffirming its sacred and universal standing.

THE GATE OF DAMASCUS

Plate 202

14th–15th April 1839

*O*ne of the most remarkable works of architecture in Jerusalem is certainly represented by the city walls, which run some two and a half miles, in part around the perimeter of the original Roman fortifications, and in part around those built during the Crusades. Built with fairly small blocks and recycled materials, the walls - which still enclose the old part of the city - were erected between 1536 and 1542 at the orders of Suleiman the Magnificent when Palestine was under Turkish rule.

The walls, which still possess the original battlements, communication trenches, and interior stairways, are punctuated by the eight gates, seven of which, massive and well proportioned, were built upon the foundations of older gates; a number of elements of these gates have also been incorporated. When David Roberts visited Jerusalem, only four gates, corresponding to the four cardinal points, were open. Of the eight gates, the most handsome and best known is the Damascus Gate, once known as Bal-el-Amud. The gate takes its modern name from the fact that

it leads to the road for Syria and the north. Built astride an ogival arch set between two imposing square towers with corner sentry-turrets, this gate is somewhat more ornate than the other seven. Today, just as when Roberts, disguised as an Arab with a train of camels and an entourage of servants, drew it, a marketplace stood nearby, with the noise of haggling and the aroma of spices wafting over all. In the nearby money-changing bureaus, one might almost expect to see the glitter of gold and silver coins on the pans of finely wrought balances; nonetheless, even though over time the precious metals have been replaced by folding bills and calculators, the mercantile tradition of the place has remained solidly anchored, seemingly deep in the stones themselves. This drawing bears the date of the 14th of April - the next day Roberts left Jerusalem and set out for Nablus. The notes written in Roberts's journal for that date inform us that on that night while sleeping in their tents, he and his entourage were alarmed at the clearly encroaching presence of jackals.

FROM JERUSALEM TO BAALBEC

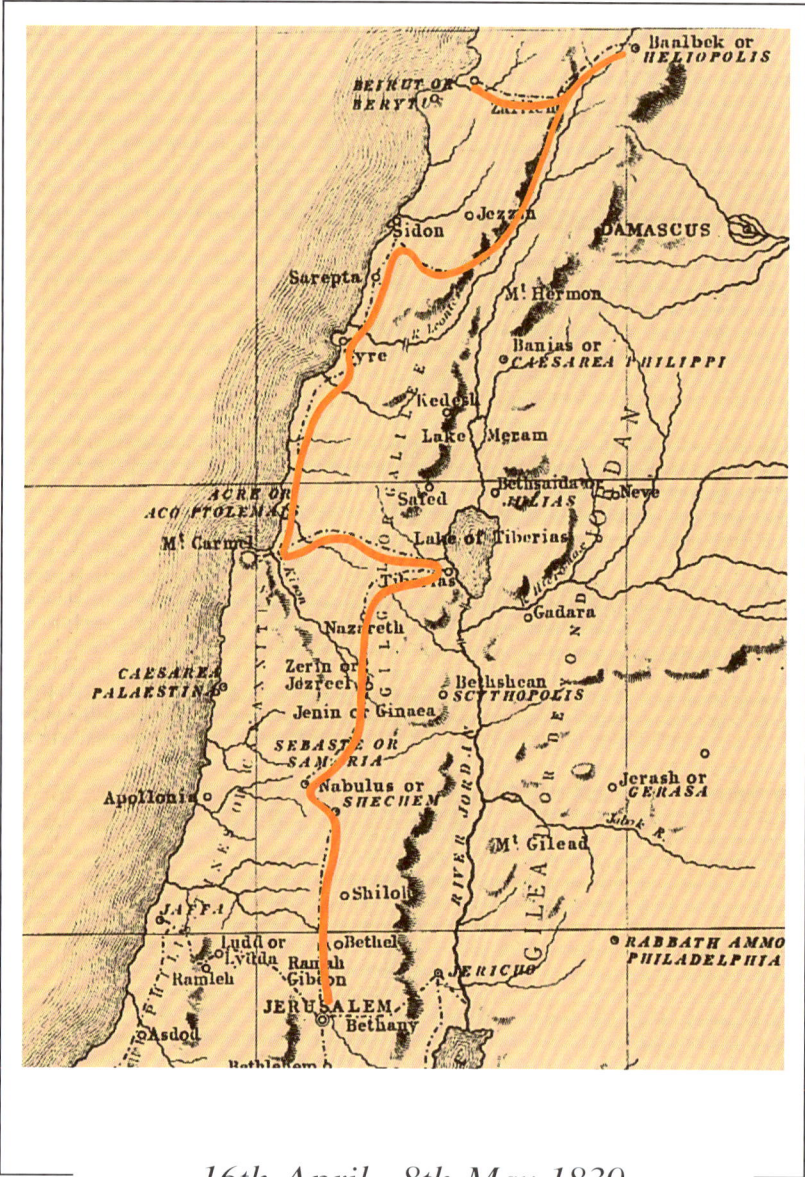

16th April - 8th May 1839

The

HOLY LAND,

Syria, Idumea, Arabia, Egypt & Nubia.

FROM DRAWINGS MADE ON THE SPOT BY

David Roberts, R.A.

WITH HISTORICAL DESCRIPTIONS, BY

THE REV.? GEORGE CROLY. L.L.D.

LITHOGRAPHED BY

LOUIS HAGHE

VOL. 2

David Roberts, R.A.

Baalbec, from the Fountain. May 4th 1839.

LONDON, F. G. MOON. 20, THREADNEEDLE STREET,
PUBLISHER IN ORDINARY TO HER MAJESTY.
MDCCCXLIII.

VIEW OF NABLUS

Plate 203

16th April 1839

Ith typically British precision, David Roberts noted that he entered Nablus around three in the afternoon on the 16th of April. Considering the date that appears on the margin of the drawing, the direction in which the caravan shown here is heading, presumably the same of Roberts himself, and the exact documentation of the journal, we should note that this illustration certainly refers to the trip away from the village, and not to the arrival in the village, as is erroneously noted on the lithograph itself. Nablus, the ancient Shechem mentioned in the Old Testament, lies between Mount Ebal and Mount Gerizim, some thirty miles to the north of Jerusalem, at the mouth of a depression that runs all the way to the Mediterranean Sea. The city,

which is today considered to be the chief trading center in all of Samaria and a major agricultural marketplace, was given its name by Titus, who rebuilt it in A.D. 70 and called it Flavia Neapolis, in honor of his father, Titus Flavius Vespasianus, or Vespasian. The valley in which it lies, made particularly fertile by an abundance of springs, appears luxuriant in contrast with the aridity of the surrounding highlands. Even in the distant past, the area was famed for its fruit orchards. It is not surprising that Roberts should have been surprised at the welcoming and orderly appearance of the town, whose inhabitants seemed to him to be among the most prosperous of all those he had seen thus far in Palestine.

From David Roberts's journal:

April 16th - The situation of the town is beautiful. It is placed between the mountains Ebal and Gerizim, and is well sheltered from the north and south winds...

Nablus, ancient Shechem

16th April 1839

The small and bustling town of Nablus, which thrives on farming and small industry, has also preserved intact the synagogue of the Samaritans, as well as the marketplace and lore of the old quarters. Just like the names of Hebron, Jericho, and other Israeli cities, the name of Shechem is familiar to a great many Jews. It was here, in fact, that the Lord promised Abraham that he would rule over the land of Canaan, it was here that the Ark of the Covenant was set down, and it was here - later - that the twelve tribes of Israel assembled to proclaim king the successor of Solomon. The sect of the Samaritans originated at Shechem around the eighth century B.C. Their origin actually dates from the deportation of the Jews from the northern kingdom by the Assyrians, when many Asiatic colonizers arrived in the region and merged with the surviving population. It was then that the Jews, returning from exodus in Babylon, set about rebuilding the Temple and the city of Jerusalem; the Samaritans offered to help but were rudely rebuffed. The Samaritans then built a temple of their own on Mount Garizim, marking their definitive break with the Jews. In 129 B.C., John Hyrcanus destroyed Shechem and the temple; the temple was not rebuilt. The religion is rejected by Orthodox Judaism because of its syncretism and because it does not recognize the authority of the Talmud. Only a few hundred Samaritans survive, living in two separate communities. One is at Holon, not far from Tel Aviv; the other is here in Nablus, and is referred to as Somerin, or "the Guardians," as they consider themselves to be faithful custodians of the Revelation. Each year, at Easter, the Samaritan faithful climb Mount Gerizim, where they celebrate the holiday in the ruins of their ancient temple.

Jacob's Well at Nablus

Plate 205

*I*n the Samaritan synagogue at Nablus, the famous codex of the Pentateuch is preserved. The Pentateuch, the first five books of the Old Testament, is the only form of the Sacred Scriptures recognized by the members of the sect. Knowledge of this Pentateuch had reached as early a writer as St. Jerome, yet the surviving transcription of the archaic Hebrew characters dates back no further than the twelfth or the eleventh century A.D. David Roberts noted in his journal that he visited the synagogue on the 17th of April and, slightly later, that he went

to see the so-called Well of Jacob, which lies just south of Nablus on the road to Jerusalem. With a sharp note of disappointment, he wrote that the holy place looked like nothing more than a heap of abandoned rubble. There were only a few fragments of columns, partly buried but still standing as mute witnesses to the church that, according to popular lore, was built by Queen Helena.

With well-reasoned considerations, Roberts goes on to show that just as the ruins of the church are in all likelihood less ancient than is commonly believed, the identification of the well as the one where Jesus met the Samaritan can be readily rejected. In the same area, in fact, there are three or four other springs that jibe perfectly with the description found in the

Gospels. Nonetheless, here too it
is wise to give credence to that
which has been accepted by
generations of the faithful as
true, as their centuries of
devotion and continuing
adoration confer a certain
historical dignity to the few
concrete bits of evidence that
survive.

From David Roberts's journal:

*April 17th - I visited the synagogue of
the ancient Samaritans, and was
shown there two very ancient MSS. of
the Pentateuch. Went to the Well of
Jacob, where the interview took place
between our Saviour and the woman
of Samaria.*

17th April 1839

Tomb of Joseph at Shechem.

THE TOMB OF JOSEPH, AT NABLUS

Plate 206

David Roberts R.A. 1839

17th April 1839

Near Nablus, in a village called Askar, is a tomb in which tradition holds that Joseph and his two sons, Ephraim and Manasseh, heads of the two tribes of Israel that bore their names, were buried. The special holiness of this place, which has never waned over the centuries, is due to the undying reverence paid to the figure of Joseph. A man who was more pious and just than any other, Joseph died in the land of Egypt in the certain belief that Palestine was the land promised to his people. When, during the Exodus, the Jews brought the body of Joseph with them, Jacob purchased, for one hundred pieces of silver, the land in which to bury him, quite close to the ancient town of Shechem, now known as Nablus. This event supposedly sanctioned in formal terms the right of the Jewish people to the land of Canaan.

In this illustration by David Roberts, who came here shortly after visiting Jacob's Well, Joseph's Tomb appears as a massive block that has been plastered over: low and squat. On one side, a shallow niche has been carved, where a number of small lamps burn, probably brought as marks of devotion by one of the faithful. The two blocks of roughly squared stone that stand on either side of the tomb are traditionally considered to be the headstones of Ephraim and Manasseh.

SEBASTE, ANCIENT SAMARIA

Plate 207

After leaving Nablus on the afternoon of the 17th, David Roberts and his travelling companions rode for two and a half hours before they sighted the ancient Samaria, now known as Sebaste. The city was founded in 925 B.C. by King Omri of Israel; it became the third capital of the kingdom, after Shechem and Tirza. Samaria was attacked repeatedly by the Arameans, Assyrians, and then Persians; it was destroyed by Alexander the Great, and then again by John Hyrcanus, and was subsequently rebuilt by Herod the Great, who named it Sebaste (i.e., Augusta, in honor of Octavian Augustus). Herod then handed the city over to the Romans.

The modern town stands on the eastern part of the hill, while the peak of the hill is occupied by an intriguing archeological zone, that was explored by American archeology teams as early as the first few decades of this century. It is possible to admire the remains of the palace of King Omri as well as the ruins of a truly splendid Roman forum, and - above all - the Church of St. John the Baptist built by the Crusaders on the foundations of a previously existing Byzantine temple. In the crypt of this church, the relics of John the Baptist and the prophets Elisha and Elijah were venerated. In his diary, Roberts noted that the valley of Sebaste, so luxuriant and tranquil, might easily have passed for a stretch of English countryside, in stark contrast with the arid desolation found in the area around Jerusalem. With a typically Romantic sensibility, the artist described the emotions that surged up in him at the sight of the ruins of Sebaste, so silent and deserted, bathed in the warm light of sunset. In the drawing, one can clearly see the impressive colonnade of the palace of Herod, which originally had the extent of three thousand feet; the function that this colonnade intended to serve is still the object of considerable speculation. Following a period of great splendor, Sebaste underwent a rapid decline in inverse proportion to the rise of nearby Nablus; by the Middle Ages, the city already lay in ruins.

In ancient Samaria April 17th 1839.

17th April 1839

RUINS OF THE CHURCH OF ST. JOHN THE BAPTIST AT SEBASTE

Plate 208

18th April 1839

*R*oberts, who had ordered the tents pitched right at the foot of the hill upon which stand the ruins of Sebaste, toured the entire area on the 17th and 18th of April, and drew up a careful description. The remains of the walls of the Church of St. John the Baptist, which was built on the site of the martyrdom and decapitation of the saint, still stood to a considerable height, and the high, narrow windows presented decorations in the Norman style. Grotesque

naves and the higher windows were more Gothic in style. The columns had the proportions of the Corinthian order; the material used in the construction of the church was chiefly the tufa quarried in the surrounding hills. At the center of the nave, which was just almost one hundred and fifty feet in length, lay the tomb of a sheik. In addition to his architectural observations, Roberts noted that, though popular tradition might hold that Queen Helena was

figures and anthropomorphic heads adorned the many stone blocks that were scattered here and there. The apse and the altar showed clear signs of Greek Orthodox influence, as did the lower windows in the apse, while the acute arches of the

responsible for the foundation of the church, the monument itself could more rightly be attributed to the Crusading Knights of St. John; the numerous crosses carved into the rock as tokens of devotion seem to support this hypothesis.

Ruins of The Church of St. John, Sabaste

From David Roberts's journal:

April 18th - In the middle of the city (if a few wretched hovels deserve such a name), rising over vast arches of hewn stone, are the ruins of a Christian church, the architecture of which must have been very perfect...

JENIN, ANCIENT JEZREEL

Plate 209

19th April 1839

From Roberts's journal, we learn that the artist's caravan left the ruins of Sebaste on the afternoon of the 18th of April, and that it was late at night by the time the caravan reached the village of Abate, which is set on the peak of a hill not far from a lake. There Roberts and his fellow travellers finally pitched their tents. The male population of the village was mostly made up of the elderly and the infirm, since most of the young men had been conscripted into the army. Roberts was especially impressed with the clothing worn by the women of the place, of which he gives us a brief but thorough description.

"The dress consists of a loose white robe, and a red sash; a red handkerchief is bound round the head; a scarf of the same colour covering the under part of the face, falls down over the back, and a string of large silver coins hangs dangling from the dark hair."

The group of travellers set out at dawn, and was quickly within sight of Jenin, a pleasant village set at the mouth of a valley that opens out onto the fertile plain of Esdraelon. Set in a luxuriant oasis, the town is now a prosperous farming center, capital of the district with the same name.

It is believed that the town occupies the site of the ancient Jezreel, but not all of the scholars are in agreement on this. The only certain information that we have is that Jenin was first mentioned around the time of the Crusades, and that its name became increasingly familiar to the pilgrims who came to Palestine. This was a result of its favorable position on the road that leads to Nazareth from Jerusalem. Roberts sketched the town, surrounded by palm groves, alongside a pleasant stream, as if to emphasize the fertility of the region.

David. Roberts. R.A.

MOUNT TABOR

Plate 210

19th April 1839

After passing through Jenin, Roberts and his travelling companions followed a track that was to take them to Nazareth, after skirting the plain of Esdraelon. Mentioned several times in the Bible, the fertile plain of Esdraelon, crossed by the Kishon River, opens out amidst the hills of northern Samaria and between Carmel to the south and Galilee to the north. Crisscrossed by ancient and important roads and routes, this plain was the site of famous battles: Barak conquered the Medianites; Ahab routed the Syrians; Saul was conquered and killed by the Philistines; Josiah was beaten by the pharaoh Necho. The land was reclaimed and improved centuries ago and today is an extremely populous and productive farm land. The highlands that overlook it are Gilboa, Hermon, and the very imposing Mount Tabor, certainly the geographic feature that most captured the imagination of David Roberts. He sketched the mountain although he did note that he found it far less grand than he had gathered from the drawings he had seen of it by others. Although the mountain is handsome and well proportioned, it long ago lost its daunting austerity because of the ongoing process of settlement and reclamation that local farmers have been carrying forward over the years, shaping the slopes and smoothing away the mountain's most jagged edges. On the other hand, Roberts concluded in his notes that this was the same fate that befell practically every mountain and hill in Palestine, where farming softens everything. The caravan shown in the foreground in the drawing was a group of Christian pilgrims returning to Jerusalem from Damascus. Roberts came upon the caravan as the pilgrims were taking their noonday rest.

from the Plain of Esdraelon
April 19th 1839

NAZARETH

Plate 211

19th April 1839

The journal notes that the trail leading to Nazareth at first wound steeply among the hills, and then descended without warning to the tiny village, which almost seemed to burrow and nestle into the protective embrace of the hills. In both Arabic and Hebrew, the name Nazareth means "The Guardian," and while this may have originally been a reference to the strategic location of the village - which overlooks the plain of Esdrelon - today it seems to have more to do with the role that history has reserved for it, of being the guardian of Christian tradition, under the watchful administration of the Franciscan brothers. Although Nazareth has been inhabited from time out of mind, the town in which Jesus was grown up has only become a full-fledged town in recent years.

The old houses with their white-plaster coats reach almost to the peak of the hill where the Church of Jesus the Adolescent now stands, while further down modern buildings stand in neat rows. The fairly heterogeneous makeup of the urban structure corresponds to an equally complex makeup in ethnic and religious terms. While the Muslims live in the old town and the Jews live in the new quarter of Illit, there are a number of other communities, such as Catholics, Greek Orthodox, Maronites, and others belonging to minor creeds. Each of these groups now possesses its own churches and other institutions. When Roberts visited here, and was greeted by the Father Superior of the Latin convent, the population of Nazareth was just three thousand.

THE CHURCH OF THE ANNUNCIATION

Plate 212

Nazareth was inhabited exclusively by Jews until the fourth century A.D. Since the Holy Scriptures state that the birth of Jesus was announced to Mary in this precise village, the earliest Christians took up residence here and began to build a church of their own. This church was in time replaced by a Byzantine basilica, and then by a church built by Crusaders - only a few fragments survive of both of these structures. Long after Saladin won the town back to Arab rule in 1187, St. Louis, King of France came and visited Nazareth in 1252. In 1363, the Mameluke sultan Baibars had all of the Christian sacred buildings in the town destroyed,

and for more than four centuries, the place was little more than an expanse of ruins. In 1620, the Franciscans built a church and a convent here, expanding them in 1730; it was around these structures that the modern town grew. The Franciscan church, finally, was knocked down in 1655 to make way for the larger and more impressive project designed by the Italian architect Giovanni Muzio.

The Church of the Annunciation is the largest Christian church in all of the Middle East; it was made possible through a grant from the State of Israel. The illustration by David Roberts clearly shows us the interior of the church as it appeared in April of 1839. The structure is articulated over three floors, which are connected by stairways.

The highest level is occupied by
the choir, and is reserved for
monks. The intermediate level
is open to the faithful, and the
lowest level conceals the ruins of
the Cave of the Annunciation.
The monument, which shows
a clear Baroque influence,
is lavishly bestrewn with
decoration - votive images,
candelabra, silver lamps,
exquisite damasks, all cover the
pillars and envelop the main altar.

20th April 1839

THE SHRINE OF THE ANNUNCIATION

Plate 213

20th April 1839

Situated beneath the Church of the Annunciation was a small subterranean chamber in which there stood an altar, supposedly marking the exact spot in which the Angel appeared before the Virgin Mary in order to announce the divine mission that awaited her.
The two columns that still stood on either side of the altar when David Roberts made his visit to Nazareth were said to have been the work of the Queen Helena, who supposedly had them erected on

the column simply levitated in midair without the slightest structural support, by divine will; nonetheless, to the mind of an unprejudiced observer, it seemed pretty clear that the fragment of column was solidly fastened to the ceiling. In fact, the upper section proved to be made of gray marble, while the lower section was without question a block of Cipolino marble.
All the same, the renown of these two columns amongst the

the site of the Annunciation because she had had a premonitory dream. One of the two columns, clearly visible in this illustration, had been shattered by a Turkish pasha who had come in avid search of hidden treasure; in the wake of such a desecration, it is said, the pasha lost his sight. The monks claimed that the upper section of

gullible pilgrims was such that each one of them would rub up against them reverently and with devotion, secure in the knowledge that such contact provided sure balm against all ills and calamities. And on the other hand, the reasoning of faith often sorely twists and mishandles the reasoning of logic, producing what could

only be called superstition; the most innocent-minded of superstitions, but superstition nonetheless.
And so tradition had it that it was precisely in the Grotto that the Virgin Mary spent a considerable portion of her youth, and above this tiny chamber stood the Holy House, which the Angels first

transported to Dalmatia, and
then to a woods near Recanati,
and finally to Loreto - all to
preserve it from profanation by
the Muslims. It should further
be noted that the earliest
author to identify the small
sanctuary of Loreto as the
"House of Nazareth" was
Pietro di Giorgio Tolomei da
Teramo, who wrote an account

in 1472 that was soon after
expanded upon by Gerolamo
Angelita, winning enormous
and widespread credence in the
popular imagination; further,
the popes that found
themselves in the situation of
conferring privileges to the
Sanctuary - Julius II and Leo
X - considered it little more
than a pious belief.

Convent of the Terra-Santa, Nazareth. April 21st 1839.

David Roberts

THE CONVENT OF THE TERRA SANTA, NAZARETH

Plate 214

20th April 1839

The town of Nazareth lies in an enchanting amphitheater of hills, embellished by olive groves, fig trees, almond trees, and cypresses; it occupies a strategic location that nearly all of the invaders of the Holy Land over the millennia have tried to occupy securely. Aside from the Church of the Annunciation, Nazareth boasts a number of other places that are holy to Christians, such as the Fountain of the Virgin, or what is commonly said to be the Workshop of Joseph, which forms part of the Franciscan Monastery of the Terra Santa. Just a mile out of town, moreover, stands the rock which has been venerated since ancient times as the site of the dramatic effort to throw Jesus down after his sermon in the Synagogue, as narrated by St. Luke.

At the foot of the rock stands a small Maronite Christian church.

In this illustration by Roberts, Nazareth appears as a tiny cluster of houses, dominated by the minaret of a mosque, and by the bulk of the Franciscan convent; the latter, built around 1632 on the foundations of an earlier church, and then partially fortified a century later, had just been restored and enjoyed a certain wealth. Nowadays, Nazareth is a sort of Christian enclave within the borders of Galilee, with a sizable Arab population.

Galilee has always been a transit spot, vulnerable to invaders, but especially a place of miracles. Only during the past few years has Galilee been rescued from the decline and neglect into which it had fallen and rescued from the encroaching elements.

If it has become the garden spot of Israel today, that is to the everlasting credit of the hard-working and caring Hebrew pioneers.

THE FOUNTAIN OF THE VIRGIN

Plate 215

20th April 1839

*T*he so-called Fountain of the Virgin, the only source of drinkable water in the area around Nazareth, was held in great respect by Christian pilgrims, because tradition held that Mary went out to draw water from it every day, during her youth. The fountain spills forth beneath the Greek Orthodox Church of the Assumption, set in a small niche beneath an arch, at the very spot where the Virgin is said to have been greeted and hailed by the Archangel

needs. The women shown in this illustration constitute an interesting documentation of the women's clothing during the first half of the nineteenth century; among other things, Roberts noted that many of them wore long bangles or chains made up of gold and silver coins, which hung on either side of their faces, forming a magnificent contrast with their long black tresses, and that the younger girls in particular were extremely lovely in appearance. Oddly enough,

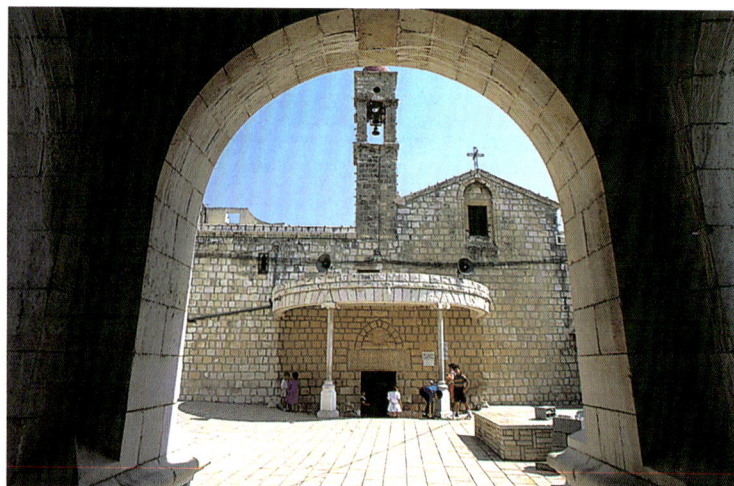

Gabriel. The basin was made out of what appeared to have originally been a sarcophagus. The spring itself, with a fairly feeble flow of water, lies at a certain distance, and the waters are conveyed to the fountain through a rough stone channel. During the summer, the source would dry up from time to time, and the inhabitants of Nazareth were then forced to go to other villages for their fresh water

although they realized that they were in the presence of a Christian, they made absolutely no effort to cover their faces. The dating of this illustration, like that of plates 91 and 94, should certainly be modified, according to what is stated in the painter's journal; here, Roberts clearly states that he was in Nazareth between the 19th and the 20th of April 1839.

Fountain of the Virgin, Nazareth. April 21. 1839.

From David Roberts's journal:

April 20th - Made two coloured drawings of the chapel, one of the Grotto or Chapel of the Annunciation, and two views of the town. Several objects of interest are pointed out to the pilgrim: the workshop of Joseph, the stone on which Christ sat with his disciples, and the fountain to which the Virgin went for water.

CANA OF GALILEE

Plate 216

21st April 1839

Roberts left Nazareth on the morning of the 21st of April, and reached Cana in Galilee around midday, after a pleasant canter that lasted a little longer than an hour. The village was formed by forty or fifty little huts, some of which were in ruins, and while its appearance might be unassuming if not actually squalid, the whole inspired him with an irrepressible sense of the holy. In Cana, in fact - according to the Gospels - Jesus performed His first miracle, changing water into wine at a wedding banquet, and, shortly thereafter, healing the son of the wealthiest man in the town who came to greet him - this upon his return from Judea. The priest of the little Greek Orthodox church that stood at the foot of the hill - and which was believed to have been built upon the remains of the home in which the miracle supposedly happened - showed Roberts a priceless relic - this, the priest said, was one of the jars in which Christ had transformed the water into wine. Not far from the church, a building lay in ruins, and it was generally indicated as the home in which Christ had lived as a guest for a certain period of time. Despite the descriptions offered by the Gospel and accepted in popular devotion, the exact location of the town of Cana is a matter of some controversy, and the current site is said to be variously Kefr Kenna, which is near Nazareth, and Kefr Qana, only a little distance off. Roberts remained in the village for only a few hours, and then continued his voyage, heading for the Sea of Galilee.

The Fountain of Cana

Plate 217

*T*he fountain shown in this illustration is believed to be the one from which Jesus is said to have drawn the water that he used in performing his first miracle; Roberts noted that the water was plentiful and remarkably pure, and that there were no other sources of fresh water for many miles around. And this fact would seem to reinforce the attribution, which was generally accepted. The large basin made of marble decorated with friezes that stood not far from the fountain was in fact a Roman sarcophagus, long since given over to use as a drinking trough for the domestic beasts, in accordance with a custom that had become fairly widespread in Palestine and in the entire Mediterranean basin. The women of Cana would go to the fountain every day, bearing jars made of the same materials, and the same size and shape as those described in the Bible. And the Christian pilgrims would often stay awhile around the fountain, quenching their thirst and participating in what almost seemed a sacred ceremony prior to entering the village. In ancient times, the miracle of the wedding banquet of Cana was depicted in the frescoes in the catacombs of Domitilla in Rome, in the mosaics of the Baptistery in Naples, and in those found in the Basilica of St. Apollinare Nuovo in Ravenna.

Afterwards, the "Wedding at Cana" was painted by Giotto in the Chapel of the Scrovegni, in Padua. During the Renaissance and the two centuries that followed it, it became a fairly common subject, used by Gérard David, by Longhi, and by Tintoretto, among others. The best known painting of the Wedding at Cana is certainly the one painted by Paolo Veronese, now at the Louvre, in which many famous personalities of the era appear as guests at the wedding banquet: Francis I, Charles V, Queen Mary I of England, better known as Bloody Mary, Suleiman the Magnificent, Titian, and Paolo Veronese himself, along with his brother.

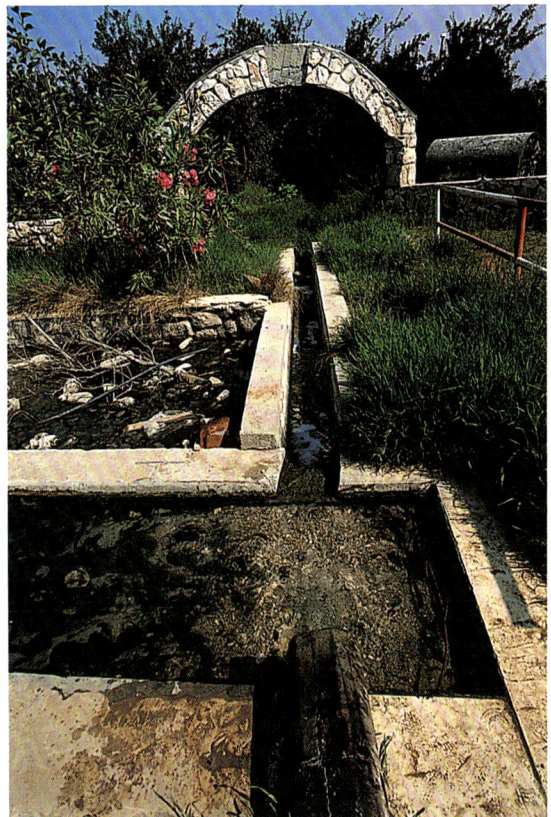

From David Roberts's journal:

21st, Sunday - ...There is a small Greek church, said to cover the place formerly occupied by the house in which the marriage took place. A ruined House is pointed out as the residence of our Saviour, and on entering the village we were shown a fountain from whence the water was said to have been taken.

21st April 1839

THE SEA OF GALILEE

Plate 218

21st April 1839

After leaving the village of Cana behind him and riding for about five hours through a pleasant landscape, Roberts finally came within sight of the Sea of Tiberias, a placid body of water upon whose enameled waters not a single vessel could be seen. From high atop the hill, at the foot of which stood the ruins of the ancient city of Tiberias - destroyed just a few years before by a terrible earthquake - the gaze of the English artist surveyed a panorama that was enchanting and at the same time majestic. Truly the jewel of Galilee, brilliant as an emerald, the Sea of Tiberias lies burrowed about six hundred fifty feet below sea level, held tight by a wreath of mountain peaks adorned with luxuriant vegetation. The lake receives the waters of the Jordan River, which rises at the foot of Mount Hermon and then runs down to the depression of the Dead Sea; one distinctive feature of this lake is its brackish water, populated by a great variety of fish. The shores of the lake were the setting for the preaching of Jesus, and the group of Apostles came into existence here.

According to the traditional interpretation of the Gospels, the miracle of the loaves and fish took place at Tabgha, while not far off is the home of St. Peter's home of Kapharnaon, as well as the Mount of the Beatitudes, where Jesus appeared before the Apostles. The ancient power that imbues the Sea of Galilee has long held sway over the imagination. Indeed, two thousand years ago the Jew historian Flavius Josephus, who wrote in Latin, was full of admiration in his description of the landscape surrounding the lake.

From David Roberts's journal:

April 21st, Sunday - Passing on through a beautiful country... we came in sight of the Sea of Galilee. Far to the left is Mount Hermon, and near to us is Safed, where the Jews expect the Messiah to reign forty years before entering Jerusalem...

THE LAKE OF TIBERIAS, VIEW TOWARDS MOUNT HERMON

Plate 219

21st April 1839

The Lake of Tiberias, also known as the Lake of Gennesareth or the Lake of Kinneret, is a small inland sea that formed toward the end of the Tertiary Period following the same tectonic depression that affected the Jordan Valley and led to the creation of the Dead Sea. The Dead Sea formed as a result of the interruption of the flow of the Jordan toward the Gulf of Aqaba. Over the millennia, the total aridity and high average temperature of the region, in combination with the shallowness and the greater surface area of the Dead Sea in comparison with the Sea of Tiberias, created a situation in which the evaporation was equal to and in some cases superior to the flow of the Jordan, so that the waters of the Dead Sea are constantly increasing in salinity and at the same time declining in volume. Regularly fed by the waters of the Jordan, which freshen the water somewhat, the Lake of Tiberias attains a depth of one hundred and sixty feet and constitutes a valuable reserve for the entire region. The remarkable location makes it subject to frequent winter tempests, an observation that is also made in the Gospels, while in the summer the surface is incessantly ruffled by a pleasant breeze. Because the water so abounds in fish, thousands of aquatic birds line the shores and the stands of reeds of this tiny "sea" just fourteen and a half miles long, with water so transparent that Roberts was dumbfounded. The artist spent much of the day at Tiberias on the 22nd of April, taking the time to tour the city and the surrounding countryside, making a few thoroughgoing sketches as he went. In this plate, Mount Hermon appears on the horizon in all its majesty, while at the foot of the hill lie the remains of the ancient town.

City of Tiberias, on the Sea of Galilee. April 22nd 1839

Town of Tiberias, looking towards Lebanon.

TIBERIAS, LOOKING TOWARD LEBANON

Plate 220

21st April 1839

*T*iberias was a Roman city famous for its curative hot springs. Today, it has become a winter spa and a well equipped tourist attraction. The city is also well known outside the narrow boundaries of Israel. It was founded in 26 B.C. by Herod Antipas, tetrarch of Galilee, the son of Herod the Great. The city's name was clearly intended to honor the emperor Tiberius. There are those, however, who attribute the name Tiberias to the Hebrew term "tabur," which means belly-button, since the lake that bears the same name has something like the shape of a belly-button. Following the destruction of the Temple of Jerusalem, a major rabbinical school was founded here. It was at that school that great scholars developed the phonetics of Hebrew writing. During the reign of Constantine, Tiberias was an episcopal see, but the city was conquered by the Arabs in A.D. 637. It then became the capital of the province of Jordan. During the First Crusade, Tiberias was occupied by the Christians and was ceded as part of the feud of Tancred. In 1187, however, it was returned to Arab rule, and four centuries later it fell under the sway of the Turks, who held the city until World War I. Each of these various occupying nations left marks of their rule in the urban fabric of the city. Two of the most intriguing monuments, however, are certainly the tomb of the Rabbi Meir Ba'al Haness and the tomb of the rabbi and martyr Akiva, both of which are sacred destinations for Jewish pilgrims. This view of the city and the lake, set beneath the snowy peaks of the mountains of Lebanon, may be visually striking, but it is also quite important in historical terms. Roberts, in fact, believed that the ruins that can be seen in the foreground were the remains of the ancient baths of Tiberias. This hypothesis is supported by the presence of numerous hot springs in the immediate vicinity. In Hebrew, these springs are called Hame Tverla, and they are said to have astonishing qualities for the treatment of rheumatism.

From David Roberts's journal:

21st April, Sunday - To the south the Jordan flows from the lake to the Dead Sea, and close to the lake lies the ancient town of Tiberias, which, with 400 of its inhabitants, was destroyed by an earthquake some years since... the ruins of a small mosque stand near the entrance to the town, and we passed to-day the foundations of more than one ancient city with excavations in the rocks.

TIBERIAS, SEEN FROM THE WALLS

Plate 221

Tiberias was largely laid waste by an earthquake in January 1837, and when Roberts visited the place it still was nothing more than an expanse of ruins, amidst which the population wandered in shock, battered by tragedy. Few buildings had survived the disaster, and the remains of a mosque were visible at the entrance to the town. Here and there amidst the rubble a few huts stood, where a number of elderly Jews lived, who had come there to spend the last days of their lives, through the generosity of their brethren scattered throughout the world. Tiberias is in fact one of the four holy cities of Judea, along with Jerusalem, Hebron, and Safed. The last named city appears in the distance in the illustration, with the mountains of Lebanon in the distance. This city, which is believed to be the site of the ancient Bethulia, became one of the greatest centers for the study of the Talmud and for Talmudic culture after the Jews were expelled from Spain, in 1492. The exiles, after founding a major rabbinical school, set up the first printing press in Israel in 1563. In Safed, great men of learning found refuge, such as Moshe Cordovero, Isaac Louria, Israel Najara, and a great many others, who devoted themselves to the study of the Holy Scriptures, developing an approach to exegesis that brought them to an understanding of the Cabala, a term used to describe a mystical Jewish system of interpretation of the Scriptures, based on the belief that every word, letter, number, and even accent of the Scriptures contains mysteries. Roberts left the Sea of Tiberias on the afternoon of the 22nd of April, headed for the coast, and spent the night camped near the only fountain that exists in the area.

From David Roberts's journal:

April 22nd - To-day I made few sketches of the town, or rather of its remains - for every part has been more or less destroyed by earthquakes. The city wall, which is Saracenic, has been built of large square stones, now thrown down and rent from top to bottom...

22nd April 1839

St. Jean d'Acre,
SEEN FROM THE SEA

Plate 222

St Jean d'Acre. April 25th 1839.

23rd April 1839

Extending along the furthest tip of land at the mouth of Haifa Bay Akko, or Acre, is one of the oldest cities in the world: silent, brooding, and enclosed by walls built by the Crusaders, it seems to be watching over the eternal vastness of the Mediterranean. Today it is Israel's most important harbor. For centuries it was coveted by invaders and interlopers for its strategic location on the gulf that bears its name. Founded in the remote eras of antiquity, Akko has been ruled by Egyptians, Assyrians, Persians, and Romans. Invaded by the Arabs in A.D. 638, it was besieged by Richard the Lion-Hearted and taken from Saladin in 1191, becoming the capital of the Crusaders' Kingdom. Its European name, St. Jean d'Acre, derives from the Hospitaler Brothers of St. John, better known as the Knights of St. John, who made it their capital. In 1291, the Muslims returned and the city quickly fell into disrepair and ruin. It was not until the eighteenth century that the Turkish emirs restored the city, and in 1799, stoutly resisted a lengthy siege laid by Napoleon; the British fleet had assisted the besieged city. Roberts reached the city during the early hours of the afternoon of the 23rd and was immediately impressed by the grandeur of the place. A large warship lay at anchor in the harbor, while the city's fortifications towered over the plain in sharp contrast with the blue of the sea, forming a panorama that, in Roberts's own words, would have satisfied the esthetic sense of Turner himself. Roberts ordered the tents pitched near the city walls and set out to wander the streets of the city where he soon realized that many of the buildings still bore evident scars from the recent war.

This lithograph by Roberts emphasizes the odd Ottoman architectural style of the city, chiefly the result of the urban planning and renovation carried out by Ahmed el Jazzar, the seventeenth-century pasha who was responsible for the construction of the mosque that bears his name, the largest in all Israel. Built in 1781, it is still a major spiritual center for the Muslim community in Israel.

From David Roberts's journal:

April 23rd - Left at half-past 8 for St. Jean d'Acre, which we came in sight of at 3 o'clock. The situation is striking - a promontory to the north of the bay, Mount Carmel rising on the south...

St. Jean d'Acre,
SEEN FROM THE LAND

<u>Plate 223</u>

23rd April 1839

The ancient stones of Akko, erected over the centuries of a history that has been stormy and often bloody - the Palace of the Knights, the subterranean crypt of the Crusaders, the Arabic caravansaries - speak eloquently of merchants and warriors, of sieges beyond count, of vast destruction followed by rebirth, and of tireless, incessant toil. In the past, among the trades plied in Akko there was the extraction and the application of purple dye, as well as the manufacture of glass. In this connection, we should note that the Roman historian Pliny considered that the city deserved credit for the invention of the techniques vital to the production of glass. Known in Roman times as Colonia Claudia Felix, the adjective "Felix," meaning happy or blessed, was a term that clearly referred to opulence or prosperity. Mentioned often in the Bible and in the papyri of the Pharaohs of Ancient Egypt, Akko had always been a center of crucial importance to the economic prosperity of the

entire region; although the city faced some extremely dire moments, it always survived with great aplomb. Roberts arrived in Akko during an extremely serious military and political crisis, and the plate we reproduce here bears witness to the military history of the period. The troops of the pasha of Egypt had taken the city in 1832, badly trouncing the Turkish army; seven years later, the same Turkish army invaded Syria, but was once again defeated at Nizip, once again frustrated in the attempt to reach the bay of Akko. The city, therefore, was held by a sizable Egyptian garrison; Roberts here portrays the garrison as it conducted military exercises before the city walls. The following year, following a renewed Egyptian rejection of the terms offered for a compromise, the fleet of Great Britain bombarded the city, and a British expeditionary force was sent into Syria. In short, the Egyptians were forced to abandon the entire region; in compensation, they were recognized to be free of the Ottoman Empire.

Haifa, looking towards Mount Carmel

Plate 224

24 April 1839

After sketching a few more views of Akko, Roberts set out for Mt. Carmel, riding along the bayshore. After crossing the riverbed of the Kishon, made famous by the song of Deborah and Barak, he reached the port of Haifa, where he was forbidden to enter as soon as he announced that he was arriving from the south. A new epidemic of the plague had in fact broken out near Jaffa. The Englishman, nevertheless, halted long enough to sketch an overall view of the city, including himself in the sketch, shown drawing while dressed in Eastern clothing. The earliest documentation of the city that we have dates from the fourth century B.C., but throughout antiquity and during the Arab occupation it was a place of no particular importance. It was not until the town was conquered by the Crusaders that it began to develop as the port of the Frankish kingdom of Palestine, with the name of Caiphas. It was destroyed in 1191 by Saladin, and it remained a humble village until the eighteenth century, when it was entirely rebuilt.

The port expanded rapidly and gained in importance during the nineteenth century. Today Haifa is the most important commercial port and destination for tourists in Israel. Here all of the products of the Jezreel Valley are brought, from an area that was once a marsh and is now the breadbasket for the entire region. The urban fabric from the trading sections of the port climbs the slopes of Mt. Carmel, luxuriant with sumptuous gardens from which one can look out over the bay as far as Akko and to the hills of Lebanon beyond. The convent that stands atop Mt. Carmel, clearly visible in this illustration, is probably where the name of the famous order of the Carmelite friars originated. Roberts was received there with great kindness and courtesy. The monks showed him, among other things the chapel, then unfinished, which was being built over the cavern in which the vision of the Virgin appeared to Elijah. After sharing a pleasant meal with his newfound friends, Roberts left the monastery at sunset and rode four hours by moonlight, and then camped for the night.

From David Roberts's journal:

April 24th - We passed on, and ascended Mount Carmel, where we were received with great kindness by the monks. They showed us the chapel, still unfinished, which, they say, covers the cave in which Elijah saw a vision of the Holy Virgin. The design is Italian, and very elegant. We saw also a statue of Elijah trampling on the priests of Baal, but they were proudest of a Virgin and Child, just received from Genoa. We ascended the belfry, from which the scene is very fine...

THE RUINS OF AN IONIC TEMPLE

Plate 225

25th-26th April 1839

An insistent and unfortunate rain forced the entire company to spend the better part of the 25th of April in their tents; in the afternoon, after making a short distance, Roberts decided to set up camp near a fountain dating from Roman times. The following morning, the caravan passed by a small village, called Nakhura, and began to follow an ancient Roman road, which for many stretches appeared still to be in excellent condition. At the peak of a slight rise, the Englishman

clear sign that the complex had been razed to the ground by one of the earthquakes that were so frequent in the area. In this connection, the artist was put out to note that neither these noble ruins nor the city that must in all likelihood have stood around the temple had a name, and that for long years they had lain in undeserved oblivion. Fragments of sculptures and the rubble of walls lay scattered over an enormous expanse of ground, now covered in part by sand dunes and patches of

ran into the ruins of a great Greek temple, the front of which must have measured one hundred ninety-seven feet across, while the depth was probably double, in obediance to the most typical classical standards. Shafts of columns and Ionic capitals, in an excellent state of preservation, were tumbled in great confusion with other, Doric columns, a

vegetation. Roberts conjectured that these might have been the last vestiges of a city founded by Alexander the Great.
Even the surrounding region appeared to have been intensely cultivated long ago.
Leaving the ruins of the temple behind them, the travellers set out again along the road to Tyre, and they were soon within sight of Cape Blanco.

Ruins called Om. El Hamed near

April 25th 1839.

David Roberts R.A.

From David Robert's journal:

*April 26th - On a height we found the
remains of an extensive Greek temple...
This building must have been at least
400 feet in length, and 200 feet in
depth, and it is singular as it has
passed unnoticed...*

CAPE BLANCO

Plate 226

26th April 1839

In the early hours of the afternoon of the 26th of April, Roberts and his travelling companions began to climb the daunting trail cut into the sheer cliff walls of Cape Blanco, also known as Ras-el-Abiad. A lowering sky hemmed in the horizon, while huge storm clouds gathered around the promontory; from far below came the dull muttering of waves breaking against the shoals, several hundred feet beneath. The steep little track was made even more perilous now and again by avalanches and landslides, and a low wall of teetering rocks was the only safeguard between the wayfarer and the void. The trail wound its way over rocks worn low by the passage of thousands of caravans and countless carts; two deep tracks had been worn into the yielding limestone. The promontory was completely exposed to the western winds,

and received the direct blast of storms blowing in from the open Mediterranean; heavy seas struck at the unprotected base of the promontory, driving the spray straight up and dousing even the steep mule track. Under ordinary conditions, Cape Blanco is certainly one of the most charming sites on the entire Lebanese coast, but on the day David Roberts visited there, the spectacle provided by the unbridled forces of nature cast a sort of spell, and the artist became determined to stay as long as was required to sketch the remarkable scene.
Climbing down the northern slope of Cape Blanco, the travellers soon reached the Phoenician plain and came to the springs called the Wells of Solomon, the waters of which were used to drive numerous waterwheels, and then to feed the aqueduct leading to the nearby city of Tyre.

494

TYRE, SEEN FROM THE ISTHMUS

Plate 227

Passing the Wells of Solomon, after roughly an hour's hike, the travellers came to the ancient city of Tyre. As they approached the site, the remains of the Phoenician city became clearer to the eye, particularly in those areas where the wind had swept away the sand. The glorious metropolis of bygone millennia had been reduced to little more than a humble collection of houses. The mosque in the town appeared to Roberts to be so tattered and shabby that he felt that the ancient prophecy - that the mosque would one day be transformed into a boulder upon which the fishermen would stretch their nets to dry - must already have come true.

The houses were in relatively good condition, however, and the streets were reasonably clean. A few ships rode at anchor in the port, but the city that had once settled colonies across the vast expanse of the Mediterranean was no more than a shadow of her former self, reduced to a petty trade in tobacco, lumber, and coal. The population had shrunk to just three thousand, and the town was huddled at the tip of the promontory, while the urban settlement on the mainland had long ago been completely abandoned. The town's supply of fresh water was amply provided by two springs that bubbled forth not far from the sea, but which were believed to be linked in some way - by some conduit running under the isthmus - to the springs of Ras-el-Ain, an hour's march away in the plain. The sole surviving ruins of the city on the mainland lay hidden under the dunes, or else had been incorporated into the breakwater that was said to have been built by Alexander the Great during the siege, and which turned the island of Tyre into a peninsula.

In this illustration by Roberts, we can clearly see, to the left, the main port and the tower that stood near the two fountains; on the opposite side, one can see the ruins of the Christian cathedral. The tower in the foreground was connected to the island by the ruins of a stone wall, and may once have formed part of a fortified complex built by the Saracens.

From David Roberts's journal:

April 26th - By-and-bye we approached the fountains called the Wells of Solomon, the water from which drives a number of mills, besides supplying the aqueduct for the use of Tyre. Another hour's ride along the sands brought us in front of ancient Tyre...

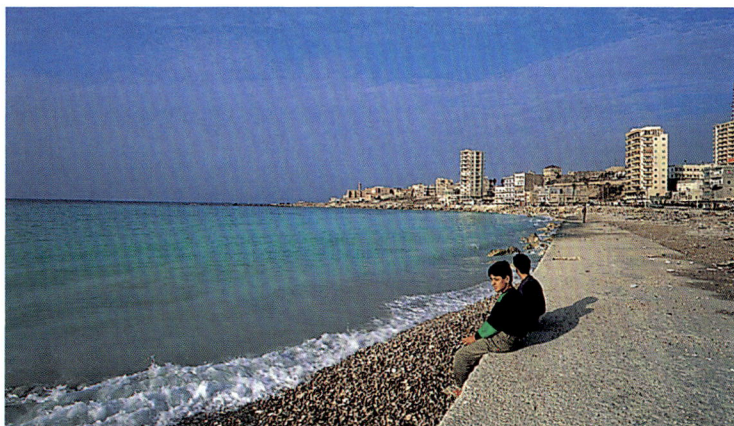

26th April 1839

The port of Tyre

Plate 228

27th April 1839

According to linguists, the modern name of Tyre - Sur - in the Semitic dialect spoken by the local population of Phoenicians origins, means rock. Today, the same term refers to a fishing village in southern Lebanon. Up until the time of Alexander the Great, the promontory upon which the modern city now stands was still made up of two islands, and was separated from the mainland by a narrow stretch of sea; in time, accumulations of sand turned this into an isthmus. Prior to the tenth century B.C., the larger island was the site of the city proper, with the port and the merchant's quarter, while on the smaller, southern island, stood a temple consecrated to a divinity which the Greeks associated with Olympian Zeus. Hiram I, King of Tyre, at last decided to join the two islands with a Cyclopean masonry; over the centuries that followed, the northern basin was enclosed with a massive breakwater, which traced a curve that ran parallel with the island's coastline. The imposing remains of this barrier, which can still be seen, just breaking the surface of the sea, are clearly shown in this illustration by Roberts, who wrote that he had been able to glimpse, at the base of the underwater wall, fragments of huge marble or stone pillars, arrayed regularly side by side; these remarkable foundation stones, which may have been made with material taken from other constructions, can be clearly seen in the plate, almost at the center of the scene.

From David Roberts's journal:

April 27th - Made some sketches. Found a ruinous tower of Saracenic construction - the stones of great size, with foundations of similar structures stretching across the isthmus, jutting into the sea.

David Roberts R.A.

Tyre. ancient Tyre. april 27th 1839.

General view of Tyre

Plate 229

27th April 1839

Founded roughly in 2800 B.C. by the Phoenicians, Tyre was for many years under the rule of the pharaohs of Egypt. It won back its independence during the reign of Rameses II, and then enjoyed a period of great prosperity. Tyre was, in fact, a city of great craftsmen who, with remarkable skill, practiced the arts of metallurgy, dyeing with the color purple, weaving, and glass manufacture. Their trade in these products extended throughout the Mediterranean, all the way into Spain and northwestern Africa, where many colonies were founded; some of these colonies later became powerful states in their own right. By the end of the eighth century B.C., Tyre was taken by the Assyrians. Though under foreign rule, the memory of the city's history and the advantages of being left politically unfettered led repeatedly to wholesale attempts at rebellion. These efforts were quashed with equal persistence, however. In the years that followed, Tyre paid tribute to Egypt, and then to the Babylonian Empire. In the wake of the decline of Babylonia, Tyre fell prey in A.D. 538 to Emperor Cyrus. The Persian ruler showed clemency and offered the city considerable freedom, thus ensuring that he was paid absolute allegiance. This was a major factor in the resistance Tyre made to the siege of Alexander the Great, who finally took the town. Once the Macedonian general died, Tyre was long fought over by the Lagids and the Seleucids. In the end, it was annexed by the Romans in 64 B.C., yet even under the Empire, it maintained its standing as a free city, though its times of great prosperity were in fact long over. In A.D. 335, it was the site of a Christian synod, and later it was handed over from Byzantine domination to Arab rule. It was then assaulted and taken by the Crusaders in 1124. Some one hundred-sixty years later the town was recaptured by Muslims who, worried that the position was tactically untenable, preferred to destroy it. Tyre was partially rebuilt over the centuries that followed, but it certainly never again attained its long-lost splendor.

SAREPTA

Plate 230

*S*etting out from the city of Tyre around eleven o'clock in the morning, Roberts and his fellow travellers continued along their way northwards, skirting the coast. After a while, they descried on the horizon what must surely be the monumental remains of a great city of the past, which they soon discovered was the noble Sarepta. Mentioned in both the Old Testament and the New Testament, the city enjoyed periods of great prosperity, under the Roman Empire and later under Arab domination; it was elevated to a bishopric during the Crusades, and in the twelfth century it was fortified and a new port was built. Later, because of the frequent Saracen raids, the coastal area was progressively abandoned, and the population took refuge inland, on a hill, where the village of Surafend now stands. Not far from the village, toward the sea, Roberts noticed a small mosque, supposedly built on the site of the house where the prophet Elias was believed to have found shelter, and where the prophet brought the widow's son back to life with prayer. In this illustration, which depicts the area surrounding the ancient Sarepta, the scenery is as different as can be from that of the earlier views of southern Palestine. The highlands have a sharper profile, and the chain of the Lebanon Mountains, covered with snow, appears on the horizon.

From David Roberts's journal:

April 27th - Leaving Tyre at 11A.M., we came upon the remains of what must have been a large town, with two beautiful little bays. The hill behind is perforated with caves.

27th April 1839

SIDON. Looking towards LEBANON

VIEW OF SIDON, TOWARDS LEBANON

Plate 231

27th April 1839

S idon can be seen on the horizon just a short way from the ruins of Sarepta, but the travellers were caught by nightfall long before they had attained their destination that day. To make things worse, a platoon of guards stopped them outside the city and ordered them to show their health certificates, since they had received word of the epidemic that swept through Palestine. Neither Roberts nor any of his travelling companions possessed any such documents; the irate Englishman made the guards understand however that he possessed a safe-conduct, given him personally by Mohammed Ali Pasha. He told them that if they continued to hinder his passage there would certainly be unpleasant consequences on the following day, as soon as he was able to inform the governor of Sidon. These words had the desired effect, and one of the guards was assigned to accompany them to a place on the beach, just south of the town. By the time they reached the beach, they were weary and worn, but to their surprise a wind storm sprang up, and it was only through the greatest of efforts that they finally succeeded in pitching their tents. Although the illustration reproduced here does not depict the episode in question, of the four plates devoted to Sidon, it certainly best describes the city as Roberts saw it, with the mountains of Lebanon in the background and the broad bay looking out to the Mediterranean.

SIDON, SEEN FROM THE SOUTH

Plate 232

28th April 1839

The escorting guard who had spent the night in the encampment on the beach conducted the Englishman and his travelling companions into the city on the 28th of April, making way for them everywhere they went and calling incessantly upon the crowd to let them pass, warning all those passing or still present that their companions were still under quarantine.

In his journal, Roberts noted that Sidon certainly enjoyed an enchanting location, perched as it was atop a high promontory overlooking the sea and boasting a stout and well-protected harbor. The city's hinterland was fertile and well cultivated; the olive groves were numerous, as was the case throughout Syria. Everywhere orange groves and vineyards alternated with fig trees and pomegranate trees. Long rows of mulberry bushes indicated that the silkworm breeding industry was quite prosperous. The city itself gave off a sense of tranquil prosperity, with clean and solidly built houses, wide streets, and well-dressed, healthy citizens.

The sole defect was the general absence of any worthy relics of the past. In fact, during his rapid tour of the city, Roberts noted only a few granite columns lying headlong in the dust and some mosaic floors. The small building that stands in the foreground in this illustration was venerated by Jews as well as Christians and Muslims as the Tomb of Zebulon, one of the ten sons of Jacob, and founder and namesake of one of the Tribes of Israel.

THE CITADEL OF SIDON

Plate 233

28th April 1839

espite the many difficulties besetting him, Roberts was quite determined to make a few sketches of the city, and one of the subjects that interested him greatly was the Citadel, a massive structure built out into the sea a few yards off the beach, connected to terra firma by a solid bridge made of stone blocks. Today, the entire fortified complex lies in almost total ruins, but at Roberts's time it was still in fairly good condition. Although this plate clearly shows a number of features without a doubt, and in all likelihood, from the time of St. Louis, who was also King Louis IX of France. Along a coastline that is notoriously scanty in good harbors and that is often swept by insidious and even violent winds, the presence of a port as safe and advantageous as Sidon was practically a title to active trade and great prosperity.

The possession of this town, therefore, was of crucial strategic importance, and was well worth the effort of establishing secure military

typical of Islamic architecture, such as the low central dome and the lobed arch on the right side of the structure, the foundation of the fortress dates back to the Crusades, defenses. This explains why the Muslims, as soon as they took the city, immediately set about restoring the Crusaders' Citadel, adopting it as their stronghold.

From David Roberts's journal:

*28th April, Sunday - ... I got one or
two splendid views of an ancient fort,
connected with the land by a bridge of
several arches. The houses of Sidon
seem large, but I could discover few
antiquities...*

SIDON

Plate 234

28th April 1839

The earliest documentation of the name Sidon appears in a number of Egyptian documents dating from the thirteenth century B.C. Governed by kings, like other Phoenician cities, Sidon skillfully maneuvered amidst the struggles between Egypt, Babylonia, and the Hittites; meanwhile it prospered greatly on the trade between the Near East and the Mediterranean basin. After Sidon fell under the domination of Nineveh, it was caught up in the struggle against the Assyrians. The latter destroyed the city in 675 B.C. When the city rose once again to renewed splendor, it first became a vassal of the Egyptians, then fell into the hands of the Babylonians, and lastly came under Persian rule. The Persians razed Sidon, but in time the city was rebuilt and, in 332 B.C. it surrendered willingly to Alexander the Great. Following the premature death of the great conqueror, the city became a vassal of first the Lagid and later the Seleucid sovereigns. In 64 B.C., it finally fell to the Romans. In ancient times, Sidon, now called Saida, had always been a city of great traders and great manufacturers. The city's merchants and businessmen sailed their ships to every port on the Mediterranean, and even ventured beyond the strait of Gibraltar, plying the Atlantic coast of Europe all the way up to Brittany and down along the shores of Africa. The colonization carried out by this Phoenician city is documented by a number of coins dating from the fifth and the sixth centuries B.C. Upon these coins, it is possible to read: "Sidon, mother of Carthage, Hippona, Cithius, Tyre." The inhabitants of ancient Sidon are also credited with having transformed the hieroglyphic system of writing practiced by the Egyptians into a purely phonetic - and hence alphabetic - system of writing, the true ancestor of modern writing. In the earliest years of Christianity, Sidon was certainly given the status of an episcopal see, and the earliest name of a bishop of Sidon that appears in an official document is that of Theodore, who in A.D. 325 took part in the First Council of Nicaea. During the Crusades, Sidon was at first ignored by the knights of Christendom, but its highly strategic location made it essential for them to take it. Sidon was repeatedly besieged by Baldwin I, the new king of Jerusalem, and it finally fell in 1111. Saladin retook it and restored it to Muslim rule, and the city changed hands again and again, undergoing bloody destruction each time that it did so. Once it had definitively become an Islamic possession, Sidon enjoyed in the seventeenth century a new period of splendor due to the tireless labors of the Druse Emir Fakhr-el-Din, who embellished the city with

magnificent palaces. As the port of Beirut gradually grew in prosperity and influence, the port of Sidon, experienced an equally rapid decline. Still Sidon conserved its opulence and the appearance of sober dignity that Roberts had an opportunity to appreciate so thoroughly.

ARRIVAL IN BAALBEC

Plate 235

O n the same day that he reached Sidon, where his stay was necessarily quite brief due to the problems mentioned above, Roberts set off once again in the direction of the fabled Baalbec. After a stretch of coastline, the small group of travellers began to climb an extension of the Mountains of Lebanon. At the peak, they camped for the night. The next day was spent crossing the difficult and tiring coastal chain, though the obstacles of the trip were in part offset by the remarkable beauty of the natural setting. The old Roman road ran through the territory of the Druse, a people that belonged to a sect of the Muslim religion. That evening, the English artist confided to the pages of his diary that, since it had been impossible to replenish their supplies at Sidon, they were running dangerously short on foodstuffs. They were completely out of tea, wine, and alcohol, they still had a little coffee but no sugar at all, and they had used up all their fuel oil. The only consolation they could afford before lying down to sleep at night was a pipeful of tobacco. On the morning of the 30th of April, the group of travellers found itself in the region inhabited by the Maronites, a local community of Christians that had preserved its independence over the course of many centuries - the fields here appeared luxuriant and well-kept, and the people were

healthy and cheerful. The earliest light of dawn on the 1st of May caught the travellers between the mountains of Lebanon and those of the Antilebanon. By noon they had reached a mountain town called Ab Elias and, by afternoon, the provincial capital, Zahleh. There, as they were taking on supplies, Roberts was told that an insurrection was under way in Baalbec.

In the most martial manner he could muster, Roberts requested an audience with the sheik of the city, and showed him his safe-conduct. The governor explained that the revolt had not yet actually broken out, but that it was expected from one moment to the next. He therefore ensured Roberts of his personal support and gave him an escort of three armed men.

At last, on the 2nd of May, Roberts came within sight of Baalbec, where he set up camp in a torrential rain.

The thunderstorms continued all night long, so that by morning Roberts's tent had almost been battered down; the artist had an incipient fever and he was compelled to stay in bed the whole following day.

29th April-3rd May 1839

BAALBEC, THE ANCIENT HELIOPOLIS

Plate 236

4th–5th May 1839

The origins and the earliest history of Baalbec are lost in obscurity. Only the name indicates a clear relationship with the god Baal and, indeed, signifies "City of Baal." It would seem, however, that the original religions of the Syrian city must have been that of Hadad, a god that was, during Hellenistic times, identified with the sun and later with Zeus. From that point onward, the town was called Heliopolis, or "City of the Sun." The cult of Heliopolitan Jupiter, whose earliest relics date from Roman times, would seem to be the result of a far more ancient transposition of religious trappings. Heliopolis is mentioned by the historian Flavius Josephus in connection with his account of the expedition of Pompey that took place in 64 B.C., as well as by Strabo. It became a Roman colony and military base at the beginning of the first century A.D., probably under Augustus, and was called Julia Augusta Felix Heliopolitana - its religious importance was recognized and even fostered by the Romans in the context of their policy at the time of friendly encouragement of neighboring religions. Because of its location, the city was not an important trading center, nor was it situated along fundamental arteries of commerce. The renown of the sanctuary of Heliopolitan Jupiter is documented by the spread of its cult to various regions of the Empire. Trajan himself, just prior to his expedition against the Parthians, in A.D. 115, supposedly consulted the oracle. The importance of the city remained quite considerable until the first half of the third century A.D. and is documented by a great many inscriptions and coins. Under Constantine and Theodosius, the city's temples were converted into Christian churches, and later became an episcopal see. Many events subsequently reduced the city to ruins and rubble: The invasion of the Arabs beginning in A.D. 634; the Crusades that transformed the temples into fortresses; the conquest by Saladin; the plunder by Tamerlane; and the earthquakes of 1664 and 1750. The earliest reports of the ruins of Baalbec came from Martin Baumgarten who visited the site in 1508. But it was not until the beginning of the nineteenth century that the ancient sanctuary city became the destination of men and women of letters and scholars. The first restoration was begun in 1870 and work was resumed with even greater fervor following the visit of the Emperor Wilhelm II. An immense and thorough task of research and published documentation was carried on first by Wiegand and later, by the French school of archeology. The modern city, located in a fertile plain at the foot of the Antilebanon, occupies only a part of the original city plan.

From David Roberts's journal:

4th - Have begun my studies of the temple, of the magnificence of which it is impossible to convey any idea, either by pencil or pen. The beauty of its form, the exquisite richness of its ornament, and the vast magnitude of its dimensions, are altogether unparalleled...
The capitals (Corinthian) are of the most exquisite proportion, and, with the ornamentation of the frieze and cornice, are so deeply and boldly cut, that I should think they must have been carved after being erected.

THE SANCTUARY OF BAALBEC

Plate 237

4th–5th May 1839

The western section of the city was largely occupied by the ruins of the great sanctuary of the triad of Heliopolis. These ruins constitute one of the most imposing architectural complexes of all antiquity to have survived in modern times. The giant structure dominated the city's skyline, even though it had been built in the plain, and it was overtopped only by the nearby hill of the Acropolis. The main temple, which was consecrated to Jupiter-Hadad, was made up of four sections arranged along an axis running from east to west. The propylaea along the frontal portico consisted of twelve columns and led into a great hexagonal vestibule some one hundred and ninety-seven feet in width surrounded, in turn, by columns. This space, the walls of which were adorned by niches, formed an intermediate feature, enclosed and self-contained, that served as a passage to the great courtyard standing before the temple proper. The courtyard was four hundred and forty-three feet in length and about three hundred and seventy feet in width. The courtyard was bounded on three sides by porticoes and exedrae, whose monolithic columns made of pink granite can now be seen in the Mosque of Baalbec. At the center of the courtyard stood a great altar in the shape of a four-story tower, with the terrace accessible through an interior stairway.

The temple was two hundred and ninety-five feet in length and one hundred and seventy-seven feet in width. A peripteral Corinthian construction with ten columns along the short sides and nineteen along the longer sides, it stood upon a giant podium that measured forty-six feet high. Of this remarkable structure, only six columns remain standing along the southern side, some ninety-two feet in height; many of the bases of the other columns are still in place. All around, the colossal ruins of the cella can be seen, with fragments of columns and trabeations.

The construction of the great sanctuary must have gone on for several centuries. In the past, it was believed that Antoninus Pius had the temple built, but it has since been determined that the great terrace of the temple dates from the beginning of the first century A.D., and that the temple itself dates from around A.D. 60, while the propylaea probably date from around the time of Septimius Severus.

The hexagonal courtyard dates from around the middle of the third century A.D.

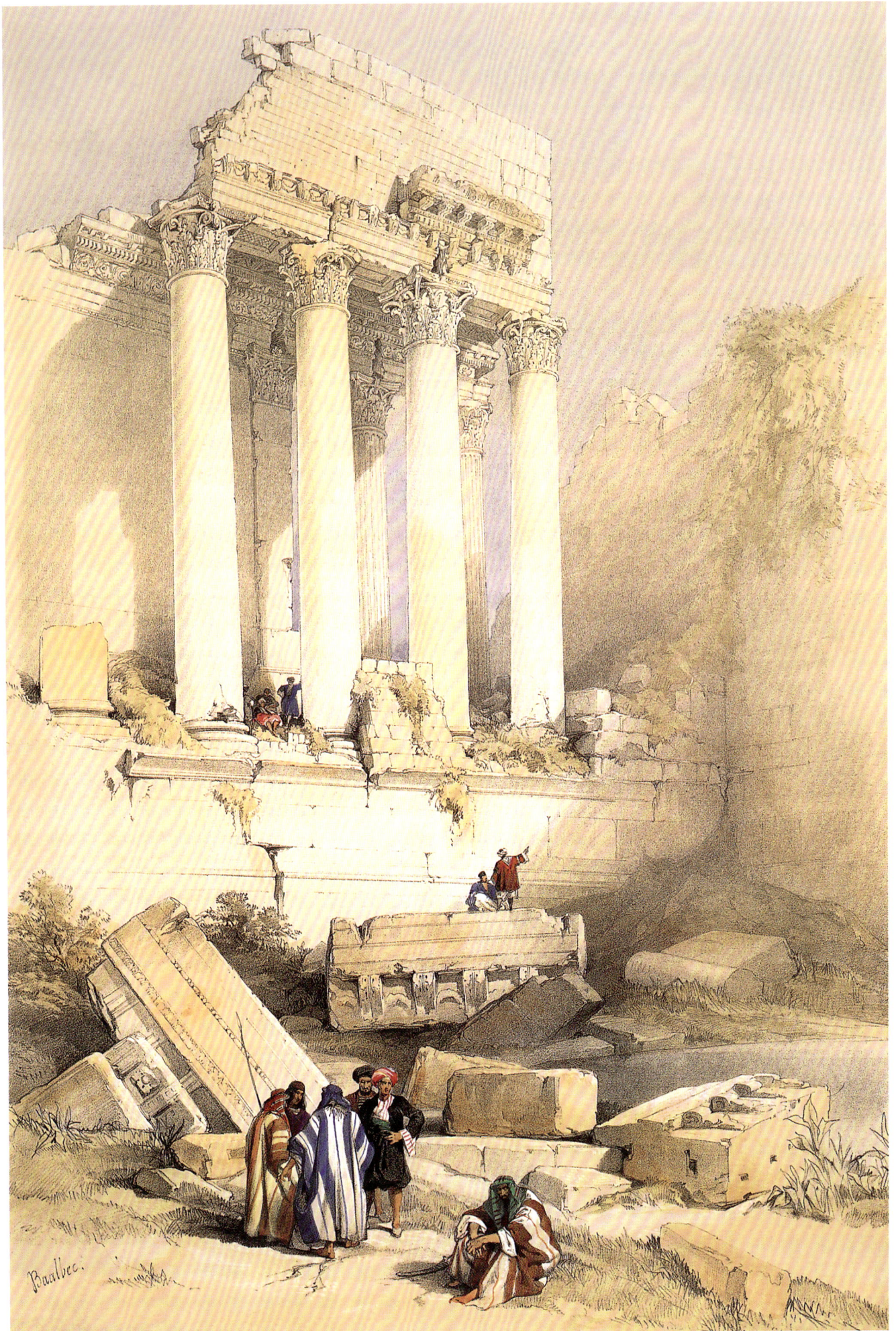

Baalbec.

THE CIRCULAR TEMPLE AT BAALBEC

Plate 238

5th May 1839

*T*his illustration portrays one of the architectural wonders of the ancient world: the Temple of Venus. Located near the great temple along the decuman - the principal road of the city - the temple is a small circular and peripteral building with six smooth Corinthian columns, set on a tall podium, and connected to the cella by five indented arcs of a circle. Before the cella, with an interior diameter of just under thirty feet, stands a tetrastile pronaos and a stairway of about twenty steps. Externally, the wall of the cella presents four niches, doubled on the inside and on two superimposed orders. The entire, remarkably elegant structure was probably covered by a small cupola.

This little temple, dedicated to Tyche or to Venus Atargatis, was lavishly decorated with high-relief friezes and statues. Of those, only the bases in the niches still survive. This illustration bears the date of the 5th of May; the same day on which a small mishap befell Roberts that was to have unforeseen consequences: early that morning a servant came to tell him that the mules of his expedition had been requisitioned for the transport of grain to feed the troops. The Englishman lost no time and immediately hastened to the residence of the local governor. The governor, reclining upon his divan, was surrounded by one of the most remarkable and picturesque courts that Roberts had seen in all his years. None of the individuals present wore the same outfit; two richly dressed Beduin chiefs in particular stood out for their sartorial splendor. Groups of attendants bustled here and there. Glittering threads and exquisite clothing could be seen everywhere, and the scene was as colorful as could be. The Englishman was invited to sit at the left hand of the lord of the house, and was able to display his safe-conduct pass only after he had been served coffee. To his enormous surprise no one gave the document a second glance as it was written in Turkish. Nonetheless, they did recognize the signature of Pasha Abbas, and the governor apologized for the misunderstanding. He gave the order to return the animals to Roberts immediately. Roberts then expressed the desire to visit Damascus, which was only a two-day ride away. The high official immediately offered him an escort soldier and a letter of presentation to the governor of that city.

THE EASTERN PORTICO OF THE TEMPLE OF BACCHUS

Plate 239

*T*o the south of the Great Temple, oriented in the same direction and in a far superior state of conservation, is the Small Temple, also said to be a temple of Bacchus. This is a peripteral building (i.e., surrounded by a single row of columns), with eight columns on each facade and fifteen columns on the longer sides, and has an elongated plan. The podium upon which the temple stands is just about sixteen feet tall, and before it is a stairway with thirty-four steps. On the interior, the cella, which is roughly almost sixty feet high, is punctuated by elegant Corinthian half-columns which frame a double order of niches. The ornamental details, particularly abundant in the portal and in the trabeation, are marked by a style quite similar to that found in the courtyard of the great sanctuary. The building, which is still imposing in appearance despite the extensive decrepitude, dates from about the middle of the second century A.D. The attribution to Bacchus was made based upon the reliefs, many of which portray racemes of grape vines. It is believed however that the temple was also dedicated to the triad of Heliopolis, and more specifically to Mercury, the Roman personification of the local deity Shamash. The main temple would thus be dedicated to the official cult, while the smaller one would be dedicated to the

mystery rites. Roberts was greatly impressed by the spectacle of the colossal ruins of Baalbec, whose magnificence in his eyes transcended any possible description. Although he was feverish, the beauty of the temples, the exquisite richness of the friezes, the incomparable proportions of the entire complex worked so overpowering an enchantment

upon him that he spent four days wandering through the ruins, sketching frantically, and noting sizes and proportions in his notebook. In this plate, in particular, it is possible to grasp the truly astonishing proportions of the Temple of Bacchus; the view of the eastern portico clearly shows the refined craftsmanship of the Corinthian capitals and of the cornices.

6th -7th May 1839

THE DOORWAY OF THE
TEMPLE OF BACCHUS

Plate 240

8th May 1839

The great doorway of the temple of Bacchus was one of the pieces of architecture that most stimulated Roberts's artistic sensibilities during his stay at Baalbec. The Englishman was not only impressed with the remarkable quality of the friezes, but also by the colossal proportions of the structure. Although the architrave had been seriously damaged by an earthquake, and the central portion was dangling in a precarious state of equilibrium, the sober elegance of the whole seemed to Roberts to be a work of incomparable beauty. The racemes and the interwoven acanthus leaves were exquisite in style, and suggested a lightness of touch that contrasted sharply with the majestic eagle, its wings spread wide, that was carved upon the lower side of the architrave. Roberts had promised himself that he would complete at least seven drawings of the ruins of Baalbec, and it is worth noting that he was elected a member of the Royal Academy, thanks to the oil-on-canvas painting upon his return to London, based upon the sketch of the great portal. Unfortunately, the stay at Baalbec was troubled by an increasingly troublesome fever, and at last the artist was forced to abandon his plans of continuing to visit Damascus and Palmyra and indeed convinced him to set out in the

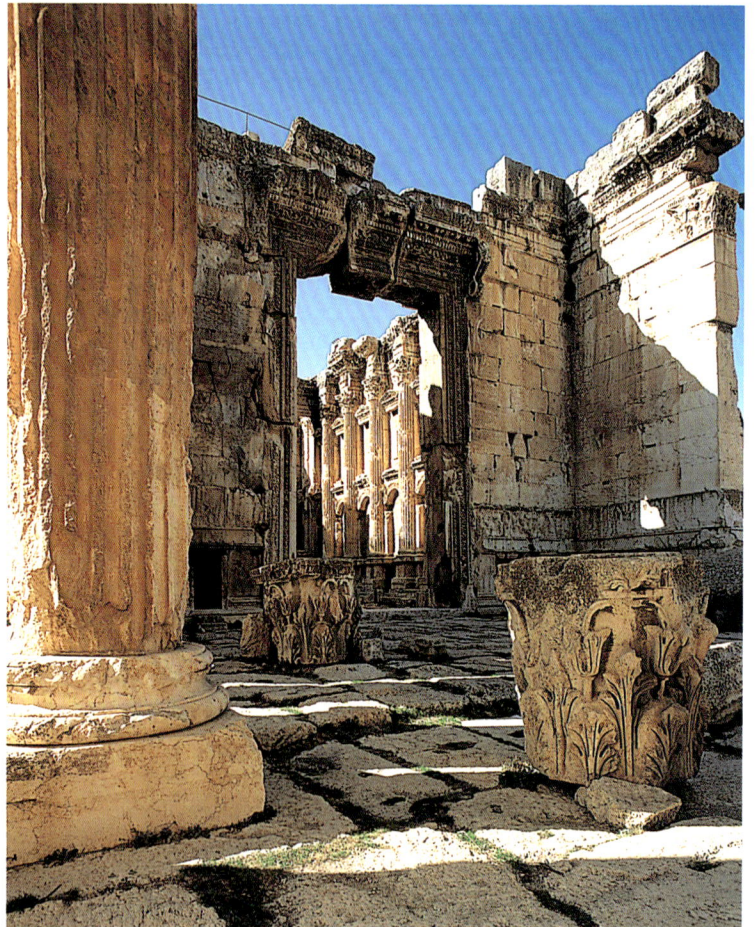

direction of Beirut, though with great misgivings. Setting out on the morning of the 8th of May, he crossed once again the mountains of Lebanon, and within days he was in sight of the great port city. In Beirut, he met up again with John Kinnear and a number of other friends, happily spending time with them and telling of his recent adventures. On the 13th of May he boarded a ship bound for Alexandria, where he arrived after a voyage of three days.

He then continued his voyage, reaching Malta, where he was obliged to spend three weeks in quarantine. Then a five-day voyage aboard the steamer "Volcano" took him to Gibraltar; after spending a week in Cadiz, as a guest of the consul, who was a friend of long acquaintance, and after a few more days in Lisbon, David Roberts finally returned to London, docking on the 21st of July, after an absence of eleven months.

LIST OF PLATES

All the photographs published in this volume are by Antonio Attini, except for the following:

Laura Accomazzo: page 53 top.

Marcello Bertinetti/Archivio White Star: pages 30, 294, 300, 315, 380, 382, 399, 415, 429, 430, 508.

Claudio Concina: pages 296, 304, 307, 312.

Duba: pages 284, 292, 394.

Cesare Gerolimetto: pages 482, 485.

Shai Ginott: page 396.

Barry Iverson: pages 209, 213 top, 220, 226 bottom, 228, 245 bottom, 262.

Gadi Kabalo: page 359.

Meir Ragwan: page 461.

J. Sahar: pages 355, 481.

Alberto Siliotti: pages 287, 289, 290, 298, 303, 309.

Giulio Veggi/Archivio White Star: pages 115 top, 130 bottom, 160, 257 bottom.

All the lithographs reproduced in this volume belong to the Library of Congress of New York, except for the following:

Dea Picture Library: page 8.

By courtesy of the Fine Art Society, London: pages 22-23.

Grundy Art Gallery, Backpool: page 9.

Library of Congress, Washington: page 12.

National Galleries of Scotland, Edimburgh: pages 20-21.

Scottish National Portrait Gallery: page 13.

Bernard Shapero/Rare Books Private collections: pages 32-33, 82-83, 112-113, 148-149, 168-169, 174-175, 178-179, 180-181, 182-183, 184-185 Sotheby's Library, London: page 19.

The Worshipful Company of Goldsmiths: page 20.

V&A Images/Victoria and Albert Museum, Londra/Foto Scala, Firenze: pages 14-15, 380-381.